Houghton
Mifflin
Harcourt

# GO MATH!

## Volume 2

© Houghton Mifflin Harcourt Publishing Company • Cover Image Credits: (Moose) ©Richard Wear/Design Pics/
Corbis; (Field, Delaware) ©Brian E. Kushner/Flickr Open/Getty Images

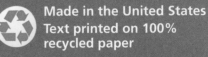

Made in the United States
Text printed on 100%
recycled paper

Houghton
Mifflin
Harcourt

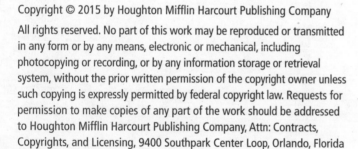

Printed in the U.S.A.

ISBN 978-0-544-43276-5

11 12 13 14  0029  22 21 20 19 18
4500713600          D E F G

Dear Students and Families,

Welcome to **Go Math!**, Grade 3! In this exciting mathematics program, there are hands-on activities to do and real-world problems to solve. Best of all, you will write your ideas and answers right in your book. In **Go Math!**, writing and drawing on the pages helps you think deeply about what you are learning, and you will really understand math!

By the way, all of the pages in your **Go Math!** book are made using recycled paper. We wanted you to know that you can Go Green with **Go Math!**

Sincerely,

The Authors

Made in the United States
Text printed on 100% recycled paper

# GO MATH!

# Authors

**Juli K. Dixon, Ph.D.**
Professor, Mathematics Education
University of Central Florida
Orlando, Florida

**Edward B. Burger, Ph.D.**
President, Southwestern University
Georgetown, Texas

**Steven J. Leinwand**
Principal Research Analyst
American Institutes for
    Research (AIR)
Washington, D.C.

## Contributor

**Rena Petrello**
Professor, Mathematics
Moorpark College
Moorpark, CA

**Matthew R. Larson, Ph.D.**
K-12 Curriculum Specialist for
    Mathematics
Lincoln Public Schools
Lincoln, Nebraska

**Martha E. Sandoval-Martinez**
Math Instructor
El Camino College
Torrance, California

## English Language Learners Consultant

**Elizabeth Jiménez**
CEO, GEMAS Consulting
Professional Expert on English
    Learner Education
Bilingual Education and
    Dual Language
Pomona, California

# VOLUME 1
# Whole Number Operations

 **Critical Area** Developing understanding of multiplication and division and strategies for multiplication and division within 100

 **Inventing Toys** . . . . . . . . . . . . . . . .**2**

 Critical Area

**GO DIGITAL**

Go online! Your math lessons are interactive. Use *i*Tools, Animated Math Models, the Multimedia eGlossary, and more.

Essential Question
How can you use properties to explain patterns on the addition table?
Start

## 1 Addition and Subtraction Within 1,000    **3**

**Domains** Operations and Algebraic Thinking
Number and Operations in Base Ten
COMMON CORE STATE STANDARDS 3.OA.D.8, 3.OA.D.9, 3.NBT.A.1, 3.NBT.A.2

**Chapter 1 Overview**

In this chapter, you will explore and discover answers to the following **Essential Questions**:

• How can you add and subtract whole numbers and decide if an answer is reasonable?

• How do you know when an estimate will be close to an exact answer?

• When do you regroup to add or subtract whole numbers?

• How might you decide which strategy to use to add or subtract?

## 2 Represent and Interpret Data    **85**

**Domains** Operations and Algebraic Thinking
Number and Operations in Base Ten
Measurement and Data
COMMON CORE STATE STANDARDS 3.OA.D.8, 3.NBT.A.2, 3.MD.B.3, 3.MD.B.4

**Chapter 2 Overview**

In this chapter, you will explore and discover answers to the following **Essential Questions**:

• How can you represent and interpret data?

• What are some ways to organize data so it is easy to use?

• How can analyzing data in graphs help you solve problems?

### Chapter 3 Overview

In this chapter, you will explore and discover answers to the following **Essential Questions**:

• How can you use multiplication to find how many in all?

• What models can help you multiply?

• How can you use skip counting to help you multiply?

• How can multiplication properties help you find products?

• What types of problems can be solved by using multiplication?

### Practice and Homework

Lesson Check and Spiral Review in every lesson

### Chapter 4 Overview

In this chapter, you will explore and discover answers to the following **Essential Questions**:

• What strategies can you use to multiply?

• How are patterns and multiplication related?

• How can multiplication properties help you find products?

• What types of problems can be solved by using multiplication?

## Use Multiplication Facts 259

**Domains** Operations and Algebraic Thinking
Number and Operations in Base Ten
COMMON CORE STATE STANDARDS 3.OA.A.4, 3.OA.D.9, 3.NBT.A.3

**Chapter 5 Overview**

In this chapter, you will explore and discover answers to the following **Essential Questions**:

• How can you use multiplication facts, place value, and properties to solve multiplication problems?

• How are patterns and multiplication related?

• How can multiplication properties help you find products?

• What types of problems can be solved by using multiplication?

## Understand Division 299

**Domain** Operations and Algebraic Thinking
COMMON CORE STATE STANDARDS 3.OA.A.2, 3.OA.A.3, 3.OA.B.5, 3.OA.B.6, 3.OA.C.7

**Chapter 6 Overview**

In this chapter, you will explore and discover answers to the following **Essential Questions**:

• How can you use division to find how many in each group or how many equal groups?

• How are multiplication and division related?

• What models can help you divide?

• How can subtraction help you divide?

## Chapter 7 Overview

In this chapter, you will explore and discover answers to the following **Essential Questions**:

- What strategies can you use to divide?
- How can you use a related multiplication fact to divide?
- How can you use factors to divide?
- What types of problems can be solved by using division?

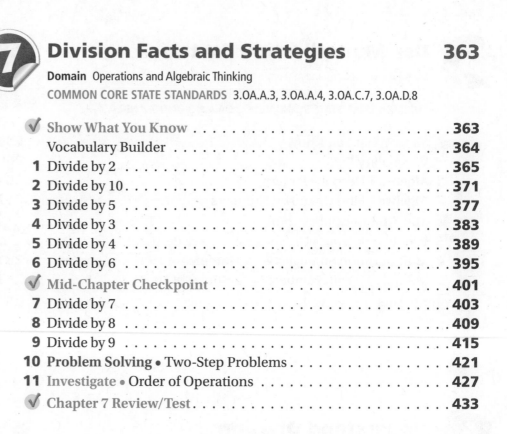

# 7 Division Facts and Strategies 363

**Domain** Operations and Algebraic Thinking

COMMON CORE STATE STANDARDS 3.OA.A.3, 3.OA.A.4, 3.OA.C.7, 3.OA.D.8

**VOLUME 2**
# Fractions

 **Critical Area** Developing understanding of fractions, especially unit fractions (fractions with numerator 1)

## ⑧ Understand Fractions      441

**Domain** Number and Operations–Fractions
COMMON CORE STATE STANDARDS 3.NF.A.1, 3.NF.A.2a, 3.NF.A.2b, 3.NF.A.3c

## ⑨ Compare Fractions      505

**Domain** Number and Operations–Fractions
COMMON CORE STATE STANDARDS 3.NF.A.3a, 3.NF.A.3b, 3.NF.A.3d

**Critical Area**

**GO DIGITAL**

Go online! Your math lessons are interactive. Use *i*Tools, Animated Math Models, the Multimedia *e*Glossary, and more.

**Essential Question**
? What are equal parts of a whole?
Start

**Chapter 8 Overview**

In this chapter, you will explore and discover answers to the following **Essential Questions**:

• How can you use fractions to describe how much or how many?

• Why do you need to have equal parts for fractions?

• How can you solve problems that involve fractions?

**Chapter 9 Overview**

In this chapter, you will explore and discover answers to the following **Essential Questions**:

• How can you compare fractions?

• What models can help you compare and order fractions?

• How can you use the size of the pieces to help you compare and order fractions?

• How can you find equivalent fractions?

# Measurement

 **Critical Area** Developing understanding of the structure of rectangular arrays and of area

# Geometry

## Critical Area

### GO DIGITAL

Go online! Your math lessons are interactive. Use *i*Tools, Animated Math Models, the Multimedia eGlossary, and more.

### Chapter **12** Overview

In this chapter, you will explore and discover answers to the following **Essential Questions**:

- What are some ways to describe and classify two-dimensional shapes?
- How can you describe the angles and sides in polygons?
- How can you use sides and angles to describe quadrilaterals and triangles?
- How can you use properties of shapes to classify them?
- How can you divide shapes into equal parts and use unit fractions to describe the parts?

**Personal Math Trainer**
Online Assessment and Intervention

# Critical Area Fractions

**Common Core**

**CRITICAL AREA** Developing understanding of fractions, especially unit fractions (fractions with numerator 1)

MISSOURI
1821
CORPS OF DISCOVERY
1804          2004
2003
E PLURIBUS UNUM

The Missouri quarter shows explorers Lewis and Clark traveling down the Missouri River. The Gateway Arch is in the background.

## Real World Project

# Coins in the U.S.

Many years ago, a coin called a *piece of eight* was sometimes cut into 8 equal parts. Each part was equal to one eighth ($\frac{1}{8}$) of the whole. Now, U.S. coin values are based on the dollar. Four quarters are equal in value to 1 dollar. So, 1 quarter is equal to one fourth ($\frac{1}{4}$) of a dollar.

## Get Started

WRITE ▸ *Math*

Work with a partner. In which year were the Missouri state quarters minted? Use the Important Facts to help you. Then write fractions to answer these questions:

1. 2 quarters are equal to what part of a dollar?
2. 1 nickel is equal to what part of a dime?
3. 2 nickels are equal to what part of a dime?

### Important Facts

- The U.S. government minted state quarters every year from 1999 to 2008 in the order that the states became part of the United States.
- 1999—Delaware, Pennsylvania, New Jersey, Georgia, Connecticut
- 2000—Massachusetts, Maryland, South Carolina, New Hampshire, Virginia
- 2001—New York, North Carolina, Rhode Island, Vermont, Kentucky
- 2002—Tennessee, Ohio, Louisiana, Indiana, Mississippi
- 2003—Illinois, Alabama, Maine, Missouri, Arkansas
- 2004—Michigan, Florida, Texas, Iowa, Wisconsin
- 2005—California, Minnesota, Oregon, Kansas, West Virginia
- 2006—Nevada, Nebraska, Colorado, North Dakota, South Dakota
- 2007—Montana, Washington, Idaho, Wyoming, Utah
- 2008—Oklahoma, New Mexico, Arizona, Alaska, Hawaii

_____

_____

_____

_____

Completed by _____

# Understand Fractions

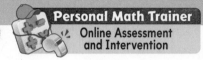

## Show What You Know

Personal Math Trainer
Online Assessment
and Intervention

Check your understanding of important skills.

Name _____

▶ **Equal Parts** Circle the shape that has equal parts. (1.G.A.3)

1.

2.

▶ **Combine Plane Shapes** Write the number of △ needed to cover the shape. (1.G.A.2)

3.

_____ triangles

4.

_____ triangles

5.

_____ triangles

▶ **Count Equal Groups** Complete. (3.OA.A.1)

6.

_____ groups

_____ in each group

7.

_____ groups

_____ in each group

Casey shared a pizza with some friends. They each ate $\frac{1}{3}$ of the pizza. How many people shared the pizza?

# Vocabulary Builder

▶ **Visualize It** ................................

**Complete the bubble map by using the words with a ✓.**

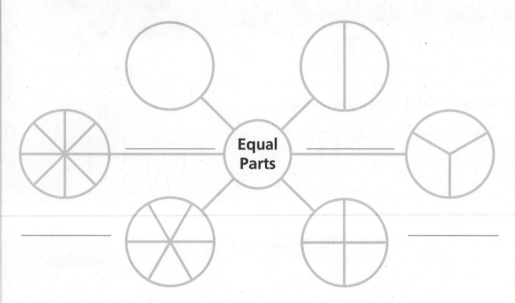

Equal Parts

**Preview Words**

denominator
✓ eighths
  equal parts
✓ fourths
  fraction
  fraction greater than 1
✓ halves
  numerator
✓ sixths
✓ thirds
  unit fraction
✓ whole

▶ **Understand Vocabulary** ................................

**Read the description. Write the preview word.**

1. It is a number that names part of a whole or part of a group. _____

2. It is the part of a fraction above the line, which tells how many parts are being counted.

   _____

3. It is the part of a fraction below the line, which tells how many equal parts there are in the whole or in the group. _____

4. It is a number that names 1 equal part of a whole and has 1 as its numerator. _____

• Interactive Student Edition
• Multimedia eGlossary

# Chapter 8 Vocabulary

**denominator**

denominador

11

**Eighths**

octavos

17

**Equal Parts**

partes iguales

21

**Fourths**

cuartos

26

**fraction**

fracción

27

**Fraction Greater than 1**

fraccíon mayor que 1

28

**Halves**

mitades

32

**numerator**

numerador

53

These are eighths

The part of a fraction below the line, which tells how many equal parts there are in the whole or in the group

Example: $\frac{1}{5}$ ← denominator

---

These are fourths

Parts that are exactly the same size

6 equal parts

---

A number which has a numerator that is greater than its denominator

Examples:

    $\frac{6}{3}$   $\frac{2}{1}$

A number that names part of a whole or part of a group

Examples:

    $\frac{1}{3}$

---

The part of a fraction above the line, which tells how many parts are being counted

Example: $\frac{1}{5}$ ← numerator

These are halves

# Chapter 8 Vocabulary

**denominator**

denominator

11

**Eighths**

octavos

17

**Equal Parts**

partes iguales

21

**Fourths**

cuartos

26

**fraction**

fracción

27

**Fraction Greater than 1**

fraccíon mayor que 1

28

**Halves**

mitades

32

**numerator**

numerador

53

These are eighths

The part of a fraction below the line, which tells how many equal parts there are in the whole or in the group

Example: $\frac{1}{5}$ ← denominator

These are fourths

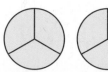

Parts that are exactly the same size

6 equal parts

A number which has a numerator that is greater than its denominator

Examples:

 $\frac{6}{3}$ $\frac{2}{1}$

A number that names part of a whole or part of a group

Examples:

 $\frac{1}{3}$

The part of a fraction above the line, which tells how many parts are being counted

Example: $\frac{1}{5}$ ← numerator

These are halves

**Sixths**

sextos

74

**Thirds**

tercios

77

**unit fraction**

fraccíon unitaria

79

**Whole**

entero

84

These are thirds

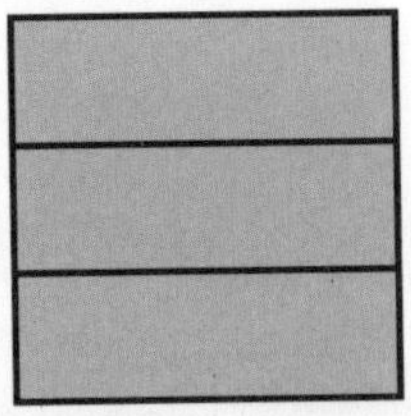

These are sixths

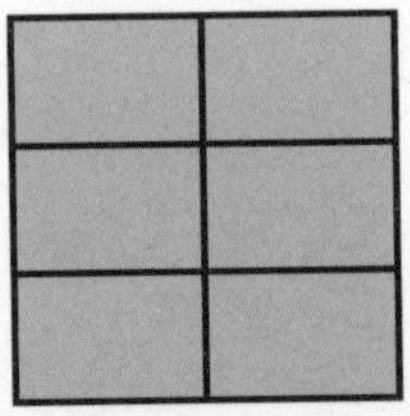

All of the parts of a shape or group

Example:

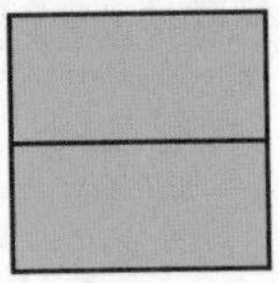

$$\frac{2}{2} = 1$$

This is one whole.

A fraction that has 1 as its top number, or numerator

Example: $\frac{1}{3}$ is a unit fraction

**Sixths**

sextos

74

**Thirds**

tercios

77

**unit fraction**

fraccíon unitaria

79

**Whole**

entero

84

These are thirds

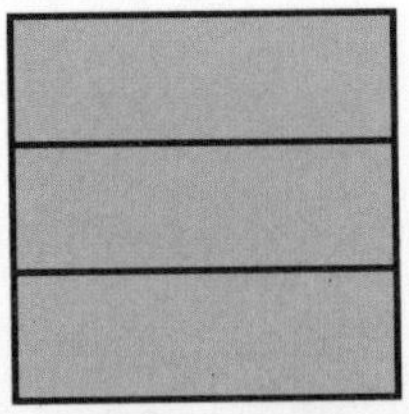

These are sixths

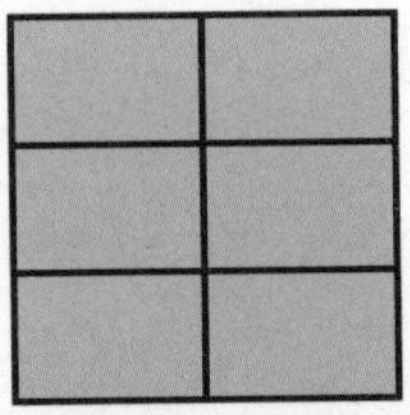

All of the parts of a shape or group

Example:

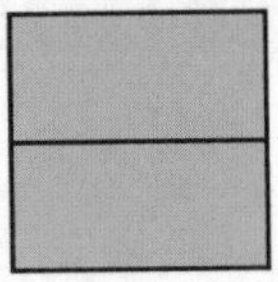

$$\frac{2}{2} = 1$$

This is one whole.

A fraction that has 1 as its top number, or numerator

Example: $\frac{1}{3}$ is a unit fraction

# Going to the Mint

For 2 to 4 players

## Materials

- 3 red playing pieces
- 3 blue playing pieces
- 3 green playing pieces
- 3 yellow playing pieces
- 1 number cube

## How to Play

1. Put your 3 playing pieces in the START circle of the same color.
2. To get a playing piece out of START, you must toss a 6 on the number cube.
   - If you toss a 6, move 1 of your playing pieces to the same colored circle on the path.
   - If you do not toss a 6, wait until your next turn.
3. Once you have a playing piece on the path, toss the number cube to take a turn. Move the playing pieces that many tan spaces. You must get all 3 of your playing pieces on the path.
4. If you land on a space with a question, answer it. If you are correct, move ahead 1 space.
5. To reach FINISH, move your playing pieces up the path that is the same color as your playing pieces. The first player to get all three playing pieces on FINISH wins.

**Word Box**

denominator
eighths
equal parts
fourths
fraction
fraction greater
  than 1
halves
numerator
sixths
thirds
unit fraction
whole

START

What is the meaning of a whole?

How many sixths does three thirds equal?

What is the name of the part of a fraction above the line?

How many fourths are in a whole?

Why is $\frac{1}{4}$ a unit fraction?

What is a fraction?

FINISH

START

Why is $\frac{4}{3}$ a fraction greater than 1?

Which is a whole: $\frac{3}{8}$ or $\frac{8}{8}$?

START

What kind of fraction is $\frac{1}{3}$?

If a whole has two equal parts, what are the equal parts called?

How many equal parts called thirds are in a whole?

What are equal parts?

What are sixths?

What kind of number has a numerator greater than its denominator?

FINISH

If there are 8 equal parts in a whole, what are the equal parts called?

What is the meaning of *denominator*?

START

# The Write Way

## Reflect

**Choose one idea. Write about it.**

- Draw and explain the ideas of *equal* and *unequal parts*. Use a separate piece of paper for your drawing.
- Tell the most important idea to understand about fractions.
- Define *numerator and denominator* so that a younger child would understand.

# Name _____

## Equal Parts of a Whole

**Essential Question** What are equal parts of a whole?

 Common Core **Number and Operations— Fractions—3.NF.A.1** *Also 3.G.A.2*

**MATHEMATICAL PRACTICES**
**MP3, MP4, MP6**

## 🗝 Unlock the Problem *Real World*

Lauren shares a sandwich with her brother. They each get an equal part. How many equal parts are there?

🔑 Each whole shape below is divided into equal parts. A **whole** is all of the parts of one shape or group. **Equal parts** are exactly the same size.

- What do you need to find?

  _____

  _____

- How many people share the

  sandwich? _____

2 **halves**

3 **thirds**

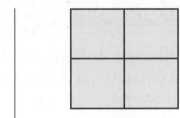

4 **fourths**

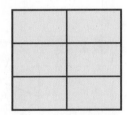

_____ **sixths**

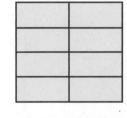

_____ **eighths**

Lauren's sandwich is divided into halves.

So, there are _____ equal parts.

- Draw a picture to show a different way Lauren's sandwich could have been divided into halves.

**Math Talk**

**MATHEMATICAL PRACTICES ③**

**Verify the Reasoning of Others** Are your halves the same shape as your classmates' halves? Explain why both halves represent the same size.

**Chapter 8    443**

**Try This!** Write whether the shape is divided into
*equal* parts or *unequal* parts.

**A**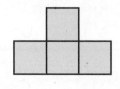

4 _____ parts
fourths

**B**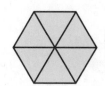

6 _____ parts
sixths

**C**

2 _____ parts
These are not halves.

**! ERROR Alert**
Be sure the parts are
equal in size.

equal      unequal

**Share and Show**  MATH BOARD

**Math Talk**    MATHEMATICAL PRACTICES ③

1. This shape is divided into 3
equal parts. What is the name
for the parts?

**Apply** How do you
determine if the shapes
are divided into equal
parts?

_____

**Write the number of equal parts. Then write the name
for the parts.**

2.

_____ equal parts

_____

3.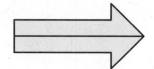

_____ equal parts

_____

✓4.

_____ equal parts

_____

**Write whether the shape is divided into *equal* parts
or *unequal* parts.**

5.

_____ parts

6.

_____ parts

✓7.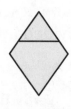

_____ parts

Name _____

**Write the number of equal parts. Then write the name for the parts.**

8.

_____ equal parts

_____

9.
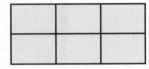

_____ equal parts

_____

10.

_____ equal parts

_____

11.
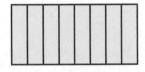

_____ equal parts

_____

12.
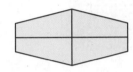

_____ equal parts

_____

13.

_____ equal parts

_____

**Write whether the shape is divided into *equal* parts or *unequal* parts.**

14.
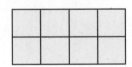

_____ parts

15.

_____ parts

16.
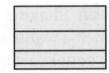

_____ parts

17. Draw lines to divide the circle into 8 eighths.

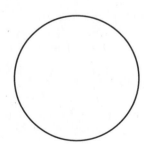

18. **GO DEEPER** Thomas wants to divide a square piece of paper into 4 equal parts. Draw two different quick pictures to show what his paper could look like.

## Problem Solving • Applications (Real World)

**Use the pictures for 19–20.**

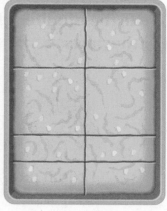

**Pan A**          **Pan B**

**19.** Mrs. Rivera made 2 pans of corn casserole for a large family dinner. She cut each pan into parts. What is the name of the parts in A?

_____

**20.** THINK SMARTER  Alex said his mom divided Pan B into eighths. Does his statement make sense? Explain.

_____

_____

**21.** MATHEMATICAL PRACTICE 6 **Explain** why the rectangle is divided into 4 equal parts.

_____

_____

**22.** GO DEEPER  Shakira cut a triangle out of paper. She wants to divide the triangle into 2 equal parts. Draw a quick picture to show what her triangle could look like.

**23.** THINK SMARTER  Parker divides a fruit bar into 3 equal parts. Circle the word that makes the sentence true.

The fruit bar is divided into | thirds / halves / fourths |.

Name _____

## Equal Parts of a Whole

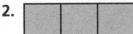 **COMMON CORE STANDARD—3.NF.A.1**
*Develop understanding of fractions as numbers.*

**Write the number of equal parts.**
**Then write the name for the parts.**

1.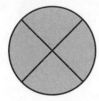

___4___ equal parts

___fourths___

2.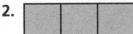

_____ equal parts

_____

**Write whether the shape is divided into *equal* parts or *unequal* parts.**

3.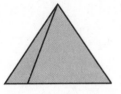

_____ parts

4.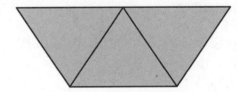

_____ parts

 **Problem Solving** ·World·

5. Diego cuts a round pizza into eight equal slices. What is the name for the parts?

_____

6. Madison is making a place mat. She divides it into 6 equal parts to color. What is the name for the parts?

_____

7. **WRITE** ▸*Math* Describe how 4 friends could share a sandwich equally.

_____

_____

## Lesson Check (3.NF.A.1)

1. How many equal parts are in this shape?

_____

2. What is the name for the equal parts of the whole?

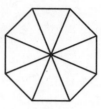

_____

## Spiral Review (3.OA.A.3, 3.OA.C.7)

3. Use a related multiplication fact to find the quotient.

$$49 \div 7 =$$

_____

4. Find the unknown factor and quotient.

$$9 \times \boxed{\phantom{0}} = 45$$

$$45 \div 9 = \boxed{\phantom{0}}$$

_____

5. There are 5 pairs of socks in one package. Matt buys 3 packages of socks. How many pairs of socks does Matt buy?

_____

6. Mrs. McCarr buys 9 packages of markers for an art project. Each package has 10 markers. How many markers does Mrs. McCarr buy?

_____

FOR MORE PRACTICE
GO TO THE
Personal Math Trainer

Name _____

# Equal Shares

**Essential Question** Why do you need to know how to make equal shares?

 Common Core  Number and Operations— Fractions—3.NF.A.1 *Also 3.G.A.2*

MATHEMATICAL PRACTICES
MP2, MP4, MP6

 **🔑 Unlock the Problem**

Four friends share 2 small pizzas equally. What are two ways the pizza could be divided equally? How much pizza will each friend get?

🔒 **Draw to model the problem.**

Draw 2 circles to show the pizzas.

• How might the two ways be different?

_____

_____

## 🔒 One Way

There are ____ friends.

So, divide each pizza into 4 slices.

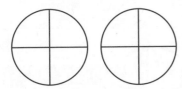

There are ____ equal parts.

Each friend can have 2 equal parts. Each friend will get 2 eighths of all the pizza.

## 🔒 Another Way

There are ____ friends.

So, divide all the pizza into 4 slices.

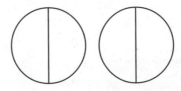

There are ____ equal parts.

Each friend can have 1 equal part. Each friend will get 1 half of a pizza.

**Math Talk**

MATHEMATICAL PRACTICES ②

**Use Reasoning** Why does dividing the pizza into different size slices still allow the friends to have an equal share?

**Try This!** Four girls share 3 oranges equally. Draw a quick picture to find out how much each girl gets.

• Draw 3 circles to show the oranges.

• Draw lines to divide the circles equally.

• Shade the part 1 girl gets.

• Describe what part of an orange each girl gets.

_____

## 🔑 Example

Melissa and Kyle are planning to share one pan of lasagna with 6 friends. They do not agree on the way to cut the pan into equal parts. Will each friend get an equal share using Melissa's way? Using Kyle's way?

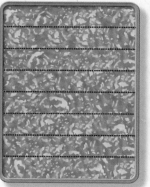 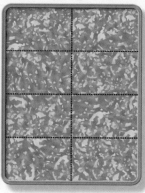

**Melissa's Way**     **Kyle's Way**

- Will Melissa's shares and Kyle's shares have the same shape? _____

- Will their shares using either way be the same size? _____

So, each friend will get an _____ share using either way.

- Explain why both ways let the friends have the same amount.

_____

_____

## Share and Show  MATH BOARD

Math Talk

MATHEMATICAL PRACTICES ⑥

Explain another way the oranges could have been divided. Tell how much each friend will get.

1. Two friends share 4 oranges equally. Use the picture to find how much each friend gets.

**Think:** There are more oranges than friends.

_____

**Draw lines to show how much each person gets. Write the answer.**

✓ 2. 8 sisters share 3 eggrolls equally.

✓ 3. 6 students share 4 bagels equally.

_____     _____

Name _____

**Draw lines to show how much each person gets. Write the answer.**

4. 3 classmates share 2 granola bars equally.

_____

5. 4 brothers share 2 sandwiches equally.

_____

**Draw to show how much each person gets. Shade the amount that one person gets. Write the answer.**

6. 8 friends share 4 sheets of construction paper equally.

_____

7. **MATHEMATICAL PRACTICE ④ Model Mathematics** 4 sisters share 3 muffins equally.

_____

8. **GO DEEPER** Maria prepared 5 quesadillas. She wants to share them equally among 8 of her neighbors. How much of a quesadilla will each neighbor get?

_____

## Unlock the Problem

9. **THINK SMARTER** Julia holds a bread-baking class. She has 4 adults and 3 children in the class. The class will make 2 round loaves of bread. If Julia plans to give each person, including herself, an equal part of the baked breads, how much bread will each person get?

a. What do you need to find? _____

_____

b. How will you use what you know about drawing equal

shares to solve the problem? _____

_____

c. Draw a quick picture to find the share of bread each person will get.

d. So, each person will get

_____ of a loaf of bread.

10. **THINK SMARTER** Lara and three girl friends share three sandwiches equally.

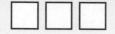

How much does each girl get? Mark all that apply.

(A) 3 fifths of a sandwich        (C) 1 whole sandwich

(B) 3 fourths of a sandwich      (D) one half and 1 fourth of a sandwich

452

Name _____

## Equal Shares

COMMON CORE STANDARD—3.NF.A.1
*Develop understanding of fractions as numbers.*

**Draw lines to show how much each person gets. Write the answer.**

1. 6 friends share 3 sandwiches equally.

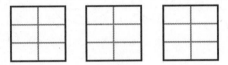

3 sixths of a sandwich
_____

_____

2. 4 teammates share 5 granola bars equally. Draw to show how much each person gets. Shade the amount that one person gets. Write the answer.

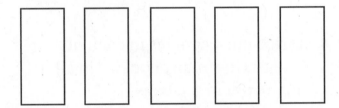

_____

© Houghton Mifflin Harcourt Publishing Company

**Problem Solving** Real World

3. Three brothers share 2 sandwiches equally. How much of a sandwich does each brother get?

_____

_____

4. Six neighbors share 4 pies equally. How much of a pie does each neighbor get?

_____

_____

5. **WRITE** ▸*Math*  Draw a diagram to show 3 pizzas shared equally among 6 friends.

_____

_____

## Lesson Check (3.NF.A.1)

**1.** Two friends share 3 fruit bars equally. How much does each friend get?

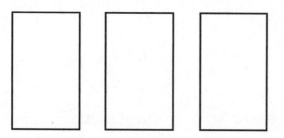

**2.** Four brothers share 3 pizzas equally. How much of a pizza does each brother get?

_____

_____

## Spiral Review (3.OA.A.3, 3.OA.C.7, 3.NBT.A.2)

**3.** Find the quotient.

$$3\overline{)27}$$

**4.** Tyrice put 4 cookies in each of 7 bags. How many cookies in all did he put in the bags?

_____

_____

**5.** Ryan earned $5 per hour raking leaves. He earned $35. How many hours did he rake leaves?

**6.** Hannah has 229 horse stickers and 164 kitten stickers. How many more horse stickers than kitten stickers does Hannah have?

_____

_____

FOR MORE PRACTICE
GO TO THE
Personal Math Trainer

# Unit Fractions of a Whole

**Essential Question** What do the top and bottom numbers of a fraction tell?

Common Core — Number and Operations—Fractions—**3.NF.A.1** *Also 3.G.A.2*

**MATHEMATICAL PRACTICES**
MP2, MP3, MP4

A **fraction** is a number that names part of a whole or part of a group.

In a fraction, the top number tells how many equal parts are being counted.

The bottom number tells how many equal parts are in the whole or in the group.

$\longrightarrow \dfrac{1}{6}$

A **unit fraction** names 1 equal part of a whole. It has 1 as its top number. $\frac{1}{6}$ is a unit fraction.

##  Unlock the Problem *Real World*

Luke's family picked strawberries. They put the washed strawberries in one part of a fruit platter. The platter had 6 equal parts. What fraction of the fruit platter had strawberries?

**1** **Find part of a whole.**

Shade 1 of the 6 equal parts.

**Read:** one sixth    **Write:** $\frac{1}{6}$

So, _____ of the platter had strawberries.

**1** **Use a fraction to find a whole.**

This shape ☐ is $\frac{1}{4}$ of the whole. Here are examples of what the whole could look like.

**Math Talk**   MATHEMATICAL PRACTICES ②

**Reason Abstractly** How can you make a whole if you know what one equal part looks like?

**A** 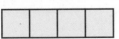   **B**    **C**

**Try This!** Look again at the examples at the bottom of page 455. Draw two other pictures of how the whole might look.

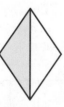

**Share and Show**

1. What fraction names the shaded part? _____

   **Think:** 1 out of 3 equal parts is shaded.

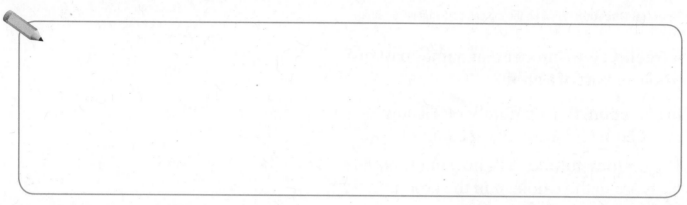

Math Talk

MATHEMATICAL PRACTICES ④

**Use Models** When using a fraction model, how do you know what the denominator of the fraction will be?

**Write the number of equal parts in the whole.**
**Then write the fraction that names the shaded part.**

2.

_____ equal parts

_____

3.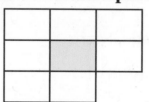

_____ equal parts

_____

4.

_____ equal parts

_____

5.

_____ equal parts

_____

6.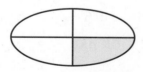

_____ equal parts

_____

7.

_____ equal parts

_____

**456**

Name _____

## On Your Own

**Write the number of equal parts in the whole.**
**Then write the fraction that names the shaded part.**

8.

_____ equal parts

_____

9.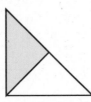

_____ equal parts

_____

10.

_____ equal parts

_____

11.

_____ equal parts

_____

12.

_____ equal parts

_____

13. GO DEEPER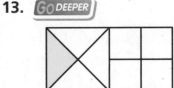

_____ equal parts

_____

MATHEMATICAL PRACTICE ④ **Use Diagrams** **Draw a picture of the whole.**

14. $\frac{1}{2}$ is

15. $\frac{1}{3}$ is [gray square]

16. $\frac{1}{6}$ is [gray rectangle]

17. $\frac{1}{4}$ is

## Problem Solving • Applications

**Use the pictures for 18–19.**

| Kylie's Lunch | Dylan's Lunch |
|---|---|
| sandwich | pizza |
| apple | fruit bar |

18. The missing parts of the pictures show what Kylie and Dylan ate for lunch. What fraction of the pizza did Dylan eat? What fraction of the fruit bar did he eat?

_____

19. What fraction of the apple did Kylie eat? Write the fraction in numbers and in words.

_____

20. **MATHEMATICAL PRACTICE 3** **Make Arguments** Diego drew lines to divide the square into 6 pieces as shown. Then he shaded part of the square. Diego says he shaded $\frac{1}{6}$ of the square. Is he correct? Explain how you know.

_____

_____

21. **THINK SMARTER** Riley and Chad each have a granola bar broken into equal pieces. They each eat one piece, or $\frac{1}{4}$, of their granola bar. How many more pieces do Riley and Chad need to eat to finish both granola bars? Draw a picture to justify your answer.

_____

22. **THINK SMARTER** What fraction names the shaded part? Explain how you know how to write the fraction.

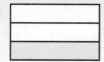

_____

## Unit Fractions of a Whole

COMMON CORE STANDARD—3.NF.A.1
*Develop understanding of fractions as numbers.*

**Write the number of equal parts in the whole.**
**Then write the fraction that names the shaded part.**

1.

_____6_____ equal parts

_____$\frac{1}{6}$_____

2.

_____ equal parts

_____

**Draw a picture of the whole.**

3. $\frac{1}{3}$ is

4. $\frac{1}{8}$ is

## Problem Solving · Real World

5. Tyler made a pan of cornbread. He cut it into 8 equal pieces and ate 1 piece. What fraction of the cornbread did Tyler eat?

_____

6. Anna cut an apple into 4 equal pieces. She gave 1 piece to her sister. What fraction of the apple did Anna give to her sister?

_____

7. **WRITE** ▸*Math*  Draw a picture to show what 1 out of 3 equal parts looks like. Then write the fraction.

_____

_____

## Lesson Check (3.NF.A.1)

**1.** What fraction names the shaded part?

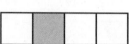

**2.** Tasha cut a fruit bar into 3 equal parts. She ate 1 part. What fraction of the fruit bar did Tasha eat?

_____

_____

## Spiral Review (3.OA.A.3, 3.OA.B.5, 3.MD.B.3)

**3.** Alex has 5 lizards. He divides them equally among 5 cages. How many lizards does Alex put in each cage?

**4.** Find the product.

$$8 \times 1 = \boxed{\phantom{0}}$$

_____

_____

**5.** Leo bought 6 chew toys for his new puppy. Each chew toy cost $4. How much did Leo spend for the chew toys?

**6.** Lilly is making a picture graph. Each picture of a star is equal to two books she has read. The row for the month of December has 3 stars. How many books did Lilly read during the month of December?

_____

_____

FOR MORE PRACTICE
GO TO THE
**Personal Math Trainer**

Name _____

# Fractions of a Whole

**Essential Question** How does a fraction name part of a whole?

Common Core
Number and Operations—
Fractions—3.NF.A.1 *Also 3.G.A.2*
MATHEMATICAL PRACTICES
MP3, MP4, MP8

 **Unlock the Problem**

The first pizzeria in America opened in New York in 1905. The pizza recipe came from Italy. Look at Italy's flag. What fraction of the flag is not red?

🔑 **Name equal parts of a whole.**

A fraction can name more than 1 equal part of a whole.

The flag is divided into 3 equal parts, and 2 parts are not red.

2 parts not red → **2** ← numerator
3 equal parts in all → **3** ← denominator

**Read:** two thirds or two parts out of three equal parts

**Write:** $\frac{2}{3}$

So, ____ of the flag is not red.

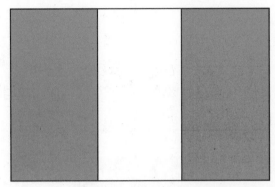

▲ Italy's flag has three equal parts.

**Math Idea**

When all the parts are shaded, one whole shape is equal to all of its parts. It represents the whole number 1.

$$\frac{3}{3} = 1$$

The **numerator** tells how many parts are being counted.

The **denominator** tells how many equal parts are in the whole or in the group.

You can count equal parts, such as sixths, to make a whole.

| $\frac{1}{6}$ | | |
|---|---|---|
| | | |

One $\frac{1}{6}$ part

$\frac{1}{6}$

| $\frac{1}{6}$ | $\frac{1}{6}$ | |
|---|---|---|
| | | |

Two $\frac{1}{6}$ parts

$\frac{2}{6}$

| $\frac{1}{6}$ | $\frac{1}{6}$ | $\frac{1}{6}$ |
|---|---|---|
| | | |

Three $\frac{1}{6}$ parts

$\frac{3}{6}$

| $\frac{1}{6}$ | $\frac{1}{6}$ | $\frac{1}{6}$ |
|---|---|---|
| $\frac{1}{6}$ | | |

Four $\frac{1}{6}$ parts

$\frac{\phantom{0}}{6}$

| $\frac{1}{6}$ | $\frac{1}{6}$ | $\frac{1}{6}$ |
|---|---|---|
| $\frac{1}{6}$ | $\frac{1}{6}$ | |

Five $\frac{1}{6}$ parts

$\frac{\phantom{0}}{6}$

| $\frac{1}{6}$ | $\frac{1}{6}$ | $\frac{1}{6}$ |
|---|---|---|
| $\frac{1}{6}$ | $\frac{1}{6}$ | $\frac{1}{6}$ |

Six $\frac{1}{6}$ parts

$\frac{\phantom{0}}{6}$

For example, $\frac{6}{6}$ = one whole, or 1.

**Try This!** Write the missing word or number to name the shaded part.

 **A**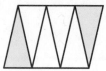

$\frac{2}{6}$

_____ sixths

**B**

$\frac{5}{8}$

_____ eighths

**C**

$\frac{\quad}{3}$

two thirds

**D**

$\frac{\quad}{6}$, or 1

six sixths, or one whole

## Share and Show  MATH BOARD

Math Talk  MATHEMATICAL PRACTICES 8

**Generalize** What do the numerator and denominator of a fraction tell you?

1. Shade two parts out of eight equal parts. Write a fraction in words and in numbers to name the shaded part.

**Think:** Each part is $\frac{1}{8}$.

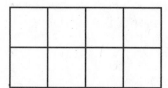

**Read:** _____ eighths      **Write:** _____

**Write the fraction that names each part. Write a fraction in words and in numbers to name the shaded part.**

2.

Each part is _____.

_____ fourths

_____

3.

Each part is _____.

_____ sixths

_____

4.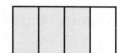

Each part is _____.

_____ fourths

_____

Name _____

**Write the fraction that names each part. Write a fraction in words and in numbers to name the shaded part.**

**5.**

Each part is ____.

_____ eighths

_____

**6.**

Each part is ____.

_____ thirds

_____

**7.**

Each part is ____.

_____ sixths

_____

**Shade the fraction circle to model the fraction. Then write the fraction in numbers.**

**8.** six out of eight

_____

**9.** three fourths

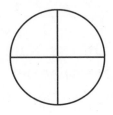

_____

**10.** three out of three

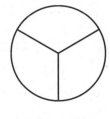

_____

**11.** A flag is divided into four equal sections. One section is white. What fraction of the flag is not white?

_____

**12.** A garden has six sections. Two sections are planted with tomatoes. Which fraction represents the part of the garden without tomatoes?

_____

**13.** Jane is making a memory quilt from some of her old favorite clothes that are too small. She will use T-shirts for the shaded squares in the pattern. What names the part of the quilt that will be made of T-shirts?

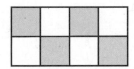

_____

# Problem Solving • Applications

**Use the diagrams for 14–15.**

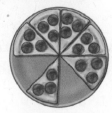  

Pepperoni      Cheese      Veggie

14. GO DEEPER  Mrs. Ormond ordered pizza. Each pizza had 8 equal slices. What fraction of the pepperoni pizza was eaten? What fraction of the cheese pizza is left?

_____

15. THINK SMARTER  **Pose a Problem**  Use the picture of the veggie pizza to write a problem that includes a fraction. Solve your problem.

_____

_____

16. MATHEMATICAL PRACTICE ❸  **Verify the Reasoning of Others**  Kate says that $\frac{2}{4}$ of the rectangle is shaded. Describe her error. Use the model to write the correct fraction for the shaded part.

_____

_____

_____

17. THINK SMARTER  Select a numerator and a denominator for the fraction that names the shaded part of the shape.

| Numerator | Denominator |
|-----------|-------------|
| ○ 2 | ○ 3 |
| ○ 3 | ○ 5 |
| ○ 5 | ○ 6 |
| ○ 6 | ○ 8 |

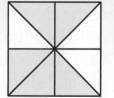

Name _____

## Fractions of a Whole

**Write the fraction that names each part. Write a fraction in words and in numbers to name the shaded part.**

**COMMON CORE STANDARD—3.NF.A.1**
*Develop understanding of fractions as numbers.*

1.

Each part is _____$\frac{1}{6}$_____.

___**three**___ sixths

___$\frac{3}{6}$___

2.

Each part is _____.

_____ eighths

_____

**Shade the fraction circle to model the fraction. Then write the fraction in numbers.**

3. four out of six

_____

4. eight out of eight

_____

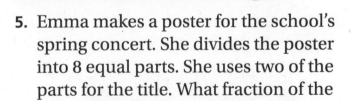

5. Emma makes a poster for the school's spring concert. She divides the poster into 8 equal parts. She uses two of the parts for the title. What fraction of the poster does Emma use for the title?

_____

6. Lucas makes a flag. It has 6 equal parts. Five of the parts are red. What fraction of the flag is red?

_____

7. **WRITE** ▸*Math* Draw a rectangle and divide it into 4 equal parts. Shade 3 parts. Then write the fraction that names the shaded part.

_____

_____

## Lesson Check (3.NF.A.1)

**1.** What fraction names the shaded part?

**2.** What fraction names the shaded part?

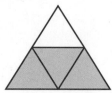

## Spiral Review (3.OA.C.7, 3.NBT.A.2, 3.MD.B.3)

**3.** Sarah biked for 115 minutes last week. Jennie biked for 89 minutes last week. How many minutes did the girls bike?

**4.** Harrison made a building using 124 blocks. Greyson made a building using 78 blocks. How many more blocks did Harrison use than Greyson?

**5.** Von buys a bag of 24 dog treats. He gives his puppy 3 treats a day. How many days will the bag of dog treats last?

**6.** How many students chose swimming?

| Favorite Activity | |
|---|---|
| Skating | ☺ ☺ |
| Swimming | ☺ ☺ ☺ ☺ ☺ |
| Biking | ☺ ☺ ☺ ☺ |
| Key: Each ☺ = 5 votes. | |

**FOR MORE PRACTICE GO TO THE**
**Personal Math Trainer**

Name _____

# Fractions on a Number Line

**Essential Question** How can you represent and locate fractions on a number line?

 Common Core
Number and Operations—
Fractions—3.NF.A.2a, 3.NF.A.2b
*Also 3.NF.A.2*
**MATHEMATICAL PRACTICES**
**MP1, MP2, MP4**

## ⚷ Unlock the Problem

Billy's family is traveling from his house to his grandma's house. They stop at gas stations when they are $\frac{1}{4}$ and $\frac{3}{4}$ of the way there. How can you represent those distances on a number line?

You can use a number line to show fractions. The length from one whole number to the next whole number represents one whole. The line can be divided into any number of equal parts, or lengths.

> **Math Idea**
> A point on a number line shows the endpoint of a length, or distance, from zero. A number or fraction can name the distance.

## 🔓 Activity Locate fractions on a number line.

**Materials** ■ fraction strips

Billy's House                                     Grandma's House
  0                                                      1

$\frac{1}{4}$

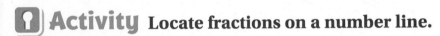

$\frac{0}{4}$                                              $\frac{4}{4}$

**STEP 1** Divide the line into four equal lengths, or fourths.
Place four $\frac{1}{4}$-fraction strips end-to-end above the line to help.

**STEP 2** At the end of each strip, draw a mark on the line.

**STEP 3** Count the fourths from zero to 1 to label the distances from zero.

**STEP 4** Think: $\frac{1}{4}$ is 1 out of 4 equal lengths.
Draw a point at $\frac{1}{4}$ to represent the distance from 0 to $\frac{1}{4}$.
Label the point *G1*.

**STEP 5** Think: $\frac{3}{4}$ is 3 out of 4 equal lengths.
Draw a point at $\frac{3}{4}$ to represent the distance from 0 to $\frac{3}{4}$.
Label the point *G2*.

Chapter 8   467

## Example Complete the number line to name the point.

Hands On

**Materials** ■ color pencils

Write the fraction that names the point on the number line.

**Think:** This number line is divided into six equal lengths, or sixths.

The length of one equal part is _____.

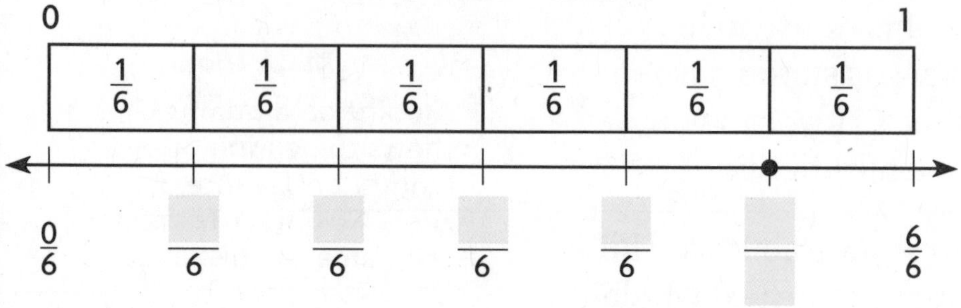


Shade the fraction strips to show the location of the point.

There are _____ out of _____ equal lengths shaded.
The shaded length shows $\frac{5}{6}$.

So, _____ names the point.

## Share and Show

MATH BOARD

1. Complete the number line. Draw a point to show $\frac{2}{3}$.

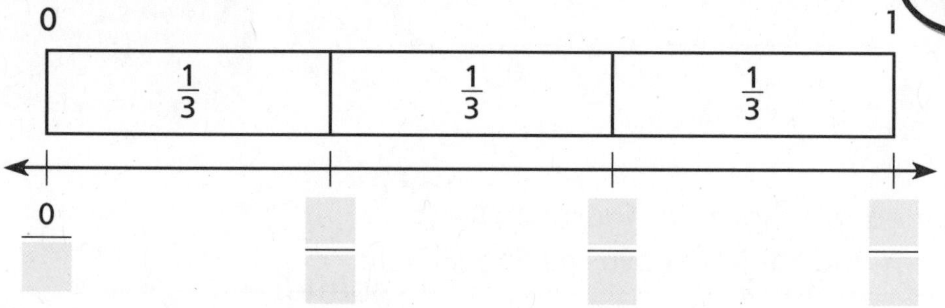


**Math Talk** MATHEMATICAL PRACTICES 4

**Use Models** What does the length between each mark on this number line represent?

**Write the fraction that names the point.**

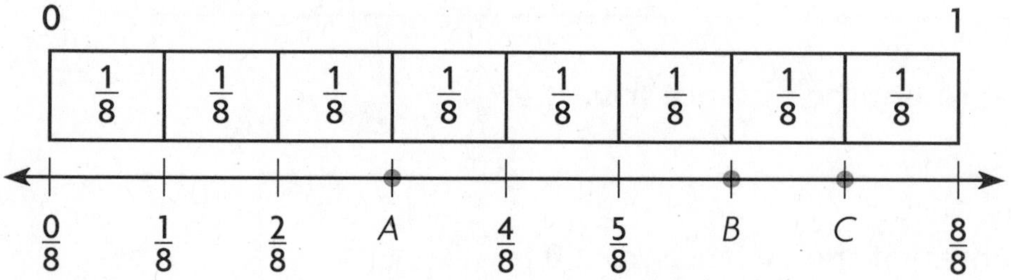


2. point *A* _____

3. point *B* _____

4. point *C* _____



© Houghton Mifflin Harcourt Publishing Company

Name _____

## On Your Own

**Use fraction strips to help you complete the number line. Then locate and draw a point for the fraction.**

**5.** $\frac{2}{6}$

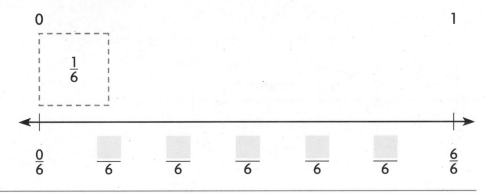

**6.** $\frac{2}{3}$

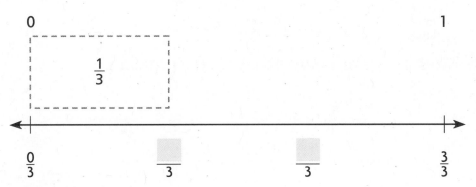

**Write the fraction that names the point.**

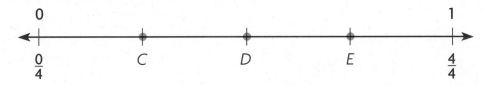

**7.** point $C$ _____    **8.** point $D$ _____    **9.** point $E$ _____

**10.** There is a walking trail at the park. Four laps around the trail is a distance of 1 mile. How many laps does it take to walk $\frac{3}{4}$ mile?

**11.** GO DEEPER A recipe for pasta makes enough for eight servings. How many servings can be made using $\frac{4}{8}$ of each ingredient in the recipe?

_____

## 🔑 Unlock the Problem

**12.** THINK SMARTER   Javia ran 8 laps around a track to run a total of 1 mile on Monday. How many laps will she need to run on Tuesday to run $\frac{3}{8}$ of a mile?

**a.** What do you need to find?

_____

_____

**b.** How will you use what you know about number lines to help you solve the problem?

_____

_____

_____

_____

**c.** MATHEMATICAL PRACTICE ④ **Use Models**  Make a model to solve the problem.

⟵————————————————⟶

**d.** Complete the sentences.

There are _____ laps in 1 mile.

Each lap represents _____ of a mile.

_____ laps represent the distance of three eighths of a mile.

So, Javia will need to run _____ laps to run $\frac{3}{8}$ of a mile.

---

**Personal Math Trainer**

**13.** THINK SMARTER + Locate and draw point *F* on the number line to represent the fraction $\frac{2}{4}$.

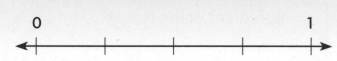

Name _____

## On Your Own

**Use fraction strips to help you complete the number line. Then locate and draw a point for the fraction.**

5. $\frac{2}{6}$

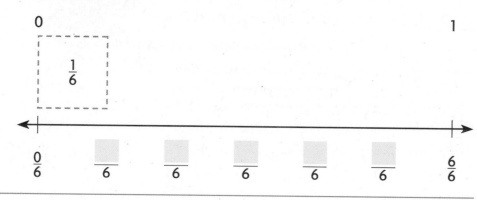

6. $\frac{2}{3}$

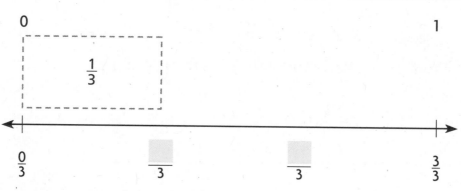

**Write the fraction that names the point.**

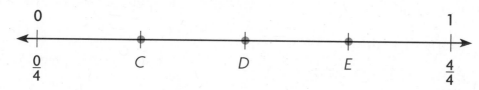

7. point $C$ _____

8. point $D$ _____

9. point $E$ _____

10. There is a walking trail at the park. Four laps around the trail is a distance of 1 mile. How many laps does it take to walk $\frac{3}{4}$ mile?

_____

11. **GO DEEPER** A recipe for pasta makes enough for eight servings. How many servings can be made using $\frac{4}{8}$ of each ingredient in the recipe?

_____

© Houghton Mifflin Harcourt Publishing Company

## 🔑 Unlock the Problem

12. **THINK SMARTER**  Javia ran 8 laps around a track to run a total of 1 mile on Monday. How many laps will she need to run on Tuesday to run $\frac{3}{8}$ of a mile?

a. What do you need to find?

_____

_____

_____

b. How will you use what you know about number lines to help you solve the problem?

_____

_____

_____

_____

c. **MATHEMATICAL PRACTICE ④** Use Models  Make a model to solve the problem.

d. Complete the sentences.

There are _____ laps in 1 mile.

Each lap represents _____ of a mile.

_____ laps represent the distance of three eighths of a mile.

So, Javia will need to run _____ laps to run $\frac{3}{8}$ of a mile.

**Personal Math Trainer**

13. **THINK SMARTER +**  Locate and draw point F on the number line to represent the fraction $\frac{2}{4}$.

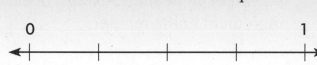

# Fractions on a Number Line

Common Core

COMMON CORE STANDARDS—3.NF.A.2a, 3.NF.A.2b *Develop understanding of fractions as numbers.*

**Use fraction strips to help you complete the number line. Then locate and draw a point for the fraction.**

1. $\frac{1}{3}$

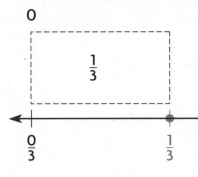

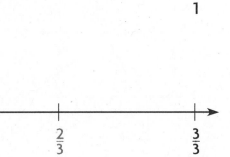

**Write the fraction that names the point.**

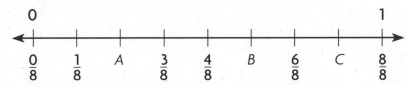

2. point $A$ _____     3. point $B$ _____     4. point $C$ _____

## Problem Solving

5. Jade ran 6 times around her neighborhood to complete a total of 1 mile. How many times will she need to run to complete $\frac{5}{6}$ of a mile?

_____

6. A missing fraction on a number line is located exactly halfway between $\frac{3}{6}$ and $\frac{5}{6}$. What is the missing fraction?

_____

7. **WRITE** ▸*Math*  Explain how showing fractions with models and a number line are alike and different.

_____

_____

## Lesson Check (3.NF.A.2a, 3.NF.A.2b)

1. What fraction names point *G* on the number line?

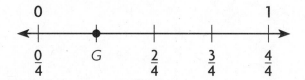

2. What fraction names point *R* on the number line?

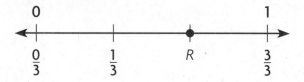

_____

_____

## Spiral Review (3.OA.B.5, 3.OA.C.7, 3.NF.A.1)

3. Each table in the cafeteria can seat 10 students. How many tables are needed to seat 40 students?

4. Use the Commutative Property of Multiplication to write a related number sentence.

$$4 \times 9 = 36$$

_____

_____

5. Pedro shaded part of a circle. What fraction names the shaded part?

6. Find the quotient.

$$8 \div 1 = \boxed{\phantom{00}}$$

_____

FOR MORE PRACTICE
GO TO THE
**Personal Math Trainer**

Name _____

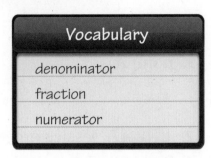

## Vocabulary

| Vocabulary |
| --- |
| denominator |
| fraction |
| numerator |

**Choose the best term from the box to complete the sentence.**

1. A _____ is a number that names part of a whole or part of a group. (p. 455)

2. The _____ tells how many equal parts are in the whole or in the group. (p. 461)

## Concepts and Skills

**Write the number of equal parts. Then write the name for the parts.** (3.NF.A.1)

3.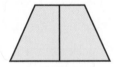

_____ equal parts

_____

4.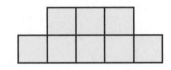

_____ equal parts

_____

5.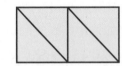

_____ equal parts

_____

**Write the number of equal parts in the whole. Then write the fraction that names the shaded part.** (3.NF.A.1)

6.

_____ equal parts

_____

7.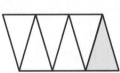

_____ equal parts

_____

8.

_____ equal parts

_____

© Houghton Mifflin Harcourt Publishing Company

Chapter 8    473

**Write the fraction that names the point.** (3.NF.A.2a, 3.NF.A.2b)

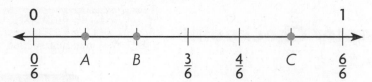

0                                      1

$\frac{0}{6}$   A   B   $\frac{3}{6}$   $\frac{4}{6}$   C   $\frac{6}{6}$

9. point A _____

10. point B _____

11. point C _____

12. 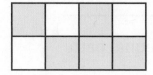 Jessica ordered a pizza. What fraction of the pizza has mushrooms? What fraction of the pizza does not have mushrooms? (3.NF.A.1)

_____

13. Which fraction names the shaded part?
(3.NF.A.1)

14. Six friends share 3 oatmeal squares equally. How much of an oatmeal square does each friend get? (3.NF.A.1)

_____

Name _____

# Relate Fractions and Whole Numbers

**Essential Question** When might you use a fraction greater than 1 or a whole number?

Common Core

**Number and Operations—Fractions—3.NF.A.3c** Also 3.NF.A.2, 3.NF.A.2b, 3.G.A.2

**MATHEMATICAL PRACTICES**
MP1, MP4, MP6, MP7

## Unlock the Problem

Steve ran 1 mile and Jenna ran $\frac{4}{4}$ of a mile. Did Steve and Jenna run the same distance?

**Locate 1 and $\frac{4}{4}$ on a number line.**

- Shade 4 lengths of $\frac{1}{4}$ and label the number line.

- Draw a point at 1 and $\frac{4}{4}$.

> **Math Idea**
> If two numbers are located at the same point on a number line, then they are equal and represent the same distance.

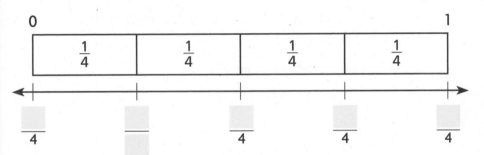

Since the distance _____ and _____ end at the same point, they are equal.

So, Steve and Jenna ran the _____ distance.

**Try This! Complete the number line. Locate and draw points at $\frac{3}{6}$, $\frac{6}{6}$, and 1.**

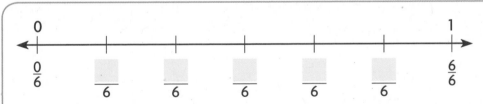

**A** Are $\frac{3}{6}$ and 1 equal? Explain.

**Think:** Do the distances end at the same point?

_____

_____

So, $\frac{3}{6}$ and 1 are _____.

**B** Are $\frac{6}{6}$ and 1 equal? Explain.

**Think:** Do the distances end at the same point?

_____

_____

So, $\frac{6}{6}$ and 1 are _____.

CONNECT The number of equal parts the whole is divided into is the denominator of a fraction. The number of parts being counted is the numerator. A **fraction greater than 1** has a numerator greater than its denominator.

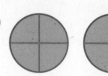 **Examples**

**Each shape is 1 whole. Write a whole number and a fraction greater than 1 for the parts that are shaded.**

Ⓐ

There are 2 wholes.

Each whole is divided into 4 equal parts, or fourths.     $2 = \frac{8}{4}$

There are _____ equal parts shaded.

Ⓑ

There are 3 wholes.

Each whole is divided into 1 equal part.     $3 = \frac{3}{1}$

There are _____ equal parts shaded.

1. Explain what *each whole is divided into 1 equal part* means in Example B.

_____

_____

**Read Math**

Read $\frac{3}{1}$ as *three ones*.

2. How do you divide a whole into 1 equal part?

_____

_____

**Try This!**

**Each shape is 1 whole. Write a whole number and a fraction greater than 1 for the parts that are shaded.**

Name _____

1. Each shape is 1 whole. Write a whole number and a fraction greater than 1 for the parts that are shaded.

There are _____ wholes.

Each whole is divided into _____ equal parts.

There are _____ equal parts shaded.

$\square = \dfrac{\square}{\square}$

**Use the number line to find whether the two numbers are equal. Write *equal* or *not equal*.**

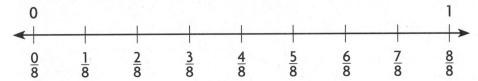

2. $\dfrac{1}{8}$ and $\dfrac{8}{8}$ _____

☑ 3. $\dfrac{8}{8}$ and 1 _____

☑ 4. 1 and $\dfrac{4}{8}$ _____

**On Your Own**

**Use the number line to find whether the two numbers are equal. Write *equal* or *not equal*.**

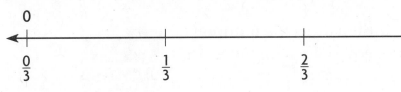

**Math Talk**

MATHEMATICAL PRACTICES ①

Evaluate How do you know whether the two fractions are equal or not equal when using a number line?

5. $\dfrac{0}{3}$ and 1 _____

6. 1 and $\dfrac{2}{3}$ _____

7. $\dfrac{3}{3}$ and 1 _____

**Each shape is 1 whole. Write a fraction for the parts that are shaded.**

8.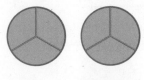

2 = _____

9.

1 = _____

10.

3 = _____

11.

2 = _____

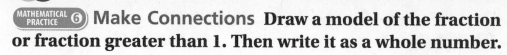
MATHEMATICAL PRACTICE 6 **Make Connections** Draw a model of the fraction or fraction greater than 1. Then write it as a whole number.

**12.** $\frac{8}{4}$ = _____

**13.** $\frac{6}{6}$ = _____

**14.** $\frac{5}{1}$ = _____

## Problem Solving • Applications (Real World)

**15.** GO DEEPER  Jeff rode his bike around a bike trail that was $\frac{1}{3}$ of a mile long. He rode around the trail 9 times. Write a fraction greater than 1 for the distance. How many miles did Jeff ride?

_____

**16.** THINK SMARTER  **What's the Error?**  Andrea drew the number line below. She said that $\frac{9}{8}$ and 1 are equal. Explain her error.

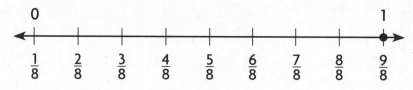

_____

**17.** THINK SMARTER  Each shape is 1 whole. Which numbers name the parts that are shaded? Mark all that apply.

(A) 4      (C) $\frac{26}{6}$      (E) $\frac{6}{4}$

(B) 6      (D) $\frac{24}{6}$

# Relate Fractions and Whole Numbers

Common Core  **COMMON CORE STANDARD—3.NF.A.3c**
*Develop an understanding of fractions as numbers.*

**Use the number line to find whether the two numbers are equal. Write *equal* or *not equal*.**

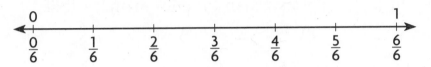

1. $\frac{0}{6}$ and 1

2. 1 and $\frac{6}{6}$

3. $\frac{1}{6}$ and $\frac{6}{6}$

_____not equal_____     _____     _____

**Each shape is 1 whole. Write a fraction for the parts that are shaded.**

4.

1 = _____

5.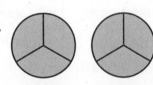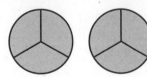

4 = _____

## Problem Solving Real World

6. Rachel jogged along a trail that was $\frac{1}{4}$ of a mile long. She jogged along the trail 8 times. How many miles did Rachel jog?

_____

7. Jon ran around a track that was $\frac{1}{8}$ of a mile long. He ran around the track 24 times. How many miles did Jon run?

_____

8. **WRITE** ▶*Math* Write a problem that uses a fraction greater than 1.

_____

_____

## Lesson Check (3.NF.A.3c)

1. Each shape is 1 whole. What fraction greater than 1 names the parts that are shaded?

_____

2. Each shape is 1 whole. What fraction greater than 1 names the parts that are shaded?

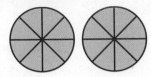

_____

## Spiral Review (3.OA.A.3, 3.OA.C.7, 3.NBT.A.2, 3.NF.A.1)

3. Tara has 598 pennies and 231 nickels. How many pennies and nickels does she have?

$$598 + 231$$

_____

_____

4. Dylan read 6 books. Kylie read double the number of books that Dylan read. How many books did Kylie read?

_____

_____

5. Alyssa divides a granola bar into halves. How many equal parts are there?

_____

6. There are 4 students in each small reading group. If there are 24 students in all, how many reading groups are there?

_____

FOR MORE PRACTICE
GO TO THE
Personal Math Trainer

# Fractions of a Group

**Essential Question** How can a fraction name part of a group?

Common Core  Number and Operations—
Fractions—3.NF.A.1
MATHEMATICAL PRACTICES
MP1, MP4, MP6

## 🔑 Unlock the Problem

Jake and Emma each have a collection of marbles.
What fraction of each collection is blue?

🔑 You can use a fraction to name part of a group.

| **Jake's Marbles** | **Emma's Marbles** |
|---|---|
|  |  |

number of
blue marbles → ☐ ← numerator
total number → 8 ← denominator
of marbles

bags of
blue marbles → ☐ ← numerator
total number → 4 ← denominator
of bags

**Read:** three eighths, or three out of eight

**Write:** $\frac{3}{8}$

**Read:** one fourth, or one out of four

**Write:** $\frac{1}{4}$

So, ____ of Jake's marbles
are blue.

So, ____ of Emma's marbles
are blue.

**Try This!** **Name part of a group.**

Draw 2 red counters and 6 yellow
counters.

Write the fraction of counters that are red.

☐ ← number of red counters

‾ ← total number of counters

Write the fraction of counters that are
not red.

☐ ← number of yellow counters

‾ ← total number of counters

So, ____ of the counters are red and ____ are not red.

## Fractions Greater Than 1

Sometimes a fraction can name more than a whole group.

Daniel collects baseballs. He has collected 8 so far. He puts them in cases that hold 4 baseballs each. What part of the baseball cases has Daniel filled?

**Think:** 1 case = 1

Daniel has two full cases of 4 baseballs each.

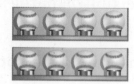

So, 2, or $\frac{8}{4}$, baseball cases are filled.

**Try This!** Complete the whole number and the fraction greater than 1 to name the part filled.

 A

**Think:** 1 pan = 1

_____, or $\dfrac{\phantom{x}}{6}$

B

**Think:** 1 box = 1

_____, or $\dfrac{\phantom{x}}{8}$

## Share and Show

1. What fraction of the counters are red? _____

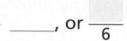

**Think:** How many red counters are there? How many counters are there in all?

**Math Talk**

MATHEMATICAL PRACTICES ⑥

Explain another way to name the fraction for Exercise 3.

**Write a fraction to name the red part of each group.**

2.     _____

3.  _____

Name _____

## Write a whole number and a fraction greater than 1 to name the part filled.

4.

Think: 1 carton = 1

_____   _____

5.

Think: 1 container = 1

_____   _____

## Write a fraction to name the blue part of each group.

6.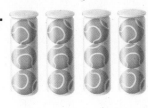

_____

7.

_____

8.

_____

9.

_____

## Write a whole number and a fraction greater than 1 to name the part filled.

10.

Think: 1 container = 1

_____   _____

11. **THINK SMARTER**

Think: 1 carton = 1

_____   _____

## Draw a quick picture on your MathBoard. Then write a fraction to name the shaded part of the group.

12. Draw 8 circles.
Shade 8 circles.

_____

13. Draw 8 triangles.
Make 4 groups.
Shade 1 group.

_____

14. Draw 4 rectangles.
Shade 2 rectangles.

_____

## Problem Solving • Applications

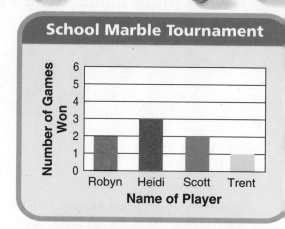

**School Marble Tournament**

**Use the graph for 15–16.**

15. **GO DEEPER**  The bar graph shows the winners of the Smith Elementary School Marble Tournament. How many games were played? What fraction of the games did Scott win?

_____    _____

16. **MATHEMATICAL PRACTICE ①** **Analyze**  What fraction of the games did Robyn NOT win?

_____

> **WRITE** ▸Math
> **Show Your Work**

17. **THINK SMARTER**  Li has 6 marbles. Of them, $\frac{1}{3}$ are blue. The rest are red. Draw a picture to show Li's marbles.

18. **WRITE** ▸Math  **What's the Question?**  A bag has 2 yellow cubes, 3 blue cubes, and 1 white cube. The answer is $\frac{1}{6}$.

_____

_____

19. **THINK SMARTER**  Makayla picked some flowers. What fraction of flowers are yellow or red? What fraction of the flowers are NOT yellow or red? Show your work.

_____

# Fractions of a Group

Write a fraction to name the shaded part
of each group.

Common Core

COMMON CORE STANDARD—3.NF.A.1
Develop understanding of fractions as
numbers.

1. 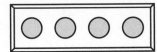  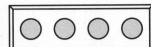 $\dfrac{6}{8}$ or $\dfrac{3}{4}$

2.

_____

Write a whole number and a fraction greater
than 1 to name the part filled. Think: 1 container = 1

3.

4.

_____     _____          _____

Draw a quick picture. Then, write a fraction
to name the shaded part of the group.

5. Draw 4 circles.
   Shade 2 circles.

6. Draw 6 circles.
   Make 3 groups.
   Shade 1 group.

_____          _____

## Problem Solving (Real World)

7. Brian has 3 basketball cards and
   5 baseball cards. What fraction of
   Brian's cards are baseball cards?

8. **WRITE** ▸ *Math*  Draw a set of objects
   where you can find a fractional part of
   the group using the total number of
   objects and by using subgroups.

_____

## Lesson Check (3.NF.A.1)

1. What fraction of the group is shaded?

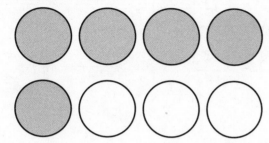

2. What fraction of the group is shaded?

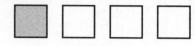

---

## Spiral Review (3.OA.A.3, 3.OA.C.7, 3.NBT.A.2)

3. What multiplication number sentence does the array represent?

☐ ☐ ☐ ☐ ☐ ☐
☐ ☐ ☐ ☐ ☐ ☐
☐ ☐ ☐ ☐ ☐ ☐

_____

_____

_____

4. Juan has 436 baseball cards and 189 football cards. How many more baseball cards than football cards does Juan have?

_____

_____

_____

5. Sydney bought 3 bottles of glitter. Each bottle of glitter cost $6. How much did Sydney spend on the bottles of glitter?

_____

6. Add.

$$\begin{array}{r} 262 \\ +\ 119 \\ \hline \end{array}$$

© Houghton Mifflin Harcourt Publishing Company

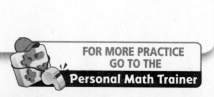

FOR MORE PRACTICE
GO TO THE
Personal Math Trainer

Name _____

# Find Part of a Group Using Unit Fractions

**Essential Question** How can a fraction tell how many are in part of a group?

 **Common Core** Number and Operations—Fractions—3.NF.A.1

**MATHEMATICAL PRACTICES**
MP3, MP4, MP6

## Unlock the Problem Real World

Audrey buys a bouquet of 12 flowers. One third of them are red. How many of the flowers are red?

- How many flowers does Audrey buy in all? _____
- What fraction of the flowers are red? _____

## Activity

**Materials** ■ two-color counters ■ MathBoard

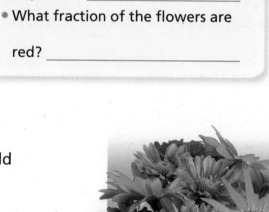

- Put 12 counters on your MathBoard.

- Since you want to find $\frac{1}{3}$ of the group, there should be _____ equal groups. Draw the counters below.

- Circle one of the groups to show _____.
  Then count the number of counters in that group.

There are _____ counters in 1 group.    $\frac{1}{3}$ of 12 = _____

So, _____ of the flowers are red.

- What if Audrey buys a bouquet of 9 flowers and one third of them are yellow? Use your MathBoard and counters to find how many of the flowers are yellow.

_____

 **Math Talk**

**MATHEMATICAL PRACTICES ③**

**Apply** How can you use the numerator and denominator in a fraction to find part of a group?

## Try This! Find part of a group.

Raul picks 20 flowers from his mother's garden. One fourth of them are purple. How many of the flowers are purple?

**STEP 1** Draw a row of 4 counters.

Think: To find $\frac{1}{4}$, make 4 equal groups.

**STEP 2** Continue to draw as many rows of 4 counters as you can until you have 20 counters.

**STEP 3** Then circle _____ equal groups.

Think: Each group represents $\frac{1}{4}$ of the flowers.

There are _____ counters in 1 group.

$\frac{1}{4}$ of 20 = _____

$$\frac{1}{4} \qquad \frac{1}{4} \qquad \frac{1}{4} \qquad \frac{1}{4}$$

So, _____ of the flowers are purple.

 **Share and Show**

**1.** Use the model to find $\frac{1}{2}$ of 8. _____

Think: How many counters are in 1 of the 2 equal groups?

**Circle equal groups to solve. Count the number of flowers in 1 group.**

**2.** $\frac{1}{4}$ of 8 = _____

✓**3.** $\frac{1}{3}$ of 6 = _____

✓**4.** $\frac{1}{6}$ of 12 = _____

Name _____

## On Your Own

**Circle equal groups to solve. Count the number of flowers in 1 group.**

**5.** $\frac{1}{4}$ of 12 = _____

**6.** $\frac{1}{3}$ of 15 = _____

**7.** $\frac{1}{4}$ of 16 = _____

**8.** $\frac{1}{6}$ of 30 = _____

**9.** $\frac{1}{3}$ of 12 = _____

**10.** THINK SMARTER

$\frac{1}{2}$ of 6 = _____

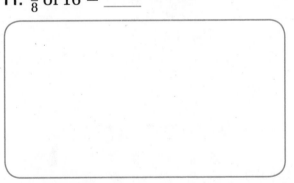

THINK SMARTER   **Draw counters. Then circle equal groups to solve.**

**11.** $\frac{1}{8}$ of 16 = _____

**12.** $\frac{1}{6}$ of 24 = _____

**13.** GO DEEPER   Gerry has 50 sports trading cards. Of those cards, $\frac{1}{5}$ of them are baseball cards, $\frac{1}{10}$ of them are football cards, and the rest are basketball cards. How many more basketball cards than baseball cards does Gerry have?

_____

**14.** GO DEEPER   Barbara has a mixed garden that has 16 rows of different flowers and vegetables. One-fourth of the rows are lettuce, $\frac{1}{8}$ of the rows are pumpkins, and $\frac{1}{2}$ of the rows are red tulips. The other rows are carrots. How many rows of carrots are in Barbara's garden?

_____

© Houghton Mifflin Harcourt Publishing Company

**Chapter 8 • Lesson 8   489**

## Problem Solving • Applications

**Use the table for 15–16.**

| Flower Seeds Bought | |
|---|---|
| Name | Number of Packs |
| Ryan | 8 |
| Brooke | 12 |
| Cole | 20 |

15. **MATHEMATICAL PRACTICE ④  Use Diagrams** One fourth of the seed packs Ryan bought are violet seeds. How many packs of violet seeds did Ryan buy? Draw counters to solve.

_____

16. **GO DEEPER** One third of Brooke's seed packs and one fourth of Cole's seed packs are daisy seeds. How many packs of daisy seeds did they buy altogether? Explain how you know.

| WRITE ▸ Math
**Show Your Work**

_____

_____

_____

17. **THINK SMARTER  Sense or Nonsense?** Sophia bought 12 pots. One sixth of them are green. Sophia said she bought 2 green pots. Does her answer make sense? Explain how you know.

_____

_____

_____

18. **THINK SMARTER +**  A florist has 24 sunflowers in a container. Mrs. Mason buys $\frac{1}{4}$ of the flowers. Mr. Kim buys $\frac{1}{3}$ of the flowers. How many sunflowers are left? Explain how you solved the problem.

Personal Math Trainer

_____

_____

_____

# Find Part of a Group Using Unit Fractions

**COMMON CORE STANDARD—3.NF.A.1**
Develop understanding of fractions as numbers.

**Circle equal groups to solve. Count the number of items in 1 group.**

1. $\frac{1}{4}$ of 12 = ___3___

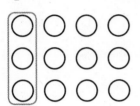

2. $\frac{1}{8}$ of 16 = _____

3. $\frac{1}{3}$ of 12 = _____

4. $\frac{1}{3}$ of 9 = _____

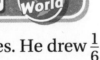

## Problem Solving (Real World)

5. Marco drew 24 pictures. He drew $\frac{1}{6}$ of them in art class. How many pictures did Marco draw in art class?

_____

6. Caroline has 16 marbles. One eighth of them are blue. How many of Caroline's marbles are blue?

_____

7. **WRITE** ▸ Math  Explain how to find which is greater: $\frac{1}{4}$ of 12 or $\frac{1}{3}$ of 12.

_____

_____

## Lesson Check (3.NF.A.1)

**1.** Ms. Davis made 12 blankets for her grandchildren. One third of the blankets are blue. How many blue blankets did she make?

○ ○ ○
○ ○ ○
○ ○ ○
○ ○ ○

_____

**2.** Jackson mowed 16 lawns. One fourth of the lawns are on Main Street. How many lawns on Main Street did Jackson mow?

○ ○ ○ ○
○ ○ ○ ○
○ ○ ○ ○
○ ○ ○ ○

_____

## Spiral Review (3.OA.A.7, 3.NBT.A.1, 3.NBT.A.2)

**3.** Find the difference.

$$\begin{array}{r} 509 \\ -175 \\ \hline \end{array}$$

_____

**4.** Find the quotient.

$$6\overline{)54}$$

_____

**5.** There are 226 pets entered in the pet show. What is 226 rounded to the nearest hundred?

**6.** Ladonne made 36 muffins. She put the same number of muffins on each of 4 plates. How many muffins did she put on each plate?

_____

_____

FOR MORE PRACTICE
GO TO THE
**Personal Math Trainer**

Name _____

# Problem Solving • Find the Whole Group Using Unit Fractions

**Essential Question** How can you use the strategy *draw a diagram* to solve fraction problems?

**Number and Operations—Fractions—3.NF.A.1**

**MATHEMATICAL PRACTICES**
MP1, MP2, MP8

## Unlock the Problem

Cameron has 4 clown fish in his fish tank. One third of the fish in the tank are clown fish. How many fish does Cameron have in his tank?

Use the graphic organizer to help you solve the problem.

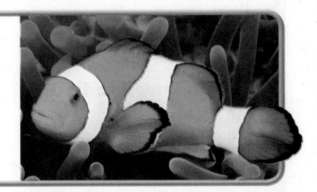

---

### Read the Problem

**What do I need to find?**

I need to find _____ are in Cameron's fish tank.

**What information do I need to use?**

Cameron has _____ clown fish.

_____ of the fish in the tank are clown fish.

**How will I use the information?**

I will use the information in the problem

to draw a _____ .

### Solve the Problem

**Describe how to draw a diagram to solve.**

The denominator in $\frac{1}{3}$ tells you

that there are _____ equal parts in the whole group. Draw 3 circles to

show _____ equal parts.

Since 4 fish are $\frac{1}{3}$ of the whole group,

draw _____ counters in the first circle.

Since there are _____ counters

in the first circle, draw _____ counters in each of the remaining circles. Then find the total number of counters.

So, Cameron has _____ fish in his tank.

Chapter 8    493

# Try Another Problem

A pet store has 2 gray rabbits. One eighth of the rabbits at the pet store are gray. How many rabbits does the pet store have?

| Read the Problem | Solve the Problem |
|---|---|
| **What do I need to find?** | |
| **What information do I need to use?** | |
| **How will I use the information?** | |

1. **MATHEMATICAL PRACTICE 8** **Draw Conclusions**  How do you know that your answer is reasonable?

   _____

   _____

2. How did your diagram help you solve the problem? _____

   _____

Math Talk

**MATHEMATICAL PRACTICES 1**

**Make Sense of Problems** Suppose $\frac{1}{2}$ of the rabbits are gray. How can you find the number of rabbits at the pet store?

Name _____

## Unlock the Problem

✓ Circle the question.
✓ Underline important facts.
✓ Put the problem in your own words.
✓ Choose a strategy you know.

1. Lily has 3 dog toys that are red. One fourth of all her dog toys are red. How many dog toys does Lily have?

   **First,** draw _____ circles to show _____ equal parts.

   **Next,** draw _____ toys in _____ circle since

   _____ circle represents the number of red toys.

   **Last,** draw _____ toys in each of the remaining circles. Find the total number of toys.

   So, Lily has _____ dog toys.

2. **THINK SMARTER** What if Lily has 4 toys that are red? How many dog toys would she have?

   _____

✓ 3. The pet store sells bags of pet food. There are 4 bags of cat food. One sixth of the bags of food are cat food. How many bags of pet food does the pet store have?

   _____

✓ 4. Rachel owns 2 parakeets. One fourth of all her birds are parakeets. How many birds does Rachel own?

   _____

© Houghton Mifflin Harcourt Publishing Company

## On Your Own

5. **THINK SMARTER** Before lunchtime, Abigail and Teresa each read some pages from different books. Abigail read 5, or one fifth, of the pages in her book. Teresa read 6, or one sixth, of the pages in her book. Whose book had more pages? How many more pages?

**WRITE** ▸ *Math* · **Show Your Work**

_____

6. **MATHEMATICAL PRACTICE ②** **Represent a Problem** Six friends share 5 meat pies. Each friend first eats half of a meat pie. How much more meat pie does each friend need to eat to finish all the meat pies and share them equally? Draw a quick picture to solve.

_____

7. **GO DEEPER** Braden bought 4 packs of dog treats. He gave 4 treats to his neighbor's dog. Now Braden has 24 treats left for his dog. How many dog treats were in each pack? Explain how you know.

_____

_____

_____

_____

8. **THINK SMARTER** Two hats are $\frac{1}{3}$ of the group. How many hats are in the whole group?

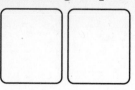

_____ hats

Name _____

# Problem Solving • Find the Whole Group Using Unit Fractions

**COMMON CORE STANDARD**—3.NF.A.1
*Develop understanding of fractions as numbers.*

**Draw a quick picture to solve.**

1. Katrina has 2 blue ribbons for her hair. One fourth of all her ribbons are blue. How many ribbons does Katrina have in all?

   _____8 ribbons_____

2. One eighth of Tony's books are mystery books. He has 3 mystery books. How many books does Tony have in all?

   _____

3. Brianna has 4 pink bracelets. One third of all her bracelets are pink. How many bracelets does Brianna have?

   _____

4. Ramal filled 3 pages in a stamp album. This is one sixth of the pages in the album. How many pages are there in Ramal's stamp album?

   _____

5. Jeff helped repair one half of the bicycles in a bike shop last week. If Jeff worked on 5 bicycles, how many bicycles did the shop repair last week?

   _____

6. **WRITE** ▸*Math* Write a problem about a group of objects in your classroom. Tell how many are in one equal part of the group. Solve your problem. Draw a diagram to help you.

   _____

   _____

## Lesson Check (3.NF.A.1)

**1.** A zoo has 2 male lions. One sixth of the lions are male lions. How many lions are there at the zoo?

_____

**2.** Max has 5 red model cars. One third of his model cars are red. How many model cars does Max have?

_____

## Spiral Review (3.OA.A.3, 3.NBT.A.1, 3.NBT.A.2, 3.NF.A.1)

**3.** There are 382 trees in the local park. What is the number of trees rounded to the nearest hundred?

**4.** The Jones family is driving 458 miles on their vacation. So far, they have driven 267 miles. How many miles do they have left to drive?

$$
\begin{array}{r}
458 \\
-\ 267 \\
\hline
\end{array}
$$

_____

_____

**5.** Ken has 6 different colors of marbles. He has 9 marbles of each color. How many marbles does Ken have in all?

**6.** Eight friends share two pizzas equally. How much of a pizza does each friend get?

_____

_____

FOR MORE PRACTICE
GO TO THE
**Personal Math Trainer**

Name _____

1. Each shape is divided into equal parts. Select the shapes that show thirds. Mark all that apply.

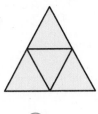  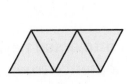 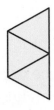

   Ⓐ          Ⓑ          Ⓒ          Ⓓ

2. What fraction names the shaded part of the shape?

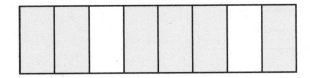

   Ⓐ    8 sixths

   Ⓑ    8 eighths

   Ⓒ    6 eighths

   Ⓓ    2 sixths

3. Omar shaded a model to show the part of the lawn that he finished mowing. What fraction names the shaded part? Explain how you know how to write the fraction.

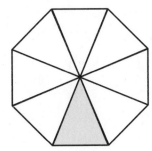

_____

_____

**4.** What fraction names point *A* on the number line?

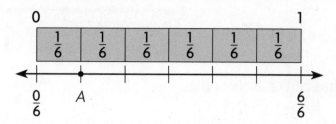

_____

**5.** Jamal folded this piece of paper into equal parts.
Circle the word that makes the sentence true.

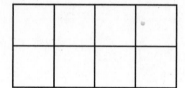

The paper is folded into
| sixths |
| --- |
| eighths |
| fourths |
.

**6.** Caleb took 18 photos at the zoo. One sixth of his
photos are of giraffes. How many of Caleb's photos are
of giraffes?

_____ photos

**7.** Three teachers share 2 packs of paper equally.

How much paper does each teacher get? Mark all
that apply.

Ⓐ   3 halves of a pack

Ⓑ   2 thirds of a pack

Ⓒ   3 sixths of a pack

Ⓓ   1 half of a pack

Ⓔ   1 third of a pack

**8.** Lilly shaded this design.

Select one number from each column to show the part of the design that Lilly shaded.

| Numerator | Denominator |
|---|---|
| ○ 1 | ○ 3 |
| ○ 3 | ○ 4 |
| ○ 5 | ○ 5 |
| ○ 6 | ○ 6 |

**9.** Marcus baked a loaf of banana bread for a party. He cut the loaf into equal size pieces. At the end of the party, there were 6 pieces left. Explain how you can find the number of pieces in the whole loaf if Marcus told you that $\frac{1}{3}$ of the loaf was left. Use a drawing to show your work.

_____

_____

_____

_____

**10.** The model shows one whole. What fraction of the model is NOT shaded?

_____

**11.** Together, Amy and Thea make up $\frac{1}{4}$ of the midfielders on the soccer team. How many midfielders are on the team? Show your work.

_____ midfielders

**12.** Six friends share 4 apples equally. How much apple does each friend get?

_____

**13.** Each shape is 1 whole.

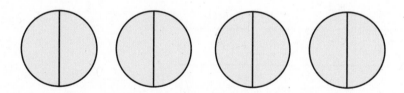

For numbers 13a–13e, choose Yes or No to show whether the number names the parts that are shaded.

13a.  4            ○ Yes        ○ No

13b.  8            ○ Yes        ○ No

13c.  $\frac{8}{2}$            ○ Yes        ○ No

13d.  $\frac{8}{4}$            ○ Yes        ○ No

13e.  $\frac{2}{8}$            ○ Yes        ○ No

**14.** Alex has 3 baseballs. He brings 2 baseballs to school. What fraction of his baseballs does Alex bring to school?

_____

**15.** GO DEEPER   Janeen and Nicole each made fruit salad for a school event.

**Part A**

Janeen used 16 pieces of fruit to make her salad. If $\frac{1}{4}$ of the fruits were peaches, how many peaches did she use? Make a drawing to show your work.

_____ peaches

**Part B**

Nicole used 24 pieces of fruit. If $\frac{1}{6}$ of them were peaches, how many peaches in all did Janeen and Nicole use to make their fruit salads? Explain how you found your answer.

_____

_____

**16.** There are 8 rows of chairs in the auditorium. Three of the rows are empty. What fraction of the rows are empty?

_____

**17.** Tara ran 3 laps around her neighborhood for a total of 1 mile yesterday. Today she wants to run $\frac{2}{3}$ of a mile. How many laps will she need to run around her neighborhood?

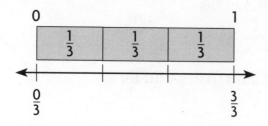

_____ laps

**18.** Gary painted some shapes.

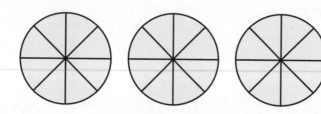

Select one number from each column to show a fraction greater than 1 that names the parts Gary painted.

| Numerator | Denominator |
|-----------|-------------|
| ○ 3 | ○ 3 |
| ○ 4 | ○ 4 |
| ○ 8 | ○ 8 |
| ○ 24 | ○ 24 |

**Personal Math Trainer**

**19.** THINK SMARTER ➕  Angelo rode his bike around a bike trail that was $\frac{1}{4}$ of a mile long. He rode his bike around the trail 8 times. Angelo says he rode a total of $\frac{8}{4}$ miles. Teresa says he is wrong and that he actually rode 2 miles. Who is correct? Use words and drawings to explain how you know.

_____

_____

_____

_____

_____

# Chapter 9 Compare Fractions

 Show What You Know

 **Personal Math Trainer** Online Assessment and Intervention

Check your understanding of important skills.

Name _____

▶ **Halves and Fourths** (1.G.A.3)

1. Find the shape that is divided into 2 equal parts. Color $\frac{1}{2}$.

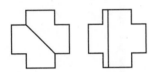

2. Find the shape that is divided into 4 equal parts. Color $\frac{1}{4}$.

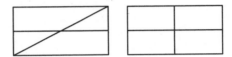

▶ **Parts of a Whole** Write the number of shaded parts and the number of equal parts. (2.G.A.2)

3.  ____ shaded parts

____ equal parts

4.  ____ shaded parts

____ equal parts

▶ **Fractions of a Whole**

Write the fraction that names the shaded part of each shape. (3.NF.A.1)

5.  ____

6. ____

7. ____

 **Math in the Real World**

Hannah keeps her marbles in bags with 4 marbles in each bag. She writes $\frac{3}{4}$ to show the number of red marbles in each bag. Find another fraction to name the number of red marbles in 2 bags.

© Houghton Mifflin Harcourt Publishing Company

**Chapter 9** 505

## Vocabulary Builder

▶ **Visualize It**

Complete the flow map by using the words with a ✓.

### Fractions and Whole Numbers

| What is it? | | What are some examples? |
|---|---|---|

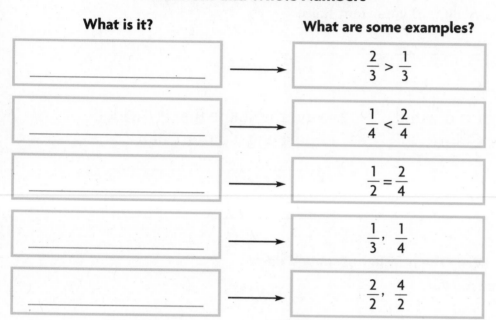

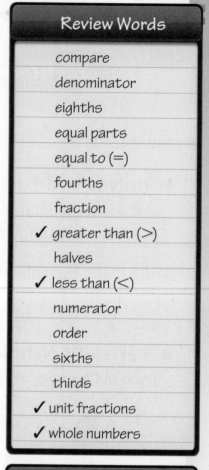

▶ **Understand Vocabulary**

Write the review word or preview word that answers the riddle.

1. We are two fractions that name the same amount.

   _____

2. I am the part of a fraction above the line. I tell how many parts are being counted.

   _____

3. I am the part of a fraction below the line. I tell how many equal parts are in the whole or in the group.

   _____

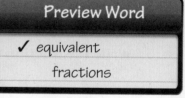

• **Interactive Student Edition**
• **Multimedia eGlossary**

# Chapter 9 Vocabulary

**denominator**

denominador

11

**Eighths**

octavos

17

**Equal Parts**

partes iguales

21

**equivalent fractions**

fracciones equivalentes

23

**greater than (>)**

mayor que

31

**less than (<)**

menor que

41

**numerator**

numerador

53

**unit fraction**

fracción unitaria

79

These are eighths

The part of a fraction below the line, which tells how many equal parts there are in the whole or in the group

Example: $\frac{1}{5}$ ← denominator

---

Two or more fractions that name the same amount

Example: $\frac{1}{2}$ and $\frac{3}{6}$ are equivalent fractions

Parts that are exactly the same size

6 equal parts

---

A symbol used to compare two numbers when the lesser number is given first

Example:
Read $3 < 7$ as "three is less than seven."

A symbol used to compare two numbers when the greater number is given first

Example:
Read $6 > 4$ as "six is greater than four."

---

A fraction that has 1 as its top number, or numerator

Example: $\frac{1}{3}$ is a unit fraction

The part of a fraction above the line, which tells how many parts are being counted

Example: $\frac{1}{5}$ ← numerator

# Pick It

**Word Box**
denominator
eighths
equal parts
equivalent
  fractions
greater than (>)
less than (<)
numerator
unit fractions

For 3 players

## Materials

• 4 sets of word cards

## How to Play

1. Each player is dealt 5 cards. The remaining cards are a draw pile.

2. To take a turn, ask any player if he or she has a word that matches one of your word cards.

3. If the player has the word, he or she gives the card to you, and you must define the word.
   • If you are correct, keep the card and put the matching pair in front of you. Take another turn.
   • If you are wrong, return the card. Your turn is over.

4. If the player does not have the word, he or she answers, "Pick it." Then you take a card from the draw pile.

5. If the card you draw matches one of your word cards, follow the directions for Step 3 above. If it does not, your turn is over.

6. The game is over when one player has no cards left. The player with the most pairs wins.

# The Write Way

### Reflect

**Choose one idea. Write about it.**

- Juan swam $\frac{3}{5}$ of a mile, and Greg swam $\frac{3}{8}$ of a mile. Explain how you know who swam farther.

- Explain how to compare two fractions.

- Write two examples of equivalent fractions and explain how you know they are equivalent.

Name _____

# Problem Solving • Compare Fractions

**Essential Question** How can you use the strategy *act it out* to solve comparison problems?

Common Core · **Number and Operations— Fractions—3.NF.A.3d** *Also 3.NF.A.1*
MATHEMATICAL PRACTICES
**MP2, MP4, MP5, MP6**

## Unlock the Problem

Mary and Vincent climbed up a rock wall at the park. Mary climbed $\frac{3}{4}$ of the way up the wall. Vincent climbed $\frac{3}{8}$ of the way up the wall. Who climbed higher?

You can act out the problem by using manipulatives to help you compare fractions.

**Remember**
$<$ is less than
$>$ is greater than
$=$ is equal to

### Read the Problem

#### What do I need to find?

_____

#### What information do I need to use?

Mary climbed _____ of the way.

Vincent climbed _____ of the way.

#### How will I use the information?

I will use _____

and _____ the lengths of

the models to find who climbed

_____.

### Solve the Problem

#### Record the steps you used to solve the problem.

| 1 |
|---|

| $\frac{1}{4}$ | $\frac{1}{4}$ | $\frac{1}{4}$ |
|---|---|---|

| $\frac{1}{8}$ | $\frac{1}{8}$ | $\frac{1}{8}$ |
|---|---|---|

Compare the lengths.

_____ ◯ _____

The length of the $\frac{3}{4}$ model is _____

than the length of the $\frac{3}{8}$ model.

So, _____ climbed higher on the rock wall.

**Math Talk**

MATHEMATICAL PRACTICES ④

**Use Models** When comparing fractions using fraction strips, how do you know which fraction is the lesser fraction?

# 🔓 Try Another Problem

Students at day camp are decorating paper circles for placemats. Tracy finished $\frac{3}{6}$ of her placemat. Kim finished $\frac{5}{6}$ of her placemat. Who finished more of her placemat?

| Read the Problem | Solve the Problem |
|---|---|
| **What do I need to find?** | **Record the steps you used to solve the problem.** |
| **What information do I need to use?** | |
| **How will I use the information?** | |

**Math Talk**

MATHEMATICAL PRACTICES ②

Use Reasoning How do you know that $\frac{5}{6}$ is greater than $\frac{3}{6}$ without using models?

1. How did your model help you solve the problem? _____

_____

2. Tracy and Kim each had a carton of milk with lunch. Tracy drank $\frac{5}{8}$ of her milk. Kim drank $\frac{7}{8}$ of her milk. Who drank more of her milk? Explain.

_____

_____

Name _____

## Unlock the Problem

✓ Circle the question.
✓ Underline important facts.
✓ Act out the problem using manipulatives.

1. At the park, people can climb a rope ladder to its top. Rosa climbed $\frac{2}{8}$ of the way up the ladder. Justin climbed $\frac{2}{6}$ of the way up the ladder. Who climbed higher on the rope ladder?

**First**, what are you asked to find?

_____

**Then**, model and compare the fractions. **Think:** Compare $\frac{2}{8}$ and $\frac{2}{6}$.

**Last**, find the greater fraction.

____ ◯ ____

So, _____ climbed higher on the rope ladder.

2. What if Cara also tried the rope ladder and climbed $\frac{2}{4}$ of the way up? Who climbed highest on the rope ladder: Rosa, Justin, or Cara? Explain how you know.

_____

_____

_____

_____

### On Your Own

3. **MATHEMATICAL PRACTICE ⑤ Use a Concrete Model** Ted walked $\frac{2}{3}$ mile to his soccer game. Then he walked $\frac{1}{3}$ mile to his friend's house. Which distance is shorter? Explain how you know.

_____

_____

**Use the table for 4–5.**

4. **GoDEEPER** Suri is spreading jam on 8 biscuits for breakfast. The table shows the fraction of biscuits spread with each jam flavor. Which flavor did Suri use on the most biscuits?

   Hint: Use 8 counters to model the biscuits.

   _____

| Suri's Biscuits | |
| --- | --- |
| Jam Flavor | Fraction of Biscuits |
| Peach | $\frac{3}{8}$ |
| Raspberry | $\frac{4}{8}$ |
| Strawberry | $\frac{1}{8}$ |

5. **WRITE** ▸Math **What's the Question?** The answer is strawberry.

   _____

   _____

· **WRITE** ▸Math · **Show Your Work** ·

6. **THINK SMARTER** Suppose Suri had also used plum jam on the biscuits. She frosted $\frac{1}{2}$ of the biscuits with peach jam, $\frac{1}{4}$ with raspberry jam, $\frac{1}{8}$ with strawberry jam, and $\frac{1}{8}$ with plum jam. Which flavor of jam did Suri use on the most biscuits?

   _____

7. Ms. Gordon has many snack bar recipes. One recipe uses $\frac{1}{3}$ cup oatmeal, $\frac{1}{4}$ cup of milk, and $\frac{1}{2}$ cup flour. Which ingredient will Ms. Gordon use the most of?

   _____

8. **THINK SMARTER** Rick lives $\frac{4}{6}$ mile from school. Noah lives $\frac{3}{6}$ mile from school.

   Use the fractions and symbols to show which distance is longer.

   $\frac{3}{6}$ , $\frac{4}{6}$ , $<$ and $>$    □ ○ □

## Problem Solving • Compare Fractions

**Common Core** COMMON CORE STANDARD—3.NF.A.3d
*Develop understanding of fractions as numbers.*

**Solve.**

1. Luis skates $\frac{2}{3}$ mile from his home to school. Isabella skates $\frac{2}{4}$ mile to get to school. Who skates farther?

   **Think:** Use fraction strips to act it out.

   _____ Luis _____

2. Sandra makes a pizza. She puts mushrooms on $\frac{2}{8}$ of the pizza. She adds green peppers to $\frac{5}{8}$ of the pizza. Which topping covers more of the pizza?

   _____

3. The jars of paint in the art room have different amounts of paint. The green paint jar is $\frac{4}{8}$ full. The purple paint jar is $\frac{4}{6}$ full. Which paint jar is less full?

   _____

4. Jan has a recipe for bread. She uses $\frac{2}{3}$ cup of flour and $\frac{1}{3}$ cup of chopped onion. Which ingredient does she use more of, flour or onion?

   _____

5. **WRITE** ▸*Math* Explain how you can find whether $\frac{5}{6}$ or $\frac{5}{8}$ is greater.

   _____

   _____

## Lesson Check (3.NF.A.3d)

1. Ali and Jonah collect seashells in identical buckets. When they are finished, Ali's bucket is $\frac{2}{6}$ full and Jonah's bucket is $\frac{3}{6}$ full. Compare the fractions using >, < or =.

$$\frac{3}{6} \bigcirc \frac{2}{6}$$

2. Rosa paints a wall in her bedroom. She puts green paint on $\frac{5}{8}$ of the wall and blue paint on $\frac{3}{8}$ of the wall. Compare the fractions using >, < or =.

$$\frac{5}{8} \bigcirc \frac{3}{8}$$

## Spiral Review (3.OA.B.6, 3.OA.D.9, 3.NF.A.1)

3. Dan divides a pie into eighths. How many equal parts are there?

_____

4. Draw lines to divide the circle into 4 equal parts.

5. Charles places 30 pictures on his bulletin board in 6 equal rows. How many pictures are in each row?

6. Describe a pattern in the table.

| Tables | 1 | 2 | 3 | 4 | 5 |
|--------|---|----|----|----|----|
| Chairs | 5 | 10 | 15 | 20 | 25 |

© Houghton Mifflin Harcourt Publishing Company

FOR MORE PRACTICE
GO TO THE
Personal Math Trainer

Name _____

# Compare Fractions with the Same Denominator

Common Core  **Number and Operations—Fractions—3.NF.A.3d** *Also 3.NF.A.1, 3.NF.A.2b*
**MATHEMATICAL PRACTICES**
MP2, MP3, MP6

**Essential Question** How can you compare fractions with the same denominator?

## Unlock the Problem (Real World)

Jeremy and Christina are each making a quilt block. Both blocks are the same size and both are made of 4 equal-size squares. $\frac{2}{4}$ of Jeremy's squares are green. $\frac{1}{4}$ of Christina's squares are green. Whose quilt block has more green squares?

* Circle the two fractions you need to compare.
* How are the two fractions alike?

_____

**Compare fractions of a whole.**

* Shade $\frac{2}{4}$ of Jeremy's quilt block.
* Shade $\frac{1}{4}$ of Christina's quilt block.
* Compare $\frac{2}{4}$ and $\frac{1}{4}$.

The greater fraction will have the larger amount of the whole shaded.

$$\frac{2}{4} \bigcirc \frac{1}{4}$$

**Jeremy's Quilt Block**  **Christina's Quilt Block**

**Math Idea**
You can compare two fractions when they refer to the same whole or to groups that are the same size.

So, _____ quilt block has more green squares.

**Compare fractions of a group.**

Jen and Maggie each have 6 buttons.

* Shade 3 of Jen's buttons to show the number of buttons that are red. Shade 5 of Maggie's buttons to show the number that are red.
* Write a fraction to show the number of red buttons in each group. Compare the fractions.

**Jen's Buttons**

**Maggie's Buttons**

There are the same number of buttons in each group, so you can count the number of red buttons to compare the fractions.

$$3 < \underline{\quad}, \text{ so } \frac{\square}{6} < \frac{\square}{6}.$$

So, _____ has a greater fraction of red buttons.

🔑 **Use fraction strips and a number line.**

At the craft store, one piece of ribbon is $\frac{2}{8}$ yard long. Another piece of ribbon is $\frac{7}{8}$ yard long. If Sean wants to buy the longer piece of ribbon, which piece should he buy?

**Compare $\frac{2}{8}$ and $\frac{7}{8}$.**

- Shade the fraction strips to show the locations of $\frac{2}{8}$ and $\frac{7}{8}$.

- Draw and label points on the number line to represent the distances $\frac{2}{8}$ and $\frac{7}{8}$.

- Compare the lengths.

  $\frac{2}{8}$ is to the left of $\frac{7}{8}$. It is closer to $\frac{0}{8}$, or _____.

  $\frac{7}{8}$ is to the _____ of $\frac{2}{8}$. It is closer to ___, or _____.

  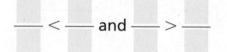

So, Sean should buy the piece of ribbon that is ___ yard long.

• On a number line, a fraction farther to the right is greater than a fraction to its left.

• On a number line, a fraction farther to the left is _____ a fraction to its right.

| $\frac{1}{8}$ | $\frac{1}{8}$ | $\frac{1}{8}$ | $\frac{1}{8}$ | $\frac{1}{8}$ | $\frac{1}{8}$ | $\frac{1}{8}$ | $\frac{1}{8}$ |
|---|---|---|---|---|---|---|---|
| $\frac{1}{8}$ | $\frac{1}{8}$ | $\frac{1}{8}$ | $\frac{1}{8}$ | $\frac{1}{8}$ | $\frac{1}{8}$ | $\frac{1}{8}$ | $\frac{1}{8}$ |

$\frac{0}{8}$        $\frac{8}{8}$

🔑 **Use reasoning.**

Ana and Omar are decorating same-size bookmarks. Ana covers $\frac{3}{3}$ of her bookmark with glitter. Omar covers $\frac{1}{3}$ of his bookmark with glitter. Whose bookmark is covered with more glitter?

**Compare $\frac{3}{3}$ and $\frac{1}{3}$.**

- When the denominators are the same, the whole is divided

  into same-size pieces. You can look at the _____ to compare the number of pieces.

- Both fractions involve third-size pieces. _____ pieces

  are more than _____ piece. 3 > _____, so ___ > ___.

So, _____ bookmark is covered with more glitter.

**Math Talk**

**Explain** how you can use reasoning to compare fractions with the same denominator.

Name _____

Math Talk

MATHEMATICAL PRACTICES ②

**Reason Abstractly** Why do fractions increase in size as you move right on the number line?

1. Draw points on the number line to show $\frac{1}{6}$ and $\frac{5}{6}$. Then compare the fractions.

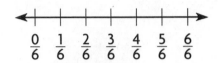

$\frac{0}{6}$ $\frac{1}{6}$ $\frac{2}{6}$ $\frac{3}{6}$ $\frac{4}{6}$ $\frac{5}{6}$ $\frac{6}{6}$

**Think:** $\frac{1}{6}$ is to the left of $\frac{5}{6}$ on the number line.

$\frac{1}{6}$ ◯ $\frac{5}{6}$

**Compare. Write <, >, or =.**

2. $\frac{4}{8}$ ◯ $\frac{3}{8}$

☑ 3. $\frac{1}{4}$ ◯ $\frac{4}{4}$

4. $\frac{1}{2}$ ◯ $\frac{1}{2}$

☑ 5. $\frac{3}{6}$ ◯ $\frac{2}{6}$

**On Your Own**

**Compare. Write <, >, or =.**

6. $\frac{2}{4}$ ◯ $\frac{3}{4}$

7. $\frac{2}{3}$ ◯ $\frac{2}{3}$

8. $\frac{4}{6}$ ◯ $\frac{2}{6}$

9. $\frac{0}{8}$ ◯ $\frac{2}{8}$

THINK SMARTER Write a fraction less than, greater than, or equal to the given fraction.

10. $\frac{1}{2} < \dfrac{\square}{\square}$

11. $\dfrac{\square}{\square} < \frac{12}{6}$

12. $\frac{8}{8} = \dfrac{\square}{\square}$

13. $\dfrac{\square}{\square} > \frac{2}{4}$

**Problem Solving • Applications**

14. Carlos finished $\frac{5}{8}$ of his art project on Monday. Tyler finished $\frac{7}{8}$ of his art project on Monday. Who finished more of his art project on Monday?

15. MATHEMATICAL PRACTICE ② **Use Reasoning** Ms. Endo made two loaves of bread that are the same size. Her family ate $\frac{1}{4}$ of the banana bread and $\frac{3}{4}$ of the cinnamon bread. Which loaf of bread had less left over?

16. **THINK SMARTER** Todd and Lisa are comparing fraction strips. Which statements are correct? Mark all that apply.

Ⓐ $\frac{1}{4} < \frac{4}{4}$     Ⓑ $\frac{5}{6} < \frac{4}{6}$     Ⓒ $\frac{2}{3} > \frac{1}{3}$     Ⓓ $\frac{5}{8} > \frac{4}{8}$

**THINK SMARTER** **What's the Error?**

17. Gary and Vanessa are comparing fractions. Vanessa models $\frac{2}{4}$ and Gary models $\frac{3}{4}$. Vanessa writes $\frac{3}{4} < \frac{2}{4}$. Look at Gary's model and Vanessa's model and describe her error.

| **Vanessa's Model** | **Gary's Model** |
|---|---|
| 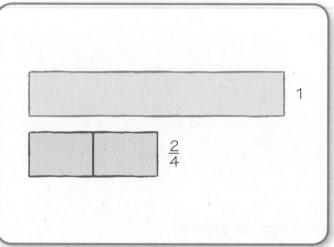 | 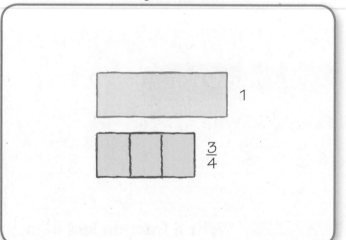 |

- Describe Vanessa's error.

_____

_____

18. **GO DEEPER** Explain how to correct Vanessa's error. Then show the correct model.

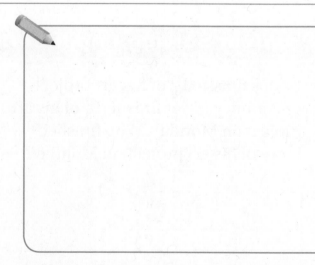

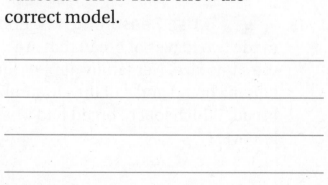

## Compare Fractions with the Same Denominator

COMMON CORE STANDARD—3.NF.A.3d
Develop understanding of fractions as numbers.

**Compare. Write <, >, or =.**

1. $\frac{3}{4} \bigodot_{>} \frac{1}{4}$

2. $\frac{3}{6} \bigcirc \frac{0}{6}$

3. $\frac{1}{2} \bigcirc \frac{1}{2}$

4. $\frac{5}{6} \bigcirc \frac{6}{6}$

5. $\frac{7}{8} \bigcirc \frac{5}{8}$

6. $\frac{2}{3} \bigcirc \frac{3}{3}$

7. $\frac{8}{8} \bigcirc \frac{0}{8}$

8. $\frac{1}{6} \bigcirc \frac{1}{6}$

9. $\frac{3}{4} \bigcirc \frac{2}{4}$

10. $\frac{1}{6} \bigcirc \frac{2}{6}$

11. $\frac{1}{2} \bigcirc \frac{0}{2}$

12. $\frac{3}{8} \bigcirc \frac{3}{8}$

13. $\frac{1}{4} \bigcirc \frac{4}{4}$

14. $\frac{5}{8} \bigcirc \frac{4}{8}$

15. $\frac{4}{6} \bigcirc \frac{6}{6}$

**Problem Solving** Real World

16. Ben mowed $\frac{5}{6}$ of his lawn in one hour. John mowed $\frac{4}{6}$ of his lawn in one hour. Who mowed less of his lawn in one hour?

17. Darcy baked 8 muffins. She put blueberries in $\frac{5}{8}$ of the muffins. She put raspberries in $\frac{3}{8}$ of the muffins. Did more muffins have blueberries or raspberries?

_____       _____

18. **WRITE** ▸Math  Explain how you can use reasoning to compare two fractions with the same denominator.

_____

_____

## Lesson Check (3.NF.A.3d)

1. Julia paints $\frac{2}{6}$ of a wall in her room white. She paints more of the wall green than white. What fraction could show the part of the wall that is green?

_____

2. Compare. Write $<$, $>$, or $=$.

$$\frac{2}{8} \bigcirc \frac{3}{8}$$

## Spiral Review (3.OA.A.3, 3.OA.B.5, 3.OA.C.7, 3.NBT.A.3)

3. Mr. Edwards buys 2 new knobs for each of his kitchen cabinets. The kitchen has 9 cabinets. How many knobs does he buy?

_____

4. Allie builds a new bookcase with 8 shelves. She can put 30 books on each shelf. How many books can the bookcase hold?

_____

5. The Good Morning Café has 28 customers for breakfast. There are 4 people sitting at each table. How many tables are filled?

_____

6. Ella wants to use the Commutative Property of Multiplication to help find the product $5 \times 4$. What number sentence can she use?

_____

FOR MORE PRACTICE
GO TO THE
**Personal Math Trainer**

Name _____

# Compare Fractions with the Same Numerator

**Essential Question** How can you compare fractions with the same numerator?

 **Common Core** Number and Operations—Fractions—3.NF.A.3d *Also 3.NF.A.1*
**MATHEMATICAL PRACTICES**
MP1, MP2, MP6

##  Unlock the Problem

Markos is at Athena's Cafe. He can sit at a table with 5 of his friends or at a different table with 7 of his friends. The same-size spinach pie is shared equally among the people at each table. At which table should Markos sit to get more pie?

**Model the problem.**

There will be 6 friends sharing Pie A or 8 friends sharing Pie B.

So, Markos will get either $\frac{1}{6}$ or $\frac{1}{8}$ of a pie.

- Shade $\frac{1}{6}$ of Pie A.
- Shade $\frac{1}{8}$ of Pie B.
- Which piece of pie is larger?
- Compare $\frac{1}{6}$ and $\frac{1}{8}$.

$$\frac{1}{6} \bigcirc \frac{1}{8}$$

So, Markos should sit at the table with _____ friends to get more pie.

- Including Markos, how many friends will be sharing pie at each table?

_____

- What will you compare?

_____

_____

**Pie A**          **Pie B**

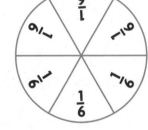          

**1.** Which pie has more pieces? _____
The *more* pieces a whole is divided into,

the _____ the pieces are.

**2.** Which pie has fewer pieces? _____
The *fewer* pieces a whole is divided into,

the _____ the pieces are.

 **Math Talk**

**MATHEMATICAL PRACTICES** ①

**Make Sense of Problems** Suppose Markos wants two pieces of one of the pies above. Is $\frac{2}{6}$ or $\frac{2}{8}$ of the pie a greater amount? Explain how you know.

## Use fraction strips.

On Saturday, the campers paddled $\frac{2}{8}$ of their planned route down the river. On Sunday, they paddled $\frac{2}{3}$ of their route down the river. On which day did the campers paddle farther?

**Compare $\frac{2}{8}$ and $\frac{2}{3}$.**

- Place a ✓ next to the fraction strips that show more parts in the whole.

- Shade $\frac{2}{8}$. Then shade $\frac{2}{3}$. Compare the shaded parts.

- $\frac{2}{8}$ ◯ $\frac{2}{3}$

| 1 |
|---|

| $\frac{1}{8}$ | $\frac{1}{8}$ | $\frac{1}{8}$ | $\frac{1}{8}$ | $\frac{1}{8}$ | $\frac{1}{8}$ | $\frac{1}{8}$ | $\frac{1}{8}$ |
|---|---|---|---|---|---|---|---|

| $\frac{1}{3}$ | $\frac{1}{3}$ | $\frac{1}{3}$ |
|---|---|---|

**Think:** $\frac{1}{8}$ is less than $\frac{1}{3}$, so $\frac{2}{8}$ is less than $\frac{2}{3}$.

So, the campers paddled farther on _____.

## Use reasoning.

For her class party, Felicia baked two trays of snacks that were the same size. After the party, she had $\frac{3}{4}$ of the carrot snack and $\frac{3}{6}$ of the apple snack left over. Was more carrot snack or more apple snack left over?

**Compare $\frac{3}{4}$ and $\frac{3}{6}$.**

- Since the numerators are the same, look at the denominators to compare the size of the pieces.    $\frac{3}{4}$  $\frac{3}{6}$

> - The *more* pieces a whole is divided into,
>
>   the _____ the pieces are.
> - The *fewer* pieces a whole is divided into,
>
>   the _____ the pieces are.

> **! ERROR Alert**
>
> When comparing fractions with the same numerator, be sure the symbol shows that the fraction with fewer pieces in the whole is the greater fraction.

- $\frac{1}{4}$ is _____ than $\frac{1}{6}$ because there are

  _____ pieces.

- $\frac{3}{4}$ ◯ $\frac{3}{6}$

So, there was more of the _____ snack left over.

Name _____

1. Shade the models to show $\frac{1}{6}$ and $\frac{1}{4}$.

   Then compare the fractions.

   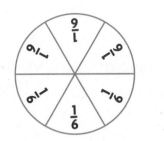 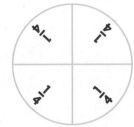

   $\frac{1}{6}$ ◯ $\frac{1}{4}$

**Compare. Write <, >, or =.**

**2.** $\frac{1}{8}$ ◯ $\frac{1}{3}$    ✓**3.** $\frac{3}{4}$ ◯ $\frac{3}{8}$    **4.** $\frac{2}{6}$ ◯ $\frac{2}{3}$

**5.** $\frac{4}{8}$ ◯ $\frac{4}{4}$    **6.** $\frac{3}{6}$ ◯ $\frac{3}{6}$    **7.** $\frac{8}{4}$ ◯ $\frac{8}{8}$

**Math Talk**  **MATHEMATICAL PRACTICES ①**

**Evaluate** Why is $\frac{1}{2}$ greater than $\frac{1}{4}$?

**On Your Own**

**Compare. Write <, >, or =.**

**8.** $\frac{1}{3}$ ◯ $\frac{1}{4}$    **9.** $\frac{2}{3}$ ◯ $\frac{2}{6}$    **10.** $\frac{4}{8}$ ◯ $\frac{4}{2}$

**11.** $\frac{6}{8}$ ◯ $\frac{6}{6}$    **12.** $\frac{1}{6}$ ◯ $\frac{1}{2}$    **13.** $\frac{7}{8}$ ◯ $\frac{7}{8}$

14. **GO DEEPER** James ate $\frac{3}{4}$ of his quesadilla. David ate $\frac{2}{3}$ of his quesadilla. Both are the same size. Who ate more of his quesadilla?

    James said he knows he ate more because he looked at the amounts left. Does his answer make sense? Shade the models. Explain.

    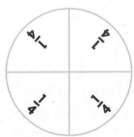 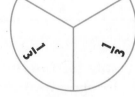

    **James**          **David**

    _____

    _____

Unlock the Problem

**15.** MATHEMATICAL PRACTICE ① **Make Sense of Problems** Quinton and Hunter are biking on trails in Katy Trail State Park. They biked $\frac{5}{6}$ mile in the morning and $\frac{5}{8}$ mile in the afternoon. Did they bike a greater distance in the morning or in the afternoon?

a. What do you need to know? _____

b. The numerator is 5 in both fractions, so compare $\frac{1}{6}$ and $\frac{1}{8}$. Explain.

_____

c. How can you solve the problem?

d. Complete the sentences.

In the morning, the boys biked

_____ mile. In the afternoon, they biked _____ mile.

So, the boys biked a greater distance

in the _____ . $\frac{5}{6}$ ◯ $\frac{5}{8}$

**16.** THINK SMARTER Zach has a piece of pie that is $\frac{1}{4}$ of a pie. Max has a piece of pie that is $\frac{1}{2}$ of a pie. Max's piece is smaller than Zach's piece. Explain how this could happen. Draw a picture to show your answer.

_____

_____

**Personal Math Trainer**

**17.** THINK SMARTER ➕ Before taking a hike, Kate and Dylan each ate part of their same-size granola bars. Kate ate $\frac{1}{3}$ of her bar. Dylan ate $\frac{1}{2}$ of his bar. Who ate more of the granola bar? Explain how you solved the problem.

_____

_____

Name _____

# Compare Fractions with the Same Numerator

Common Core
**COMMON CORE STANDARD—3.NF.A.3d**
*Develop understanding of fractions as numbers.*

**Compare. Write <, >, or =.**

1. $\frac{1}{8}$ $\boxed{<}$ $\frac{1}{2}$

2. $\frac{3}{8}$ ◯ $\frac{3}{6}$

3. $\frac{2}{3}$ ◯ $\frac{2}{4}$

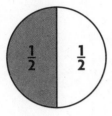

4. $\frac{2}{8}$ ◯ $\frac{2}{3}$

5. $\frac{3}{6}$ ◯ $\frac{3}{4}$

6. $\frac{1}{2}$ ◯ $\frac{1}{6}$

7. $\frac{5}{6}$ ◯ $\frac{5}{8}$

8. $\frac{4}{8}$ ◯ $\frac{4}{8}$

9. $\frac{6}{8}$ ◯ $\frac{6}{6}$

## Problem Solving (Real World)

10. Javier is buying food in the lunch line. The tray of salad plates is $\frac{3}{8}$ full. The tray of fruit plates is $\frac{3}{4}$ full. Which tray is more full?

_____

11. Rachel bought some buttons. Of the buttons, $\frac{2}{4}$ are yellow and $\frac{2}{8}$ are red. Rachel bought more of which color buttons?

_____

12. **WRITE** ▸*Math* Explain how the number of pieces in a whole relates to the size of each piece.

_____

_____

## Lesson Check (3.NF.A.3d)

1. What symbol makes the statement true? Write <, >, or =.

$\frac{3}{4}$ ◯ $\frac{3}{8}$

2. What symbol makes the statement true? Write <, >, or =.

$\frac{2}{4}$ ◯ $\frac{2}{3}$

## Spiral Review (3.OA.C.7, 3.NF.A.1)

3. Anita divided a circle into 6 equal parts and shaded 1 of the parts. What fraction names the part she shaded?

_____

4. What fraction names the shaded part of the rectangle?

_____

5. Chip worked at the animal shelter for 6 hours each week for several weeks. He worked for a total of 42 hours. How many weeks did Chip work at the animal shelter?

6. Mr. Jackson has 20 quarters. If he gives 4 quarters to each of his children, how many children does Mr. Jackson have?

_____          _____

FOR MORE PRACTICE
GO TO THE
**Personal Math Trainer**

Name _____

# Compare Fractions

**Essential Question** What strategies can you use to compare fractions?

 **Common Core** Number and Operations—Fractions—3.NF.A.3d *Also 3.NF.A.1, 3.NF.A.3*

**MATHEMATICAL PRACTICES**
MP1, MP2, MP4, MP6

##  Unlock the Problem

Luka and Ann are eating the same-size small pizzas. One plate has $\frac{3}{4}$ of Luka's cheese pizza. Another plate has $\frac{5}{6}$ of Ann's mushroom pizza. Whose plate has more pizza?

- Circle the numbers you need to compare.
- How many pieces make up each whole pizza?

_____

 Compare $\frac{3}{4}$ and $\frac{5}{6}$.

**Missing Pieces Strategy**
- You can compare fractions by comparing pieces missing from a whole.

- Shade $\frac{3}{4}$ of Luka's pizza and $\frac{5}{6}$ of Ann's pizza. Each fraction represents a whole that is missing one piece.

- Since $\frac{1}{6}$ ◯ $\frac{1}{4}$, a smaller piece is missing from Ann's pizza.

- If a smaller piece is missing from Ann's pizza, she must have more pizza.

So, _____ plate has more pizza.

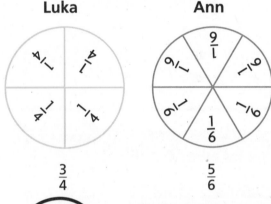

**Luka**          **Ann**

$\frac{3}{4}$          $\frac{5}{6}$

 **Math Talk**    MATHEMATICAL PRACTICES ②

**Reason Abstractly** How does knowing that $\frac{1}{4}$ is less than $\frac{1}{3}$ help you compare $\frac{3}{4}$ and $\frac{2}{3}$?

---

Morgan ran $\frac{2}{3}$ mile. Alexa ran $\frac{1}{3}$ mile. Who ran farther?

 Compare $\frac{2}{3}$ and $\frac{1}{3}$.

$\frac{\phantom{0}}{3} > \frac{\phantom{0}}{3}$

**Same Denominator Strategy**
- When the denominators are the same, you can compare only the number of pieces, or the numerators.

So, _____ ran farther.

Ms. Davis is making a fruit salad with $\frac{3}{4}$ pound of cherries and $\frac{3}{8}$ pound of strawberries. Which weighs less, the cherries or the strawberries?

 Compare $\frac{3}{4}$ and $\frac{3}{8}$.

**Same Numerator Strategy**
• When the numerators are the same, look at the denominators to compare the size of the pieces.

**Think:** $\frac{1}{8}$ is smaller than $\frac{1}{4}$ because there are more pieces.

$$\frac{3}{\boxed{\phantom{x}}} < \frac{3}{\boxed{\phantom{x}}}$$

So, the _____ weigh less.

## Share and Show    MATH BOARD

1. Compare $\frac{7}{8}$ and $\frac{5}{6}$.

   **Think:** What is missing from each whole?

   Write <, >, or =. $\frac{7}{8} \bigcirc \frac{5}{6}$

**Compare. Write <, >, or =. Write the strategy you used.**

2. $\frac{1}{2} \bigcirc \frac{2}{3}$

   _____

3. $\frac{3}{4} \bigcirc \frac{2}{4}$

   _____

4. $\frac{3}{8} \bigcirc \frac{3}{6}$

   _____

5. $\frac{3}{4} \bigcirc \frac{7}{8}$

   _____

**Math Talk**    MATHEMATICAL PRACTICES ①

Make Sense of Problems
How do the missing pieces in Exercise 1 help you compare $\frac{7}{8}$ and $\frac{5}{6}$?

Name _____

## On Your Own

**Compare. Write <, >, or =. Write the strategy you used.**

6. $\frac{1}{2}$ ◯ $\frac{2}{2}$

_____

7. $\frac{1}{3}$ ◯ $\frac{1}{4}$

_____

8. $\frac{2}{3}$ ◯ $\frac{5}{6}$

_____

9. $\frac{4}{6}$ ◯ $\frac{4}{2}$

_____

**Name a fraction that is less than or greater than the given fraction. Draw to justify your answer.**

10. less than $\frac{5}{6}$ _____

11. greater than $\frac{3}{8}$ _____

12. **GO DEEPER**  Luke, Seth, and Anja have empty glasses. Mr. Gabel pours $\frac{3}{6}$ cup of orange juice in Seth's glass. Then he pours $\frac{1}{6}$ cup of orange juice in Luke's glass and $\frac{2}{6}$ cup of orange juice in Anja's glass. Who gets the most orange juice?

_____

13. **THINK SMARTER**  **What's the Error?**  Jack says that $\frac{5}{8}$ is greater than $\frac{5}{6}$ because the denominator 8 is greater than the denominator 6. Describe Jack's error. Draw a picture to explain your answer.

_____

_____

_____

_____

##  Unlock the Problem Real World

**14.** **MATHEMATICAL PRACTICE ①** **Analyze** Tracy is making blueberry muffins. She is using $\frac{4}{4}$ cup of honey and $\frac{4}{2}$ cups of flour. Does Tracy use more honey or more flour?

**a.** What do you need to know?

_____

**b.** What strategy will you use to compare the fractions?

_____

**c.** Show the steps you used to solve the problem.

**d.** Complete the comparison.

So, Tracy uses more _____.

---

**15.** **THINK SMARTER** Compare the fractions. Circle a symbol that makes the statement true.

$\frac{2}{8}$ $\boxed{\begin{array}{c} > \\ < \\ = \end{array}}$ $\frac{2}{4}$          $\frac{1}{4}$ $\boxed{\begin{array}{c} > \\ < \\ = \end{array}}$ $\frac{4}{8}$

## Compare Fractions

Common Core
**COMMON CORE STANDARD—3.NF.A.3d**
*Develop an understanding of fractions as numbers.*

**Compare. Write <, >, or =. Write the strategy you used.**

1. $\frac{3}{8}$ $<$ $\frac{3}{4}$

   **Think:** The numerators are the same. Compare the denominators. The greater fraction will have the lesser denominator.

   <u>same numerator</u>

2. $\frac{2}{3}$ ○ $\frac{7}{8}$

   _____

3. $\frac{3}{4}$ ○ $\frac{1}{4}$

   _____

**Name a fraction that is less than or greater than the given fraction. Draw to justify your answer.**

4. greater than $\frac{1}{3}$ —

5. less than $\frac{3}{4}$ —

**Problem Solving** Real World

6. At the third-grade party, two groups each had their own pizza. The blue group ate $\frac{7}{8}$ pizza. The green group ate $\frac{2}{8}$ pizza. Which group ate more of their pizza?

   _____

7. Ben and Antonio both take the same bus to school. Ben's ride is $\frac{7}{8}$ mile. Antonio's ride is $\frac{3}{4}$ mile. Who has a longer bus ride?

   _____

8. **WRITE** ▸ *Math* Explain how to use the missing pieces strategy to compare two fractions. Include a diagram with your explanation.

_____

## Lesson Check (3.NF.A.3d)

1. Compare $\frac{2}{3}$ and $\frac{7}{8}$. Write <, >, or =.

2. What symbol makes the statement true? Write <, >, or =.

## Spiral Review (3.OA.A.4, 3.NBT.A.3, 3.NF.A.3c)

3. Cam, Stella, and Rose each picked 40 apples. They put all their apples in one crate. How many apples are in the crate?

4. Each shape is 1 whole. What fraction is represented by the shaded part of the model?

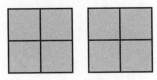

_____

_____

5. What related multiplication fact can you use to find $16 \div \blacksquare = 2$?

6. What is the unknown factor?

$$9 \times \blacksquare = 36$$

_____

_____

_____

_____

FOR MORE PRACTICE
GO TO THE
**Personal Math Trainer**

Name _____

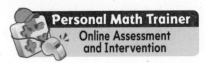
**Personal Math Trainer**
Online Assessment
and Intervention

## Concepts and Skills

1. When two fractions refer to the same whole, explain why the fraction with a lesser denominator has larger pieces than the fraction with a greater denominator. (3.NF.A.3d)

_____

_____

_____

2. When two fractions refer to the same whole and have the same denominators, explain why you can compare only the numerators. (3.NF.A.3d)

_____

_____

_____

**Compare. Write $<$, $>$, or $=$.** (3.NF.A.3d)

3. $\frac{1}{6} \bigcirc \frac{1}{4}$

4. $\frac{1}{8} \bigcirc \frac{1}{8}$

5. $\frac{2}{8} \bigcirc \frac{2}{3}$

6. $\frac{4}{2} \bigcirc \frac{1}{2}$

7. $\frac{7}{8} \bigcirc \frac{3}{8}$

8. $\frac{5}{6} \bigcirc \frac{2}{3}$

9. $\frac{2}{4} \bigcirc \frac{3}{4}$

10. $\frac{6}{6} \bigcirc \frac{6}{8}$

11. $\frac{3}{4} \bigcirc \frac{7}{8}$

**Name a fraction that is less than or greater than the given fraction. Draw to justify your answer.** (3.NF.A.3d)

12. greater than $\frac{2}{6}$ _____

13. less than $\frac{2}{3}$ _____

14. Two walls in Tiffany's room are the same size. Tiffany paints $\frac{1}{4}$ of one wall. Roberto paints $\frac{1}{8}$ of the other wall. Who painted a greater amount in Tiffany's room? (3.NF.A.3d)

_____

15. Matthew ran $\frac{5}{8}$ mile during track practice. Pablo ran $\frac{5}{6}$ mile. Who ran farther? (3.NF.A.3d)

_____

16. Mallory bought 6 roses for her mother. Two-sixths of the roses are red and $\frac{4}{6}$ are yellow. Did Mallory buy fewer red roses or yellow roses? (3.NF.A.3d)

_____

17. GO DEEPER Lani used $\frac{2}{3}$ cup of raisins, $\frac{3}{8}$ cup of cranberries, and $\frac{3}{4}$ cup of oatmeal to bake cookies. Which ingredient did Lani use the least amount of? (3.NF.A.3d)

_____

# Compare and Order Fractions

**Essential Question** How can you compare and order fractions?

 **Common Core** Number and Operations—
Fractions—3.NF.A.3d *Also 3.NF.A.1*
**MATHEMATICAL PRACTICES**
MP4, MP5, MP6, MP8

## Unlock the Problem

Sierra, Tad, and Dale ride their bikes to school. Sierra rides $\frac{3}{4}$ mile, Tad rides $\frac{3}{8}$ mile, and Dale rides $\frac{3}{6}$ mile. Compare and order the distances from least to greatest.

- Circle the fractions you need to use.
- Underline the sentence that tells you what you need to do.

## Activity 1 Order fractions with the same numerator.

**Materials** ■ color pencil

You can order fractions by reasoning about the size of unit fractions.

| 1 | | | |
|---|---|---|---|
| $\frac{1}{4}$ | $\frac{1}{4}$ | $\frac{1}{4}$ | $\frac{1}{4}$ |

| $\frac{1}{8}$ | $\frac{1}{8}$ | $\frac{1}{8}$ | $\frac{1}{8}$ | $\frac{1}{8}$ | $\frac{1}{8}$ | $\frac{1}{8}$ | $\frac{1}{8}$ |

| $\frac{1}{6}$ | $\frac{1}{6}$ | $\frac{1}{6}$ | $\frac{1}{6}$ | $\frac{1}{6}$ | $\frac{1}{6}$ |

**Remember**
- The *more* pieces a whole is divided into, the smaller the pieces are.
- The *fewer* pieces a whole is divided into, the larger the pieces are.

**STEP 1** Shade one unit fraction for each fraction strip.

_____ is the longest unit fraction.

_____ is the shortest unit fraction.

**STEP 2** Shade one more unit fraction for each fraction strip.

Are the shaded fourths still the longest? _____

Are the shaded eighths still the shortest? _____

**STEP 3** Continue shading the fraction strips so that three unit fractions are shaded for each strip.

Are the shaded fourths still the longest? _____

Are the shaded eighths still the shortest? _____

$\frac{3}{4}$ mile is the _____ distance. $\frac{3}{8}$ mile is the _____ distance. $\frac{3}{6}$ mile is *between* the other two distances.

So, the distances in order from least to greatest are

_____ mile, _____ mile, _____ mile.

© Houghton Mifflin Harcourt Publishing Company

**Try This!** Order $\frac{2}{6}$, $\frac{2}{3}$, and $\frac{2}{4}$ from greatest to least.

Order the fractions $\frac{2}{6}$, $\frac{2}{3}$, and $\frac{2}{4}$ by thinking about the length of the unit fraction strip. Then label the fractions *shortest*, *between*, or *longest*.

| Fraction | Unit Fraction | Length |
|---|---|---|
| $\frac{2}{6}$ | | |
| $\frac{2}{3}$ | | |
| $\frac{2}{4}$ | | |

**Math Talk**

MATHEMATICAL PRACTICES ⑧

**Generalize** When ordering three fractions, what do you know about the third fraction when you know which fraction is the shortest and which fraction is the longest? Explain your answer.

- When the numerators are the same, think about the

  _____ of the pieces to compare and order fractions.

So, the order from greatest to least is _____, _____, _____.

## 🔓 Activity 2 Order fractions with the same denominator.

**Materials** ■ color pencil

Shade fraction strips to order $\frac{5}{8}$, $\frac{8}{8}$, and $\frac{3}{8}$ from least to greatest.

| 1 |
|---|

| $\frac{1}{8}$ | $\frac{1}{8}$ | $\frac{1}{8}$ | $\frac{1}{8}$ | $\frac{1}{8}$ | $\frac{1}{8}$ | $\frac{1}{8}$ | $\frac{1}{8}$ | Shade $\frac{5}{8}$. |

| $\frac{1}{8}$ | $\frac{1}{8}$ | $\frac{1}{8}$ | $\frac{1}{8}$ | $\frac{1}{8}$ | $\frac{1}{8}$ | $\frac{1}{8}$ | $\frac{1}{8}$ | Shade $\frac{8}{8}$. |

| $\frac{1}{8}$ | $\frac{1}{8}$ | $\frac{1}{8}$ | $\frac{1}{8}$ | $\frac{1}{8}$ | $\frac{1}{8}$ | $\frac{1}{8}$ | $\frac{1}{8}$ | Shade $\frac{3}{8}$. |

- When the denominators are the same, the size of the pieces is the _____.

  So, think about the _____ of pieces to compare and order fractions.

  _____ is the shortest. _____ is the longest.

  _____ is between the other two fractions.

So, the order from least to greatest is _____, _____, _____.

Name _____

1. Shade the fraction strips to order $\frac{4}{6}$, $\frac{4}{4}$, and $\frac{4}{8}$ from least to greatest.

**Math Talk** MATHEMATICAL PRACTICES ⑤

**Use a Concrete Model** Why does using fraction strips help you order fractions with unlike denominators?

| 1 | | | | | |
|---|---|---|---|---|---|
| $\frac{1}{6}$ | $\frac{1}{6}$ | $\frac{1}{6}$ | $\frac{1}{6}$ | $\frac{1}{6}$ | $\frac{1}{6}$ |

| $\frac{1}{4}$ | $\frac{1}{4}$ | $\frac{1}{4}$ | $\frac{1}{4}$ |
|---|---|---|---|

| $\frac{1}{8}$ | $\frac{1}{8}$ | $\frac{1}{8}$ | $\frac{1}{8}$ | $\frac{1}{8}$ | $\frac{1}{8}$ | $\frac{1}{8}$ | $\frac{1}{8}$ |
|---|---|---|---|---|---|---|---|

_____ is the shortest. _____ is the longest.

_____ is between the other two lengths.   _____, _____, _____

**Write the fractions in order from least to greatest.**

2. $\frac{1}{2}, \frac{0}{2}, \frac{2}{2}$  _____, _____, _____

3. $\frac{1}{6}, \frac{1}{2}, \frac{1}{3}$  _____, _____, _____

## On Your Own

**Write the fractions in order from greatest to least.**

4. $\frac{6}{6}, \frac{2}{6}, \frac{5}{6}$  _____, _____, _____

5. $\frac{1}{8}, \frac{1}{4}, \frac{1}{2}$  _____, _____, _____

**Write the fractions in order from least to greatest.**

6. *THINK SMARTER*
$\frac{6}{3}, \frac{6}{2}, \frac{6}{8}$  _____, _____, _____

7. *THINK SMARTER*
$\frac{4}{2}, \frac{2}{2}, \frac{8}{2}$  _____, _____, _____

8. MATHEMATICAL PRACTICE ⑥ **Compare** Pam is making biscuits.
She needs $\frac{2}{6}$ cup of oil, $\frac{2}{3}$ cup of water, and $\frac{2}{4}$ cup of milk.
Write the ingredients from greatest to least amount.

_____, _____, _____

## Problem Solving • Applications

**9.** In fifteen minutes, Greg's sailboat went $\frac{3}{6}$ mile, Gina's sailboat went $\frac{6}{6}$ mile, and Stuart's sailboat went $\frac{4}{6}$ mile. Whose sailboat went the longest distance in fifteen minutes?

_____

Whose sailboat went the shortest distance?

_____

**10.** GO DEEPER   Look back at Problem 9. Write a similar problem by changing the fraction of a mile each sailboat traveled, so the answers are different from Problem 9. Then solve the problem.

_____

_____

_____

_____

WRITE ▸ Math • **Show Your Work**

**11.** THINK SMARTER   Tom has three pieces of wood. The length of the longest piece is $\frac{3}{4}$ foot. The length of the shortest piece is $\frac{3}{8}$ foot. What might be the length of the third piece of wood?

_____

**12.** THINK SMARTER   Jesse ran $\frac{2}{4}$ mile on Monday, $\frac{2}{3}$ mile on Tuesday, and $\frac{2}{8}$ mile on Wednesday. Order the fractions from least to greatest.

$\frac{2}{4}$ , $\frac{2}{3}$ and $\frac{2}{8}$   ☐ ☐ ☐

## Compare and Order Fractions

Common Core **COMMON CORE STANDARD—3.NF.A.3d**
*Develop understanding of fractions as numbers.*

**Write the fractions in order from greatest to least.**

1. $\frac{4}{4}, \frac{1}{4}, \frac{3}{4}$    $\frac{4}{4}$ , $\frac{3}{4}$ , $\frac{1}{4}$

   **Think:** The denominators are the same, so compare the numerators: $4 > 3 > 1$.

2. $\frac{2}{8}, \frac{5}{8}, \frac{1}{8}$  _____ , _____ , _____

3. $\frac{1}{3}, \frac{1}{6}, \frac{1}{2}$  _____ , _____ , _____

4. $\frac{2}{3}, \frac{2}{6}, \frac{2}{8}$  _____ , _____ , _____

**Write the fractions in order from least to greatest.**

5. $\frac{2}{4}, \frac{4}{4}, \frac{3}{4}$  _____ , _____ , _____

6. $\frac{4}{6}, \frac{5}{6}, \frac{2}{6}$  _____ , _____ , _____

 **Problem Solving** Real World

7. Mr. Jackson ran $\frac{7}{8}$ mile on Monday. He ran $\frac{3}{8}$ mile on Wednesday and $\frac{5}{8}$ mile on Friday. On which day did Mr. Jackson run the shortest distance?

8. Delia has three pieces of ribbon. Her red ribbon is $\frac{2}{4}$ foot long. Her green ribbon is $\frac{2}{3}$ foot long. Her yellow ribbon is $\frac{2}{6}$ foot long. She wants to use the longest piece for a project. Which color ribbon should Delia use?

_____     _____

9. **WRITE** ▸*Math* Describe how fraction strips can help you order fractions.

_____

_____

_____

## Lesson Check (3.NF.A.3d)

1. Write the fractions in order from least to greatest.

$$\frac{1}{8}, \frac{1}{3}, \frac{1}{6}$$

2. Write the fractions in order from greatest to least.

$$\frac{3}{6}, \frac{3}{4}, \frac{3}{8}$$

## Spiral Review (3.OA.B.5, 3.NF.A.1, 3.MD.B.3)

3. What fraction of the group of cars is shaded?

4. Wendy has 6 pieces of fruit. Of these, 2 pieces are bananas. What fraction of Wendy's fruit is bananas?

5. Toby collects data and makes a bar graph about his classmates' pets. He finds that 9 classmates have dogs, 2 classmates have fish, 6 classmates have cats, and 3 classmates have gerbils. What pet will have the longest bar on the bar graph?

6. The number sentence is an example of which multiplication property?

$$6 \times 7 = (6 \times 5) + (6 \times 2)$$

FOR MORE PRACTICE
GO TO THE
Personal Math Trainer

Name _____

# Model Equivalent Fractions

**Essential Question** How can you use models to find equivalent fractions?

**Common Core** Number and Operations—Fractions—
**3.NF.A.3a** Also 3.NF.A.1, 3.NF.A.2a, 3.NF.A.2b, 3.NF.A.3, 3.NF.A.3b, 3.NF.A.3c, 3.G.A.2
MATHEMATICAL PRACTICES
MP2, MP6, MP7

## Investigate

**Hands On**

**Materials** ■ sheet of paper ■ crayon or color pencil

Two or more fractions that name the same amount are called **equivalent fractions**. You can use a sheet of paper to model fractions equivalent to $\frac{1}{2}$.

**A.** First, fold a sheet of paper into two equal parts. Open the paper and count the parts.

There are ____ equal parts. Each part is ____ of the paper.

Shade one of the halves. Write $\frac{1}{2}$ on each of the halves.

**B.** Next, fold the paper in half two times. Open the paper.

Now there are ____ equal parts. Each part is

____ of the paper.

Write $\frac{1}{4}$ on each of the fourths.

Look at the shaded parts. $\frac{1}{2} = \frac{\phantom{0}}{4}$

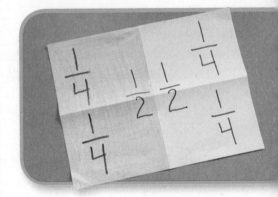

**C.** Last, fold the paper in half three times.

Now there are ____ equal parts. Each part is

____ of the paper.

Write $\frac{1}{8}$ on each of the eighths.

Find the fractions equivalent to $\frac{1}{2}$ on your paper.

So, $\frac{1}{2}$, ____ , and ____ are equivalent.

1. Explain how many $\frac{1}{8}$ parts are equivalent to one $\frac{1}{4}$ part on your paper.

_____

_____

> **Math Idea**
> Two or more numbers that have the same value or name the same amount are *equivalent*.

2. **THINK SMARTER** What do you notice about how the numerators changed for the shaded part as you folded the paper? _____

What does this tell you about the change in the number of parts? _____

How did the denominators change for the shaded part as you folded? _____

What does this tell you about the change in the size of the parts? _____

## Make Connections

> **Math Talk**
> MATHEMATICAL PRACTICES ②
> **Use Reasoning** Explain how the number of sixths in a distance on the number line is related to the number of thirds in the same distance.

You can use a number line to find equivalent fractions.

**Find a fraction equivalent to $\frac{2}{3}$.**

**Materials** ■ fraction strips

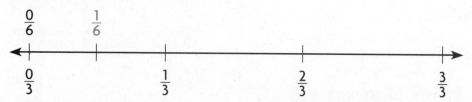

**STEP 1** Draw a point on the number line to represent the distance $\frac{2}{3}$.

_____

**STEP 2** Use fraction strips to divide the number line into sixths. At the end of each strip, draw a mark on the number line and label the marks to show sixths.

_____

**STEP 3** Identify the fraction that names the same point as $\frac{2}{3}$. _____

So, $\frac{2}{3} = \dfrac{\phantom{0}}{6}$.

Name _____

Shade the model. Then divide the pieces to find the equivalent fraction.

1.

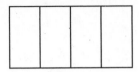

$$\frac{1}{4} = \frac{\square}{8}$$

2.

$$\frac{2}{3} = \frac{\square}{6}$$

Use the number line to find the equivalent fraction.

3.

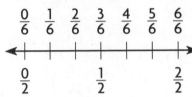

$$\frac{1}{2} = \frac{\square}{6}$$

4.

$$\frac{3}{4} = \frac{\square}{8}$$

**Problem Solving • Applications** (Real World)

5. MATHEMATICAL PRACTICE ⑥ **Explain** why $\frac{2}{2} = 1$. Write another fraction that is equal to 1. Draw to justify your answer.

_____

_____

_____

**Personal Math Trainer**

6. _THINK SMARTER +_  For numbers 6a–6d, select True or False to tell whether the fractions are equivalent.

6a.  $\frac{6}{6}$ and $\frac{3}{3}$      ○ True    ○ False

6b.  $\frac{4}{6}$ and $\frac{1}{3}$      ○ True    ○ False

6c.  $\frac{2}{3}$ and $\frac{3}{6}$      ○ True    ○ False

6d.  $\frac{1}{3}$ and $\frac{2}{6}$      ○ True    ○ False

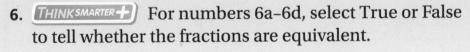

## Connect to Reading

### Summarize

You can *summarize* the information in a problem by underlining it or writing the information needed to answer a question.

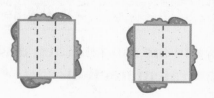

Read the problem. Underline the important information.

7. **THINK SMARTER** Mrs. Akers bought three sandwiches that were the same size. She cut the first one into thirds. She cut the second one into fourths and the third one into sixths. Marian ate 2 pieces of the first sandwich. Jason ate 2 pieces of the second sandwich. Marcos ate 3 pieces of the third sandwich. Which children ate the same amount of a sandwich? Explain.

| | | |
|---|---|---|
| The first sandwich was cut into _____. | The second sandwich was cut into _____. | The third sandwich was cut into _____. |
| Marian ate _____ pieces of the sandwich. Shade the part Marian ate. | Jason ate _____ pieces of the sandwich. Shade the part Jason ate. | Marcos ate _____ pieces of the sandwich. Shade the part Marcos ate. |
| Marian ate — of the first sandwich. | Jason ate — of the second sandwich. | Marcos ate — of the third sandwich. |

Are all the fractions equivalent? _____

Which fractions are equivalent? — = —

So, _____ and _____ ate the same amount of a sandwich.

542

# Model Equivalent Fractions

COMMON CORE STANDARD—3.NF.A.3a
Develop understanding of fractions as numbers.

**Shade the model. Then divide the pieces to find the equivalent fraction.**

1.

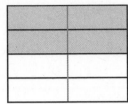

$$\frac{2}{4} = \frac{4}{8}$$

**Use the number line to find the equivalent fraction.**

2.

$$\frac{3}{4} = \frac{\phantom{0}}{8}$$

## Problem Solving · Real World

3. Mike says that $\frac{3}{3}$ of his fraction model is shaded blue. Ryan says that $\frac{6}{6}$ of the same model is shaded blue. Are the two fractions equivalent? If so, what is another equivalent fraction?

4. Brett shaded $\frac{4}{8}$ of a sheet of notebook paper. Aisha says he shaded $\frac{1}{2}$ of the paper. Are the two fractions equivalent? If so, what is another equivalent fraction?

_____

_____

5. **WRITE** ▸Math   Draw a number line that shows two equivalent fractions. Label your number line and explain how you know the fractions are equivalent.

_____

## Lesson Check (3.NF.A.3b)

1. Name a fraction equivalent to $\frac{2}{3}$.

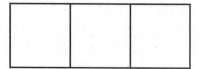

_____

2. Find the fraction equivalent to $\frac{1}{4}$.

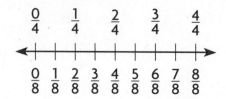

_____

## Spiral Review (3.OA.A.3, 3.OA.C.7, 3.NF.A.1)

3. Eric practiced piano and guitar for a total of 8 hours this week. He practiced the piano for $\frac{1}{4}$ of that time. How many hours did Eric practice the piano this week?

_____

4. Kylee bought a pack of 12 cookies. One-third of the cookies are peanut butter. How many of the cookies in the pack are peanut butter?

_____

5. There are 56 students going to the game. The coach puts 7 students in each van. How many vans are needed to take the students to the game?

_____

_____

6. Write a division equation for the picture.

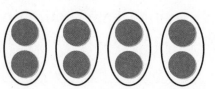

_____

_____

FOR MORE PRACTICE
GO TO THE
**Personal Math Trainer**

Name _____

# Equivalent Fractions

**Essential Question** How can you use models to name equivalent fractions?

**Common Core** **Number and Operations—Fractions—3.NF.A.3b** *Also 3.NF.A.1, 3.NF.A.3, 3.NF.A.3a, 3.G.A.2*

**MATHEMATICAL PRACTICES**
**MP2, MP3, MP4**

## Unlock the Problem *Real World*

Cole brought a submarine sandwich to the picnic. He shared the sandwich equally with 3 friends. The sandwich was cut into eighths. What are two ways to describe the part of the sandwich each friend ate?

Cole grouped the smaller pieces into twos. Draw circles to show equal groups of two pieces to show what each friend ate.

• How many people shared the sandwich?

_____

There are 4 equal groups. Each group is $\frac{1}{4}$ of the whole sandwich. So, each friend ate $\frac{1}{4}$ of the whole sandwich.

How many eighths did each friend eat? _____

$\frac{1}{4}$ and _____ are equivalent fractions since they both name

the _____ amount of the sandwich.

So, $\frac{1}{4}$ and _____ of the sandwich are two ways to describe the part of the sandwich each friend ate.

**Try This!** Circle equal groups. Write an equivalent fraction for the shaded part of the whole.

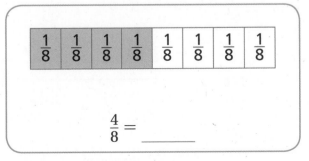

| $\frac{1}{8}$ | $\frac{1}{8}$ | $\frac{1}{8}$ | $\frac{1}{8}$ | $\frac{1}{8}$ | $\frac{1}{8}$ | $\frac{1}{8}$ | $\frac{1}{8}$ |
|---|---|---|---|---|---|---|---|

$\frac{4}{8} =$ _____

**Math Talk**   **MATHEMATICAL PRACTICES ③**

**Apply** What is a different way you could have circled the equal groups?

© Houghton Mifflin Harcourt Publishing Company

**Chapter 9** 545

## 🔑 Example  Model the problem.

Heidi ate $\frac{3}{6}$ of her fruit bar. Molly ate $\frac{4}{8}$ of her fruit bar, which is the same size. Which girl ate more of her fruit bar?

Shade $\frac{3}{6}$ of Heidi's fruit bar and $\frac{4}{8}$ of Molly's fruit bar.

- Is $\frac{3}{6}$ greater than, less than, or equal to $\frac{4}{8}$? _____

So, both girls ate the _____ amount.

Heidi

| $\frac{1}{6}$ | $\frac{1}{6}$ | $\frac{1}{6}$ |
|---|---|---|
| $\frac{1}{6}$ | $\frac{1}{6}$ | $\frac{1}{6}$ |

Molly

| $\frac{1}{8}$ | $\frac{1}{8}$ | $\frac{1}{8}$ | $\frac{1}{8}$ |
|---|---|---|---|
| $\frac{1}{8}$ | $\frac{1}{8}$ | $\frac{1}{8}$ | $\frac{1}{8}$ |

**Try This!**  Each shape is 1 whole. Write an equivalent fraction for the shaded part of the models.

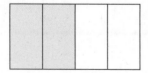

$$\frac{6}{3} = \frac{\boxed{\phantom{0}}}{6}$$

## Share and Show  MATH BOARD

**Math Talk**  MATHEMATICAL PRACTICES ②

Use Reasoning Explain why equivalent fractions name the same amount.

1. Each shape is 1 whole. Use the model to find the equivalent fraction.

$$\frac{2}{4} = \frac{\boxed{\phantom{0}}}{2}$$

**Each shape is 1 whole. Shade the model to find the equivalent fraction.**

2.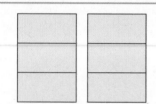

$$\frac{2}{4} = \frac{\boxed{\phantom{0}}}{8}$$

3.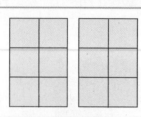

$$\frac{12}{6} = \frac{\boxed{\phantom{0}}}{3}$$

4. Andy swam $\frac{8}{8}$ mile in a race. Use the number line to find a fraction that is equivalent to $\frac{8}{8}$.

$$\frac{8}{8} = \frac{\boxed{\phantom{0}}}{\boxed{\phantom{0}}}$$

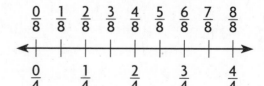

Name _____

**Circle equal groups to find the equivalent fraction.**

☑ **5.**

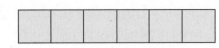

$$\frac{3}{6} = \frac{\boxed{\phantom{x}}}{2}$$

**6.**

$$\frac{6}{6} = \frac{\boxed{\phantom{x}}}{3}$$

**On Your Own**

**Each shape is 1 whole. Shade the model to find the equivalent fraction.**

**7.**

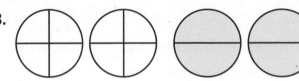

$$\frac{1}{2} = \frac{2}{\boxed{\phantom{x}}} = \frac{\boxed{\phantom{x}}}{8}$$

**8.**

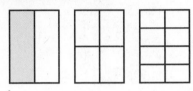

$$\frac{8}{\boxed{\phantom{x}}} = \frac{4}{2}$$

**Circle equal groups to find the equivalent fraction.**

**9.**

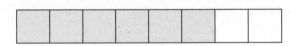

$$\frac{6}{8} = \frac{\boxed{\phantom{x}}}{4}$$

**10.**

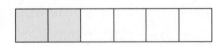

$$\frac{2}{6} = \frac{\boxed{\phantom{x}}}{3}$$

**11.** Write the fraction that names the shaded part of each circle.

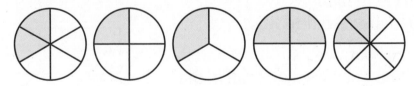

____   ____   ____   ____   ____

Which pairs of fractions are equivalent? _____

**12.** **MATHEMATICAL PRACTICE ③ Apply** Matt cut his small pizza into 6 equal pieces and ate 4 of them. Josh cut his small pizza, which is the same size, into 3 equal pieces and ate 2 of them. Write fractions for the amount they each ate. Are the fractions equivalent? Draw to explain.

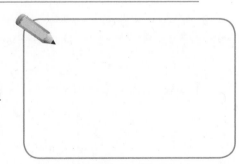

_____

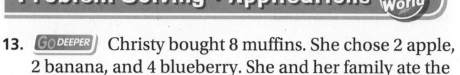

**13.** GO DEEPER  Christy bought 8 muffins. She chose 2 apple, 2 banana, and 4 blueberry. She and her family ate the apple and banana muffins for breakfast. What fraction of the muffins did they eat? Write an equivalent fraction. Draw a picture.

_____

**14.** THINK SMARTER  After dinner, $\frac{2}{3}$ of the corn bread is left. Suppose 4 friends want to share it equally. What fraction names how much of the whole pan of corn bread each friend will get? Use the model on the right. Explain your answer.

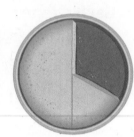

_____

_____

**15.** There are 16 people having lunch. Each person wants $\frac{1}{4}$ of a pizza. How many whole pizzas are needed? Draw a picture to show your answer.

_____

**16.** Lucy has 5 oatmeal bars, each cut in half. What fraction names all of the oatmeal bar halves? $\frac{\phantom{0}}{2}$

What if Lucy cuts each part of the oatmeal bar into 2 equal pieces to share with friends? What fraction names all of the

oatmeal bar pieces now? $\frac{\phantom{0}}{4}$

$\frac{\phantom{0}}{2}$ and $\frac{\phantom{0}}{4}$ are equivalent fractions.

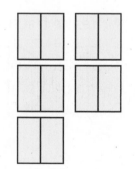

**17.** THINK SMARTER  Mr. Peters made a pizza. There is $\frac{4}{8}$ of the pizza left over. Select the fractions that are equivalent to the part of the pizza that is left over. Mark all that apply.

(A) $\frac{5}{8}$    (B) $\frac{3}{4}$    (C) $\frac{2}{4}$    (D) $\frac{1}{2}$

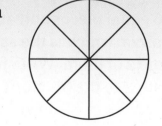

## Equivalent Fractions

Common Core  **COMMON CORE STANDARD—3.NF.A.3b**
*Develop understanding of fractions as numbers.*

**Each shape is 1 whole. Shade the model to find the equivalent fraction.**

1.
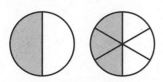

$$\frac{1}{2} = \frac{\boxed{3}}{6}$$

2.
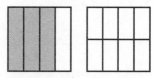

$$\frac{3}{4} = \frac{6}{\boxed{\phantom{0}}}$$

**Circle equal groups to find the equivalent fraction.**

3.
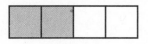

$$\frac{2}{4} = \frac{\boxed{\phantom{0}}}{2}$$

4.
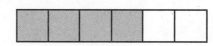

$$\frac{4}{6} = \frac{\boxed{\phantom{0}}}{3}$$

![Problem Solving Real World]

5. May painted 4 out of 8 equal parts of a poster board blue. Jared painted 2 out of 4 equal parts of a same-size poster board red. Write fractions to show which part of the poster board each person painted.

_____

6. **WRITE** *Math* Explain how you can find a fraction that is equivalent to $\frac{1}{4}$.

_____

_____

## Lesson Check (3.NF.A.3b)

**1.** What fraction is equivalent to $\frac{6}{8}$?

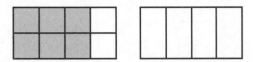

_____

**2.** What fraction is equivalent to $\frac{1}{3}$?

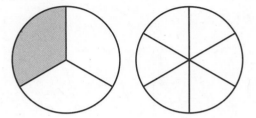

_____

## Spiral Review (3.OA.B.5, 3.OA.B.6, 3.OA.C.7)

**3.** What division number sentence is shown by the array?

_____

_____

**4.** Cody put 4 plates on the table. He put 1 apple on each plate. What number sentence can be used to find the total number of apples on the table?

_____

_____

**5.** Write a division number sentence that is a related fact to $7 \times 3 = 21$.

_____

_____

**6.** Find the quotient.

$$4\overline{)36}$$

_____

_____

**FOR MORE PRACTICE GO TO THE Personal Math Trainer**

Name _____

1. Alexa and Rose read books that have the same number of pages. Alexa's book is divided into 8 equal chapters. Rose's book is divided into 6 equal chapters. Each girl has read 3 chapters of her book.

   Write a fraction to describe what part of the book each girl read. Then tell who read more pages. Explain.

   _____

   _____

   _____

2. David, Maria, and Simone are shading same-sized index cards for a science project. David shaded $\frac{2}{4}$ of his index card. Maria shaded $\frac{2}{8}$ of her index card and Simone shaded $\frac{2}{6}$ of her index card.

   For 2a–2d, choose Yes or No to indicate whether the comparisons are correct.

   2a.  $\frac{2}{4} > \frac{2}{8}$        ○ Yes        ○ No

   2b.  $\frac{2}{8} > \frac{2}{6}$        ○ Yes        ○ No

   2c.  $\frac{2}{6} < \frac{2}{4}$        ○ Yes        ○ No

   2d.  $\frac{2}{8} = \frac{2}{4}$        ○ Yes        ○ No

3. Dan and Miguel are working on the same homework assignment. Dan has finished $\frac{1}{4}$ of the assignment. Miguel has finished $\frac{3}{4}$ of the assignment. Which statement is correct? Mark all that apply.

   Ⓐ Miguel has completed the entire assignment.

   Ⓑ Dan has not completed the entire assignment.

   Ⓒ Miguel has finished more of the assignment than Dan.

   Ⓓ Dan and Miguel have completed equal parts of the assignment.

**Assessment Options**
**Chapter Test**

**4.** Bryan cut two peaches that were the same size for lunch. He cut one peach into fourths and the other into sixths. Bryan ate $\frac{3}{4}$ of the first peach. His brother ate $\frac{5}{6}$ of the second peach. Who ate more peach? Explain the strategy you used to solve the problem.

_____

_____

_____

**5.** A nature center offers 2 guided walks. The morning walk is $\frac{2}{3}$ mile. The evening walk is $\frac{3}{6}$ mile. Which walk is shorter? Explain how you can use the model to find the answer.

| $\frac{1}{3}$ | | $\frac{1}{3}$ | | $\frac{1}{3}$ | |
|---|---|---|---|---|---|
| $\frac{1}{6}$ | $\frac{1}{6}$ | $\frac{1}{6}$ | $\frac{1}{6}$ | $\frac{1}{6}$ | $\frac{1}{6}$ |

_____

_____

**6.** Chun lives $\frac{3}{8}$ mile from school. Gail lives $\frac{5}{8}$ mile from school.

Use the fractions and symbols to show which distance is longer.

| $\frac{3}{8}$ | $\frac{5}{8}$ | $<$ | $>$ |

▢ ◯ ▢

Name _____

**7.**  Mrs. Reed baked four pans of lasagna for a family party. Use the rectangles to represent the pans.

☐ ☐ ☐ ☐

### Part A

Draw lines to show how Mrs. Reed could cut one pan of lasagna into thirds, one into fourths, one into sixths, and one into eighths.

### Part B

At the end of the dinner, equivalent amounts of lasagna in two pans were left. Use the models to show the lasagna that might have been left over. Write two pairs of equivalent fractions to represent the models.

_____

**8.** Tom rode his horse for $\frac{4}{6}$ mile. Liz rode her horse for an equal distance. What is an equivalent fraction that describes how far Liz rode? Use the models to show your work.

_____

**9.** Avery prepares 2 equal-size oranges for the bats at the zoo. One dish has $\frac{3}{8}$ of an orange. Another dish has $\frac{2}{8}$ of an orange. Which dish has more orange? Show your work.

_____

10. Jenna painted $\frac{1}{8}$ of one side of a fence. Mark painted $\frac{1}{6}$ of the other side of the same fence. Use >, =, or < to compare the parts that they painted.

_____

11. Bill used $\frac{1}{3}$ cup of raisins and $\frac{2}{3}$ cup of banana chips to make a snack.

   For 11a–11d, select True or False for each comparison.

   11a.  $\frac{1}{3} > \frac{2}{3}$        ○ True      ○ False

   11b.  $\frac{2}{3} = \frac{1}{3}$        ○ True      ○ False

   11c.  $\frac{1}{3} < \frac{2}{3}$        ○ True      ○ False

   11d.  $\frac{2}{3} > \frac{1}{3}$        ○ True      ○ False

12. **GO DEEPER**   Jorge, Lynne, and Crosby meet at the playground. Jorge lives $\frac{5}{6}$ mile from the playground. Lynne lives $\frac{4}{6}$ mile from the playground. Crosby lives $\frac{7}{8}$ mile from the playground.

   **Part A**

   Who lives closer to the playground, Jorge or Lynne? Explain how you know.

   _____

   _____

   _____

   **Part B**

   Who lives closer to the playground, Jorge or Crosby? Explain how you know.

   _____

   _____

   _____

Name _____

**13.** Ming needs $\frac{1}{2}$ pint of red paint for an art project. He has
6 jars that have the following amounts of red paint in
them. He wants to use only 1 jar of paint. Mark all of the
jars of paints that Ming could use.

Ⓐ $\frac{2}{3}$ pint

Ⓑ $\frac{1}{4}$ pint

Ⓒ $\frac{4}{6}$ pint

Ⓓ $\frac{3}{4}$ pint

Ⓔ $\frac{3}{8}$ pint

Ⓕ $\frac{2}{6}$ pint

**14.** There are 12 people having lunch. Each person wants
$\frac{1}{3}$ of a sub sandwich. How many whole sub sandwiches
are needed? Use the models to show your answer.

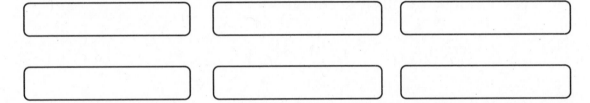

_____ sub sandwiches

**15.** Mavis mixed $\frac{2}{4}$ quart of apple juice with $\frac{1}{2}$ quart
of cranberry juice. Compare the fractions. Choose the
symbol that makes the statement true.

$$\frac{2}{4} \quad \boxed{\begin{array}{c} < \\ = \\ > \end{array}} \quad \frac{1}{2}$$

**16.** Pat has three pieces of fabric that measure $\frac{3}{6}$, $\frac{5}{6}$, and
$\frac{2}{6}$ yards long. Write the lengths in order from least
to greatest.

_____

**17.** Cora measures the heights of three plants. Draw a line to match each height on the left to the word on the right that describes its place in the order of heights.

$\frac{4}{6}$ foot •                          • least

$\frac{4}{4}$ foot •                          • between

$\frac{4}{8}$ foot •                          • greatest

**18.** Danielle drew a model to show equivalent fractions.

Use the model to complete the number sentence.

$\frac{1}{2} = $ _____ $ = $ _____

**19.** Floyd caught a fish that weighed $\frac{2}{3}$ pound. Kira caught a fish that weighed $\frac{7}{8}$ pound. Whose fish weighed more? Explain the strategy you used to solve the problem.

_____

_____

_____

_____

**20.** Sam went for a ride on a sailboat. The ride lasted $\frac{3}{4}$ hour.

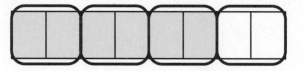

What fraction is equivalent to $\frac{3}{4}$?

_____

Measurement

 CRITICAL AREA Developing understanding of the structure of rectangular arrays and of area

Measurement tools and data are used to design and build a safe and enjoyable playground.

557

**Real World Project**

# Plan a Playground

Is there a playground at your school, in your neighborhood, or in a nearby park? Playgrounds provide a fun and safe outdoor space for you to climb, swing, slide, and play.

## Get Started   **WRITE** *Math*

Suppose you want to help plan a playground for a block in your neighborhood.

- Draw a large rectangle on the grid paper to show a fence around your playground. Find the distance around your playground by counting the number of units on each side. Record the distance.

- Use the Important Facts to help you decide on features to have in your playground. Shade parts of your playground to show each feature's location. Then find the number of unit squares the feature covers and record it on your plan.

### Important Facts

## Playground Features
- Bench
- Jungle Gym
- Playhouse
- Sandbox
- Seesaw
- Slide
- Swing Set
- Water Fountain

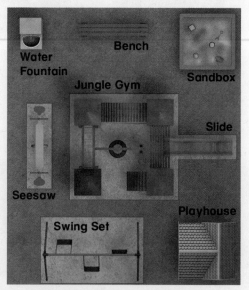

▲ This drawing shows a plan for a playground.

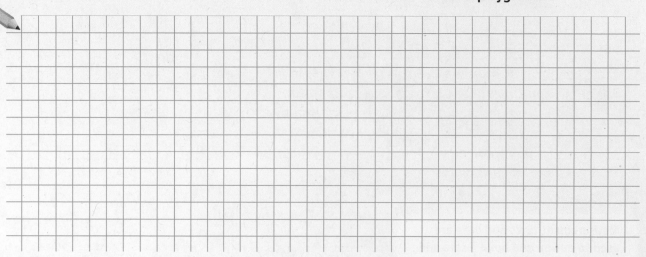

Completed by _____

© Houghton Mifflin Harcourt Publishing Company

# Time, Length, Liquid Volume, and Mass

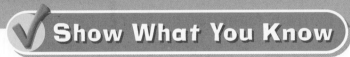

## ✓ Show What You Know

Check your understanding of important skills.

Name _____

▶ **Time to the Half Hour** **Read the clock. Write the time.** (1.MD.B.3)

1.  _____

2.  _____

▶ **Skip Count by Fives**

**Skip count by fives. Write the missing numbers.** (2.NBT.A.2)

3. 5, 10, 15, ____, 25, ____, 35

4. 55, 60, ____, 70, ____, ____, 85

▶ **Inches** **Use a ruler to measure the length to the nearest inch.** (2.MD.A.1)

5.

about _____ inches

6.

about _____ inch

### Math in the Real World

You can look at the time the sun rises and sets to find the amount of daylight each day. The table shows the time the sun rose and set from January 10 to January 14 in Philadelphia, Pennsylvania. Find which day had the least daylight and which day had the most daylight.

**Sunrise and Sunset Times**

| Date | Sunrise | Sunset |
|---|---|---|
| Jan 10 | 7:22 A.M. | 4:55 P.M. |
| Jan 11 | 7:22 A.M. | 4:56 P.M. |
| Jan 12 | 7:22 A.M. | 4:57 P.M. |
| Jan 13 | 7:21 A.M. | 4:58 P.M. |
| Jan 14 | 7:21 A.M. | 4:59 P.M. |

## Vocabulary Builder

▶ **Visualize It** ••••••••••••••••••••••••••

Complete the graphic organizer by using the words with a ✓. Write the words in order from the greatest to the least length of time.

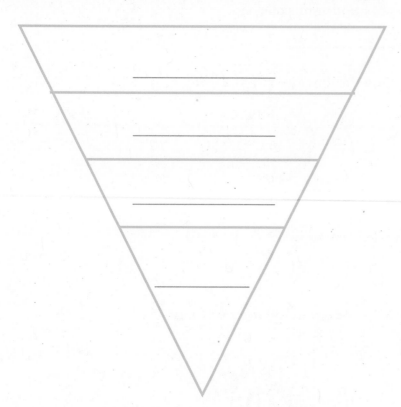

▶ **Understand Vocabulary** •••••••••••••••••••••••••

Write the word that answers the riddle.

1. I am written with times after midnight and before noon.

    _____

2. I am the time when it is 12:00 in the daytime.

    _____

3. I am the amount of liquid in a container.

    _____

4. I am the time that passes from the start of an activity to the end of that activity.

    _____

5. I am the amount of matter in an object.

    _____

GO DIGITAL
• Interactive Student Edition
• Multimedia eGlossary

# Chapter 10 Vocabulary

**A.M.**

A.M.

1

**Elapsed Time**

tiempo transcurrido

18

**gram (g)**

gramo (g)

30

**Halves**

mitades

32

**kilogram (kg)**

kilogramo (kg)

39

**liquid volume**

volumen de un líquido

45

**liter (L)**

litro (L)

46

**mass**

masa

47

The time that passes from the start of an activity to the end of that activity

So, the elapsed time is 43 minutes.

The time after midnight and before noon

After Midnight and Before Noon

These are halves

A metric unit used to measure mass
1 kilogram = 1,000 grams

A small paper clip has a mass of about 1 gram.

The amount of liquid in a container

A metric unit used to measure mass
1 kilogram = 1,000 grams

1,000 Paper clips

A box of 1,000 paper clips has a mass of about 1 kilogram.

The amount of matter in an object

A metric unit used to measure liquid volume

1 liter

**Midnight**

medianoche

48

**minute**

minuto

49

**Noon**

mediadía

52

**P.M.**

P.M.

63

A unit used to measure short amounts of time; in one minute, the minute hand on an analog clock moves from one mark to the next

minute

12:00 at night

Midnight

The time after noon and before midnight

P.M.

12:00 in the day

Noon

# Going to the Playground

**For 2 players**

## Materials

- 1 red playing piece
- 1 blue playing piece
- 1 number cube

## How to Play

1. Each player chooses a playing piece and puts it on START.
2. Toss the number cube to take a turn. Move your playing piece that many spaces.
3. If you land on these spaces, follow the instructions.

   **White Space** Tell the meaning of the math term, or use it in a sentence. If your answer is correct, jump to the next space with the same term. If your answer is not correct, stay where you are.

   **Green Space** Follow the directions printed in the space. If there are no directions, stay where you are.

4. The first player to reach FINISH wins.

| Word Box |
| --- |
| A.M. |
| elapsed time |
| gram (g) |
| kilogram (kg) |
| liquid volume |
| liter (L) |
| mass |
| midnight |
| minute |
| noon |
| P.M. |

**HOW TO PLAY**
1. Each player chooses a playing piece and puts it on START.
2. Toss the number cube to take a turn. Move your playing piece that many spaces.
3. If you land on these spaces, follow the instructions.
   • White Space: Tell the meaning of the math term, or use it in a sentence. If your answer is correct, jump to the next space with the same term. If your answer is not correct, stay where you are.
   • Green Space: Follow the directions printed in the space. If there are no directions, stay where you are.
4. The first player to reach FINISH wins.

**MATERIALS**
• 1 red playing piece
• 1 blue playing piece
• 1 number cube

FINISH

| minute | midnight | mass | liter |

| kilogram | liquid volume | liter | Go back to | mass |

| gram | elapsed time | | A.M. | P.M. |

| midnight | minute | noon | P.M. | A.M. |

| mass | liter | Go back to | kilogram | gram |

START | A.M. | elapsed time | gram | kilogram |

Game

Go back to

liquid volume

kilogram

gram

elapsed time

midnight

minute

noon

P.M.

A.M.

noon

minute

midnight

mass

Go back to

elapsed time

gram

kilogram

liquid volume

elapsed time

A.M.

noon

minute

liquid volume

liter

mass

midnight

# The Write Way

**Reflect**

## Choose one idea. Write about it.

- Write a paragraph that uses at least **three** of these words or phrases.

  gram    kilogram    liter    mass    liquid volume

- Explain how you solve one kind of measurement problem.

- Write two questions you have about telling time or finding time intervals.

Name _____

# Time to the Minute

**Essential Question** How can you tell time to the nearest minute?

Common Core  Measurement and Data—
3.MD.A.1
MATHEMATICAL PRACTICES
MP2, MP3, MP6

## 🔑 Unlock the Problem

Groundhog Day is February 2. People say that if a groundhog can see its shadow on that morning, winter will last another 6 weeks. The clock shows the time when the groundhog saw its shadow. What time was it?

- Underline the question.
- Where will you look to find the time?

_____

## 🔑 Example

Look at the time on this clock face.

- What does the hour hand tell you?

_____

- What does the minute hand tell you?

_____

In 1 **minute**, the minute hand moves from one mark to the next on a clock. It takes 5 minutes for the minute hand to move from one number to the next on a clock.

You can count on by fives to tell time to five minutes. Count zero at the 12.

0, 5, 10, 15, _____, _____, _____, _____

So, the groundhog saw its shadow at _____.

**Write:** 7:35

**Read:**

- seven _____

- thirty-five minutes after _____

**MATHEMATICAL PRACTICES ②**

**Reason Abstractly** How does skip counting by fives help you tell the time when the minute hand points to a number?

- Is 7:35 a reasonable answer? Explain. _____

_____

## Time to the Minute

Count by fives and ones to help you.

### 🔑 One Way **Find minutes after the hour.**

Look at the time on this clock face.

- What does the hour hand tell you?

  _____

- What does the minute hand tell you?

  _____

Count on by fives and ones from the 12 on the clock to where the minute hand is pointing. Write the missing counting numbers next to the clock.

When a clock shows 30 or fewer minutes after the hour, you can read the time as a number of minutes *after* the hour.

**Write:** _____

**Read:**

- twenty-three minutes after _____

- one _____

### 🔑 Another Way **Find minutes before the hour.**

Look at the time on this clock face.

- What does the hour hand tell you?

  _____

- What does the minute hand tell you?

  _____

Now count by fives and ones from the 12 on the clock back to where the minute hand is pointing. Write the missing counting numbers next to the clock.

When a clock shows 31 or more minutes after the hour, you can read the time as a number of minutes *before* the next hour.

**Write:** 2:43

**Read:**

- seventeen _____ before three

- two _____

**ERROR Alert**

Remember that time *after* the hour uses the previous hour, and time *before* the hour uses the next hour.

Name _____

1. How would you use counting and the minute hand to find the time shown on this clock? Write the time.

_____

**Write the time. Write one way you can read the time.**

2.

_____

_____

3.

_____

_____

4. 

**10:45**

_____

_____

Math Talk

MATHEMATICAL PRACTICES ③

**Apply** How do you know when to stop counting by fives and start counting by ones when counting minutes after an hour?

**On Your Own**

**Write the time. Write one way you can read the time.**

5. 

**3:12**

_____

_____

6.

_____

_____

7.

_____

_____

MATHEMATICAL PRACTICE ② **Represent a Problem** Write the time another way.

8. 34 minutes after 5

_____

9. 11 minutes before 6

_____

10. 22 minutes after 11

_____

11. 5 minutes before 12

_____

## Problem Solving • Applications

**Use the clocks for 12–13.**

**Time of Day the Groundhog Saw Its Shadow**

NY    PA

12. How many minutes later in the day did the groundhog in Pennsylvania see its shadow than the groundhog in New York?

_____

13. GO DEEPER  What if the groundhog in Pennsylvania saw its shadow 5 minutes later? What time would this be?

_____

14. If you look at your watch and the hour hand is between the 8 and the 9 and the minute hand is on the 11, what time is it?

_____

15. THINK SMARTER  What time is it when the hour hand and the minute hand are both pointing to the same number? Aiden says it is 6:30. Camilla says it is 12:00. Who is correct? Explain.

_____

_____

16. MATHEMATICAL PRACTICE ③ **Verify the Reasoning of Others**  Lucy said the time is 4:46 on her digital watch. Explain where the hands on an analog clock are pointing when it is 4:46.

_____

_____

17. THINK SMARTER  Write the time that is shown on the clock. Then write the time another way.

_____

Name _____

# Time to the Minute

**COMMON CORE STANDARD—3.MD.A.1**
*Solve problems involving measurement and estimation of intervals of time, liquid volumes, and masses of objects.*

## Write the time. Write one way you can read the time.

**1.**

1:16; sixteen minutes

after one

**2.**

_____

_____

**3.**

4:13

_____

_____

**4.**

_____

_____

**5.**

7:24

_____

_____

**6.**

_____

_____

## Write the time another way.

**7.** 23 minutes after 4

_____

**8.** 18 minutes before 11

_____

**Problem Solving** *Real World*

**9.** What time is it when the hour hand is a little past the 3 and the minute hand is pointing to the 3?

_____

**10.** Pete began practicing at twenty-five minutes before eight. What is another way to write this time?

_____

**11.** ▌WRITE ▶*Math* Draw a clock showing a time to the nearest minute. Write the time as many different ways you can.

_____

_____

## Lesson Check (3.MD.A.1)

1. What is another way to write 13 minutes before 10?

2. What time does the clock show?

_____

_____

## Spiral Review (3.OA.A.1, 3.OA.A.2, 3.OA.A.4, 3.OA.B.6)

3. Each bird has 2 wings. How many wings do 5 birds have?

4. Find the unknown factor.

$$8 \times \blacksquare = 56$$

_____

_____

5. Mr. Wren has 56 paintbrushes. He places 8 paintbrushes on each of the tables in the art room. How many tables are in the art room?

6. What number completes the equations?

$$4 \times \blacktriangle = 20 \quad 20 \div 4 = \blacktriangle$$

_____

_____

© Houghton Mifflin Harcourt Publishing Company

FOR MORE PRACTICE
GO TO THE
**Personal Math Trainer**

Name _____

# A.M. and P.M.

**Essential Question** How can you tell when to use A.M. and P.M. with time?

Common Core  Measurement and Data—
3.MD.A.1
MATHEMATICAL PRACTICES
MP1, MP2, MP6

## Unlock the Problem

Lauren's family is going hiking tomorrow at 7:00. How should Lauren write the time to show that they are going in the morning, not in the evening?

- Circle the helpful information that tells about the hiking time.
- What do you need to find?

_____

_____

You can use a number line to show the sequence or order of events. It can help you understand the number of hours in a day.

**Think:** The distance from one mark to the next mark represents one hour.

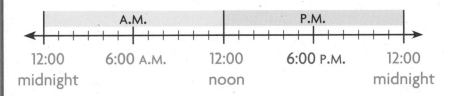

| A.M. | | P.M. | |
|---|---|---|---|
| 12:00 midnight | 6:00 A.M. | 12:00 noon | 6:00 P.M. | 12:00 midnight |

**1** **Tell time after midnight.**

**Midnight** is 12:00 at night.

The times after midnight and before noon are written with **A.M.**

7:00 in the morning is written as

7:00 _____

So, Lauren should write the hiking time as 7:00 _____

After Midnight and Before Noon

A.M.

- Find the mark that shows 7:00 A.M. on the number line above. Circle the mark.

**Math Talk**

MATHEMATICAL PRACTICES ❸

**Compare Representations** How are the number line on this page and the clock face alike? How are they different?

© Houghton Mifflin Harcourt Publishing Company • Image Credits: ©Michael Halbersta ©Steve Mason/Photodisc/Getty Images

**Chapter 10** 567

**Tell time after noon.**

Callie's family is going for a canoe ride at 3:00 in the afternoon. How should Callie write the time?

**Noon** is 12:00 in the daytime.

The times after noon and before midnight are written with **P.M.**

3:00 in the afternoon is written as 3:00 _____

After Noon and Before Midnight

So, Callie should write the time as 3:00 _____

## Share and Show MATH BOARD

1. Name two things you do in the A.M. hours.
   Name two things you do in the P.M. hours.

   _____

   _____

**Write the time for the activity. Use A.M. or P.M.**

2. ride a bicycle

   _____

3. make a sandwich

   _____

4. get ready for bed

   _____

5. This morning Sam woke up at the time shown on this clock. Write the time using A.M. or P.M. _____

**Math Talk** MATHEMATICAL PRACTICES ③

**Apply** How do you decide whether to use A.M. or P.M. when you write the time?

Name _____

**Write the time for the activity. Use A.M. or P.M.**

6. eat breakfast

_____

7. have science class

_____

8. play softball

_____

**Write the time. Use A.M. or P.M.**

9. quarter after 9:00 in the morning

_____

10. 6 minutes after 7:00 in the morning

_____

11. Mark is taking a trip on an airplane. His flight leaves at 24 minutes before 9 in the morning. Using A.M. or P.M., at what time does Mark's flight leave?

_____

12. Jennie's class ate lunch at 18 minutes before noon each day. Using A.M. or P.M., write the time that Jennie's class ate lunch.

_____

13. Daylight saving time begins on the second Sunday in March at 2:00 in the morning. Write the time.

Use A.M. or P.M. _____

14. GO DEEPER Jane and her dad are using their new telescope to look at the stars. They start looking at the stars at 23 minutes after 9 and stopped looking at the stars at 10 minutes after 10. Using A.M. or P.M., at what time did they start and stop looking at the stars?

_____

15. THINK SMARTER From midnight to noon each day, how many times does the minute hand on a clock pass 6? Explain how you found your answer.

_____

_____

## 🔑 Unlock the Problem (Real World)

**16.** Lea and her father arrived at the scenic overlook 15 minutes before noon and left 12 minutes after noon. Using A.M. or P.M., write the time when Lea and her father arrived at the scenic overlook and the time when they left.

a. What do you need to find? _____

_____

_____

b. What do you need to find first? _____

c. **MATHEMATICAL PRACTICE ⑥ Describe a Method** Show the steps you used to solve the problem.

d. They arrived at _____ _____.M.

They left at _____ _____.M.

---

**17.** **THINK SMARTER** The Davis family spent the day at the lake. Write the letter for each activity next to the time they did it.

Ⓐ Went swimming soon after lunch.              ☐ 9:50 A.M.

Ⓑ Ate breakfast at home.                        ☐ 7:00 P.M.

Ⓒ Watched the sunset over the lake.             ☐ 12:15 P.M.

Ⓓ Got to the lake cabin in the morning.         ☐ 1:30 P.M.

Ⓔ Had sandwiches for lunch.                     ☐ 7:00 A.M.

# A.M. and P.M.

**Common Core**

**COMMON CORE STANDARD—3.MD.A.1**
*Solve problems involving measurement and estimation of intervals of time, liquid volumes, and masses of objects.*

**Write the time for the activity. Use A.M. or P.M.**

**1.** eat lunch

12:20 P.M.

**2.** go home after school

**3.** see the sunrise

**4.** go for a walk

**5.** go to school

**6.** get ready for art class

**Write the time. Use A.M. or P.M.**

**7.** one half hour past midnight

**8.** one-half hour after 4:00 in the morning

## Problem Solving (Real World)

**9.** Jaime is in math class. What time is it? Use A.M. or P.M.

**10.** Pete began practicing his trumpet at fifteen minutes past three. Write this time using A.M. or P.M.

**11.** **WRITE** ▸*Math* Write your schedule for today. List each activity with its starting time. Write A.M. or P.M. for each time.

# Lesson Check (3.MD.A.1)

1. Steven is doing his homework. What time is it? Use A.M. or P.M.

   ```
    4:35
   ```

2. After he finished breakfast, Mr. Edwards left for work at fifteen minutes after seven. What time is this? Use A.M. or P.M.

## Spiral Review (3.OA.B.6, 3.NBT.A.2, 3.NBT.A.3, 3.NF.A.3d)

3. What division equation is related to the multiplication equation

   $$4 \times 6 = 24?$$

4. There are 50 toothpicks in each box. Jaime buys 4 boxes for her party platter. How many toothpicks does Jaime buy?

5. A pet store sold 145 bags of beef-flavored dog food and 263 bags of cheese-flavored dog food. How many bags of dog food were sold?

6. Compare. Write <, >, or =.

   $$\frac{3}{6} \bigcirc \frac{4}{6}$$

FOR MORE PRACTICE
GO TO THE
Personal Math Trainer

# Measure Time Intervals

**Essential Question** How can you measure elapsed time in minutes?

 **Common Core** Measurement and Data—
3.MD.A.1
MATHEMATICAL PRACTICES
MP2, MP3, MP4

## Unlock the Problem (Real World)

Alicia and her family visited the Kennedy Space Center. They watched a movie that began at 4:10 P.M. and ended at 4:53 P.M. How long did the movie last?

- Circle the times the movie began and ended.
- Underline the question.

To find **elapsed time**, find the amount of time that passes from the start of an activity to the end of the activity.

### One Way Use a number line.

**STEP 1** Find the time on the number line that the movie began.

**STEP 2** Count on to the ending time, 4:53. Count on by tens for each 10 minutes. Count on by ones for each minute. Write the times below the number line.

**STEP 3** Draw the jumps on the number line to show the minutes from 4:10 to 4:53. Record the minutes. Then add them.

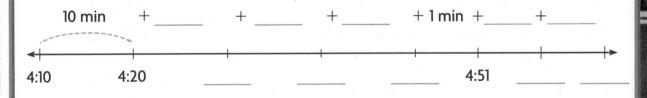

10 min  + _____  + _____  + _____  + 1 min + _____  + _____

4:10        4:20        _____     _____        4:51     _____   _____

10 + 10 + 10 + 10 + 1 + 1 + 1 = _____

The elapsed time from 4:10 P.M. to

4:53 P.M. is _____ minutes.

So, the movie lasted _____ minutes.

 **Math Talk**

MATHEMATICAL PRACTICES ④

**Use Models** What is another way you can use jumps on the number line to find the elapsed time from 4:10 P.M. to 4:53 P.M?

## 🔒 Other Ways

Start time: 4:10 P.M. End time: 4:53 P.M.

### Ⓐ Use an analog clock.

**STEP 1** Find the starting time on the clock.

**STEP 2** Count the minutes by counting on by fives and ones to 4:53 P.M. Write the missing counting numbers next to the clock.

So, the elapsed time is _____ minutes.

### Ⓑ Use subtraction.

**STEP 1** Write the ending time. Then write the starting time so that the hours and minutes line up.

**STEP 2** The hours are the same, so subtract the minutes.

$$
\begin{array}{r}
4 : \boxed{\phantom{00}} \quad \leftarrow \text{end time} \\
-\,4 : \boxed{\phantom{00}} \quad \leftarrow \text{start time} \\
\hline
\boxed{\phantom{00}} \quad \leftarrow \text{elapsed time}
\end{array}
$$

---

**Try This!** **Find the elapsed time in minutes two ways.**

Start time: 10:05 A.M. End time: 10:30 A.M.

### Ⓐ Use a number line.

**STEP 1** Find 10:05 on the number line. Count on from 10:05 to 10:30. Draw marks and record the times on the number line. Then draw and label the jumps.

**Think:** Count on using longer amounts of time that make sense.

10:05

**STEP 2** Add to find the total minutes from 10:05 to 10:30.

From 10:05 A.M. to _____ is _____ minutes.

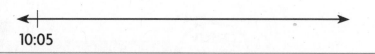

So, the elapsed time is _____ minutes.

### Ⓑ Use subtraction.

**Think:** The hours are the same, so subtract the minutes.

$$
\begin{array}{r}
10 : 30 \\
-10 : 05 \\
\hline
\boxed{\phantom{00}}
\end{array}
$$

Math Talk

© Houghton Mifflin Harcourt Publishing Company

MATHEMATICAL PRACTICES ❸

**Compare Strategies** Which method do you prefer to use to find elapsed time?

Name _____

1. Use the number line to find the elapsed time

   from 1:15 P.M. to 1:40 P.M. _____

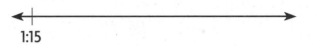

1:15

**Find the elapsed time.**

2. Start: 11:35 A.M.    End: 11:54 A.M.

_____

3. Start: 4:20 P.M.    End: 5:00 P.M.

_____

**Math Talk**    MATHEMATICAL PRACTICES ④

**Use a Model** How would you use a number line to find the elapsed time from 11:10 A.M. until noon?

**On Your Own**

MATHEMATICAL PRACTICE ⑤ **Use Appropriate Tools** **Find the elapsed time.**

4. Start: 8:35 P.M.    End: 8:55 P.M.

_____

5. Start: 10:10 A.M.    End: 10:41 A.M.

_____

6. Start: 9:25 A.M.    End: 9:43 A.M.

_____

7. Start: 2:15 P.M.    End: 2:52 P.M.

_____

## Problem Solving • Applications (Real World)

**8.** John started reading his book about outer space at quarter after nine in the morning. He read until quarter to ten in the morning. How long did John read his book?

_____

**9.** **MATHEMATICAL PRACTICE ②** **Use Reasoning** Tim and Alicia arrived at the rocket display at 3:40 P.M. Alicia left the display at 3:56 P.M. Tim left at 3:49 P.M. If the answer is Alicia, what is the question?

_____

_____

· WRITE ▸ _Math_ · **Show Your Work** · · · ·

**10.** _GO DEEPER_ At the space center, Karen bought a model of a shuttle. She started working on the model the next day at 11:13 A.M. She worked until leaving for lunch at 11:51 A.M. After lunch, she worked on the model again from 1:29 P.M. until 1:48 P.M. How long did Karen work on the model?

_____

**11.** _THINK SMARTER_ Aiden arrived at the rocket display at 3:35 P.M. and left at 3:49 P.M. Ava arrived at the rocket display at 3:30 P.M. and left at 3:56 P.M. Ava spent how many more minutes at the rocket display than Aiden?

_____

**12.** _THINK SMARTER_ Kira got on the tour bus at 5:15 P.M. She got off the bus at 5:37 P.M. How long was Kira on the bus?

Select the number to make the sentence true.

Kira was on the bus for _____ minutes.

| 15 |
|----|
| 22 |
| 37 |
| 52 |

# Measure Time Intervals

COMMON CORE STANDARD—3.MD.A.1
*Solve problems involving measurement and
estimation of intervals of time, liquid volumes,
and masses of objects.*

## Find the elapsed time.

**1.** Start: 8:10 A.M.    End: 8:45 A.M.

**35 minutes**

**2.** Start: 6:45 P.M.    End: 6:54 P.M.

**3.** Start: 3:00 P.M.    End: 3:37 P.M.

**4.** Start: 5:20 A.M.    End: 5:47 A.M.

## Problem Solving Real World

**5.** A show at the museum starts at
7:40 P.M. and ends at 7:57 P.M.
How long is the show?

**6.** The first train leaves the station at
6:15 A.M. The second train leaves
at 6:55 A.M. How much later does the
second train leave the station?

**7.** **WRITE** ▸*Math* Describe two different methods to find
the elapsed time from 2:30 P.M. to 2:58 P.M.

_____

_____

## Lesson Check (3.MD.A.1)

1. Marcus began playing basketball at 3:30 P.M. and stopped playing at 3:55 P.M. For how many minutes did he play basketball?

2. The school play started at 8:15 P.M. and ended at 8:56 P.M. How long was the school play?

## Spiral Review (3.OA.A.1, 3.OA.B.6, 3.NBT.A.2, 3.NBT.A.3)

3. Each car has 4 wheels. How many wheels do 7 cars have?

4. What number completes the equations?

$$3 \times \blacksquare = 27 \quad 27 \div 3 = \blacksquare$$

5. There are 20 napkins in each package. Kelli bought 8 packages for her party. How many napkins did Kelli buy in all?

6. Mr. Martin drove 290 miles last week. This week he drove 125 miles more than last week. How many miles did Mr. Martin drive this week?

FOR MORE PRACTICE
GO TO THE
Personal Math Trainer

Name _____

# Use Time Intervals

**Essential Question** How can you find a starting time or an ending time when you know the elapsed time?

Common Core  **Measurement and Data—**
**3.MD.A.1** *Also 3.NBT.A.2*
**MATHEMATICAL PRACTICES**
**MP2, MP3, MP4**

## ? Unlock the Problem

Javier begins working on his oceans project at 1:30 P.M. He spends 42 minutes painting a model of Earth and labeling the oceans. At what time does Javier finish working on his project?

- Circle the information you need.
- What time do you need to find?

_____

### One Way Use a number line to find the ending time.

**STEP 1** Find the time on the number line when Javier started working on the project.
_____

**STEP 2** Count forward on the number line to add the elapsed time. Draw and label the jumps to show the minutes.

Think: I can break apart 42 minutes into shorter amounts of time.
_____

**STEP 3** Write the times below the number line.

**Math Talk** MATHEMATICAL PRACTICES ④

**Model Mathematics** When finding times on the number line, how do you know what size jumps to make?

←————————————————————→
    1:30 P.M.

The jumps end at _____

So, Javier finishes working on his project at _____

### Another Way Use a clock to find the ending time.

**STEP 1** Find the starting time on the clock.
_____

**STEP 2** Count on by fives and ones for the elapsed time of 42 minutes. Write the missing counting numbers next to the clock.

So, the ending time is _____

© Houghton Mifflin Harcourt Publishing Company

## Find Starting Times

Whitney went swimming in the ocean for
25 minutes. She finished swimming at 11:15 A.M.
At what time did Whitney start swimming?

### 🔓 One Way Use a number line to find the starting time.

**STEP 1** Find the time on the number line when Whitney finished
swimming in the ocean.

**STEP 2** Count back on the number line to subtract the elapsed
time. Draw and label the jumps to show the minutes.

**STEP 3** Write the times below the number line.

11:15 A.M.

You jumped back to _____

So, Whitney started swimming at _____

### 🔓 Another Way Use a clock to find the starting time.

**STEP 1** Find the ending time on the clock.

**STEP 2** Count back by fives for the elapsed time of 25 minutes.
Write the missing counting numbers next to the clock.

So, the starting time is _____

 **Share and Show**

1. Use the number line to find the starting time if the

   elapsed time is 35 minutes. _____

**Math Talk** MATHEMATICAL PRACTICES ②

Use Reasoning How do you find the starting time when you know the ending time and the elapsed time?

5:10 P.M.

Name _____

**Find the ending time.**

2. Starting time: 1:40 P.M.
   Elapsed time: 33 minutes

   ⟵————————————⟶

   _____

3. Starting time: 9:55 A.M.
   Elapsed time: 27 minutes

   _____

**Find the starting time.**

4. Ending time: 3:05 P.M.
   Elapsed time: 40 minutes

   ⟵————————————⟶

   _____

5. Ending time: 8:06 A.M.
   Elapsed time: 16 minutes

   _____

**Problem Solving • Applications** Real World

6. **THINK SMARTER** Suzi began fishing at 10:30 A.M. and fished until 11:10 A.M. James finished fishing at 11:45 A.M. He fished for the same length of time as Suzi. At what time did James start fishing? **Explain.**

   _____

   _____

7. **GO DEEPER** Jessica starts cleaning her room at 5:50 P.M. and finishes at 6:44 P.M. Her sister Norah finishes cleaning her room at 7:12 P.M. She cleans for the same amount of time as Jessica. At what time does Norah start cleaning?

   _____

8. **THINK SMARTER +**   Dante's surfing lesson began at
2:35 P.M. His lesson lasted 45 minutes.

Draw hands on the clock to show the time Dante's
surfing lesson ended.

## Connect to Science

### Tides

If you have ever been to the beach, you have
seen the water rise and fall along the shore every
day. This change in water level is called the tide.
Ocean tides are mostly caused by the pull of the
moon and the sun's gravity. High tide is when
the water is at its highest level. Low tide is when
the water is at its lowest level. In most places on
Earth, high tide and low tide each occur about
twice a day.

**Use the table for 9–10.**

9. **GO DEEPER**   The first morning, Courtney walked
on the beach for 20 minutes. She finished
her walk 30 minutes before high tide. At what
time did Courtney start her walk?

_____

10. **MATHEMATICAL PRACTICE ② Use Reasoning**   The third
afternoon, Courtney started collecting
shells at low tide. She collected shells for
35 minutes. At what time did Courtney
finish collecting shells?

_____

| Tide Times Atlantic City, NJ | | |
|---|---|---|
| | Low Tide | High Tide |
| Day 1 | 2:12 A.M. | 9:00 A.M. |
| | 2:54 P.M. | 9:00 P.M. |
| Day 2 | 3:06 A.M. | 9:36 A.M. |
| | 3:36 P.M. | 9:54 P.M. |
| Day 3 | 4:00 A.M. | 10:12 A.M. |
| | 4:30 P.M. | 10:36 P.M. |

## Use Time Intervals

Common Core

**COMMON CORE STANDARD—3.MD.A.1**
Solve problems involving measurement and
estimation of intervals of time, liquid volumes,
and masses of objects.

**Find the starting time.**

**1.** Ending time: 4:29 P.M.
   Elapsed time: 55 minutes

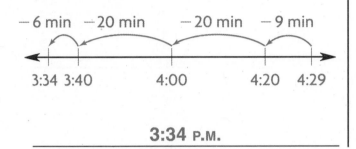

3:34 3:40   4:00   4:20 4:29

**3:34 P.M.**

**2.** Ending time: 10:08 A.M.
   Elapsed time: 30 minutes

_____

**Find the ending time.**

**3.** Starting time: 2:15 A.M.
   Elapsed time: 45 minutes

_____

**4.** Starting time: 6:57 P.M.
   Elapsed time: 47 minutes

_____

## Problem Solving Real World

**5.** Jenny spent 35 minutes doing research on the Internet. She finished at 7:10 P.M. At what time did Jenny start her research?

_____

**6.** Clark left for school at 7:43 A.M. He got to school 36 minutes later. At what time did Clark get to school?

_____

**7.** **WRITE** ▸*Math*  Describe a situation in your life when you need to know how to find a starting time.

_____

_____

## Lesson Check (3.MD.A.1)

**1.** Cody and his friends started playing a game at 6:30 P.M. It took them 37 minutes to finish the game. At what time did they finish?

**2.** Delia worked for 45 minutes on her oil painting. She took a break at 10:35 A.M. At what time did Delia start working on the painting?

## Spiral Review (3.OA.A.2, 3.OA.C.7, 3.MD.A.1)

**3.** Sierra has 30 collector's pins. She wants to put an equal number of pins in each of 5 boxes. How many pins should she put in each box?

| ? | ? | ? | ? | ? |
|---|---|---|---|---|

30 pins

**4.** What time is shown on the clock?

**5.** Ricardo has 32 books to put on 4 shelves. He puts the same number of books on each shelf. How many books does Ricardo put on each shelf?

**6.** Jon started playing a computer game at 5:35 P.M. He finished the game at 5:52 P.M. How long did Jon play the game?

FOR MORE PRACTICE
GO TO THE
**Personal Math Trainer**

Name _____

# Problem Solving • Time Intervals

**Essential Question** How can you use the strategy *draw a diagram* to solve problems about time?

 **Common Core** Measurement and Data— 3.MD.A.1 *Also 3.OA.D.8, 3.NBT.A.2*
**MATHEMATICAL PRACTICES**
MP1, MP3, MP6

## Unlock the Problem

Zach and his family are going to New York City. Their airplane leaves at 9:15 A.M. They need to arrive at the airport 60 minutes before their flight. It takes 15 minutes to get to the airport. The family needs 30 minutes to get ready to leave. At what time should Zach's family start getting ready?

## Read the Problem

| What do I need to find? | What information do I need to use? | How will I use the information? |
|---|---|---|
| I need to find what _____ Zach's family should start _____. | the time the _____ leaves; the time the family needs to arrive at the _____ ; the time it takes to get to the _____ ; and the time the family needs to _____ | I will use a number line to find the answer. |

## Solve the Problem

• Find 9:15 A.M. on the number line. Draw the jumps to show the time.

• Count back _____ minutes to find the time they need to arrive at the airport.

←————————————————————————|
9:15 A.M.

• Count back _____ minutes to find the time they need to leave for the airport.

• Count back _____ minutes to find the time they need to start getting ready.

So, Zach's family should start getting ready at _____ _____.M.

 Math Talk
**MATHEMATICAL PRACTICES ①**
**Analyze** How can you check your answer by starting with the time the family starts getting ready?

## ⬛ Try Another Problem

Bradley gets out of school at 2:45 P.M. It takes him 10 minutes to walk home. Then he spends 10 minutes eating a snack. He spends 8 minutes putting on his soccer uniform. It takes 20 minutes for Bradley's father to drive him to soccer practice. At what time does Bradley arrive at soccer practice?

### Read the Problem

| What do I need to find? | What information do I need to use? | How will I use the information? |
|---|---|---|
| | | |

### Solve the Problem

**Draw a diagram to help you explain your answer.**

$$\longleftrightarrow$$

**1.** At what time does Bradley arrive at soccer practice? _____

**2.** How do you know your answer is reasonable?

_____

_____

_____

**Math Talk**

MATHEMATICAL PRACTICES ①

**Analyze** Do you need to draw jumps on the number line in the same order as the times in the problem?

Name _____

## Unlock the Problem
√ Circle the question.
√ Underline important facts.
√ Choose a strategy you know.

**Share and Show**  MATH BOARD

1. Patty went to the shopping mall at 11:30 A.M. She shopped for 25 minutes. She spent 40 minutes eating lunch. Then she met a friend at a movie. At what time did Patty meet her friend?

First, begin with _____ on the number line.

Then, count forward _____ and _____.

**Think:** I can break apart the times into shorter amounts of time that make sense.

11:30 A.M.

So, Patty met her friend at _____ _____ M.

2. What if Patty goes to the mall at 11:30 A.M. and meets a friend at a movie at 1:15 P.M.? Patty wants to shop and have 45 minutes for lunch before meeting her friend. How much time can Patty spend shopping?

_____

3. Avery got on the bus at 1:10 P.M. The trip took 90 minutes. Then she walked for 32 minutes to get home. At what time did Avery arrive at home?

_____

**On Your Own**

4. **GO DEEPER** Kyle and Josh have a total of 64 CDs. Kyle has 12 more CDs than Josh. How many CDs does each boy have?

_____

© Houghton Mifflin Harcourt Publishing Company

5. Jamal spent 60 minutes using the computer. He spent a half hour of the time playing games and the rest of the time researching his report. How many minutes did Jamal spend researching his report?

_____

6. THINK SMARTER  When Caleb got home from school, he worked on his science project for 20 minutes. Then he studied for a test for 30 minutes. He finished at 4:35 P.M. At what time did Caleb get home from school?

_____

7. MATHEMATICAL PRACTICE 6  Miguel played video games each day for a week. On Monday, he scored 83 points. His score went up 5 points each day. On what day did Miguel score 103 points? **Explain** how you found your answer.

_____

_____

8. THINK SMARTER  When Laura arrived at the library, she spent 40 minutes reading a book. Then she spent 15 minutes reading a magazine. She left the library at 4:15 P.M.

Circle the time that makes the sentence true.

Laura arrived at the library at

3:20 P.M.

3:35 P.M.

5:10 P.M.

## Problem Solving • Time Intervals

**Common Core** COMMON CORE STANDARD—3.MD.A.1
Solve problems involving measurement and estimation of intervals of time, liquid volumes, and masses of objects.

### Solve each problem. Show your work.

1. Hannah wants to meet her friends downtown. Before leaving home, she does chores for 60 minutes and eats lunch for 20 minutes. The walk downtown takes 15 minutes. Hannah starts her chores at 11:45 A.M. At what time does she meet her friends?

60 min  + 20 min + 15 min

11:45        12:45    1:05    1:20

_____ **1:20** P.M. _____

2. Katie practiced the flute for 45 minutes. Then she ate a snack for 15 minutes. Next, she watched television for 30 minutes, until 6:00 P.M. At what time did Katie start practicing the flute?

_____

3. Nick gets out of school at 2:25 P.M. He has a 15-minute ride home on the bus. Next, he goes on a 30-minute bike ride. Then he spends 55 minutes doing homework. At what time does Nick finish his homework?

_____

4. **WRITE** ▸*Math* Write a multistep word problem that has at least two amounts of elapsed time. The problem may require finding a starting time or ending time. Include a solution.

_____

_____

## Lesson Check (3.MD.A.1)

1. Gloria went to the mall and spent 50 minutes shopping. Then she had lunch for 30 minutes. If Gloria arrived at the mall at 11:00 A.M., at what time did she finish lunch?

2. The ball game begins at 2:00 P.M. It takes Ying 30 minutes to get to the ballpark. At what time should Ying leave home to get to the game 30 minutes before it starts?

## Spiral Review (3.OA.A.2, 3.OA.A.4, 3.NF.A.2, 3.NF.A.3d)

3. Write the fractions $\frac{2}{4}$, $\frac{2}{8}$, and $\frac{2}{6}$ in order from least to greatest.

4. Find the unknown factor.

$$6 \times \blacksquare = 36$$

5. There were 405 books on the library shelf. Some books were checked out. Now there are 215 books left on the shelf. How many books were checked out?

6. Savannah has 48 photos. She places 8 photos on each page of her photo album. How many pages in the album does she use?

FOR MORE PRACTICE
GO TO THE
Personal Math Trainer

Name _____

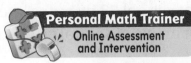

## Vocabulary

**Choose the best term from the box.**

| Vocabulary |
| --- |
| A.M. |
| minute |
| P.M. |

1. In one _____, the minute hand moves from one mark to the next on a clock. (p. 561)

2. The times after noon and before midnight are written

   with _____. (p. 568)

## Concepts and Skills

**Write the time for the activity. Use A.M. or P.M.** (3.MD.A.1)

3. play ball

_____

4. eat breakfast

_____

5. do homework

_____

6. sleep

_____

**Find the elapsed time.** (3.MD.A.1)

7. Start: 10:05 A.M.     End: 10:50 A.M.

10:05

_____

8. Start: 5:30 P.M.
   End: 5:49 P.M.

_____

**Find the starting time or the ending time.** (3.MD.A.1)

9. Starting time: _____
   Elapsed time: 50 minutes
   Ending time: 9:05 A.M.

9:05 A.M.

10. Starting time: 2:46 P.M.
    Elapsed time: 15 minutes

    Ending time: _____

**11.** Veronica started walking to school at 7:45 A.M. She arrived at school 23 minutes later. At what time did Veronica arrive at school? (3.MD.A.1)

_____

**12.** GO DEEPER  The clock shows the time the art class ends. At what time does it end? If the class started 37 minutes before the time shown, at what time did the class start?

(3.MD.A.1)

_____

**13.** Matt went to his friend's house. He arrived at 5:10 P.M. He left at 5:37 P.M. How long was Matt at his friend's house? (3.MD.A.1)

_____

**14.** Brenda's train leaves at 7:30 A.M. She needs to arrive 10 minutes early to buy her ticket. It takes her 20 minutes to get to the train station. At what time should Brenda leave her house? (3.MD.A.1)

_____

**15.** Write the time you get home from school. (3.MD.A.1)

_____

Name _____

# Measure Length

**Essential Question** How can you generate measurement data and show the data on a line plot?

Common Core  Measurement and Data—3.MD.B.4
MATHEMATICAL PRACTICES
MP3, MP5, MP6

**CONNECT** You have learned how to measure length to the nearest inch. Sometimes the length of an object is not a whole unit. For example, a paper clip is more than 1 inch but less than 2 inches.

You can measure length to the nearest half inch or fourth inch. The half-inch markings on a ruler divide each inch into two equal parts. The fourth-inch markings divide each inch into four equal parts.

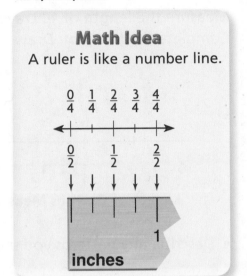

**Math Idea**
A ruler is like a number line.

$$\frac{0}{4} \quad \frac{1}{4} \quad \frac{2}{4} \quad \frac{3}{4} \quad \frac{4}{4}$$

$$\frac{0}{2} \quad \frac{1}{2} \quad \frac{2}{2}$$

inches

## Unlock the Problem Real World

### Example 1 Use a ruler to measure the glue stick to the nearest half inch.

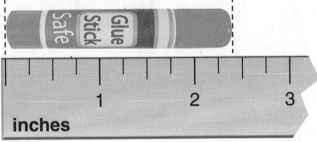

inches

- Line up the left end of the glue stick with the zero mark on the ruler.

- The right end of the glue stick is between the half-inch marks for

  _____ and _____.

- The mark that is closest to the right end of the glue stick is for _____ inches.

So, the length of the glue stick to the

nearest half inch is _____ inches.

### Example 2 Use a ruler to measure the paper clip to the nearest fourth inch.

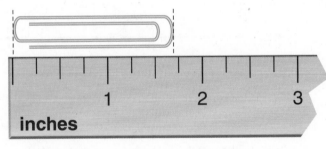

inches

- Line up the left end of the paper clip with the zero mark on the ruler.

- The right end of the paper clip is between the fourth-inch marks for

  _____ and _____.

- The mark that is closest to the right end of the paper clip is for _____ inches.

So, the length of the paper clip to the

nearest fourth inch is _____ inches.

## 🔑 Activity  Make a line plot to show measurement data.

**Materials** ▪ inch ruler ▪ 10 crayons

Measure the length of 10 crayons to the nearest half inch.
Complete the line plot. Draw an ✗ for each length.

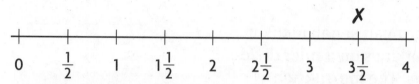

**Length of Crayons Measured to the Nearest Half Inch**

• Describe any patterns you see in your line plot.

_____

_____

**Try This!** Measure the length of your fingers to the
nearest fourth inch. Complete the line plot. Draw an
✗ for each length.

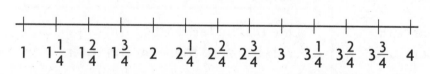

**Length of Fingers Measured to the Nearest Fourth Inch**

> **Math Talk**
>
> MATHEMATICAL PRACTICES ❸
>
> **Compare Representations**
> How do you think your
> line plot compares to
> line plots your classmates
> made?

 **Share and Show**  **MATH BOARD**

✅ **1.** Measure the length to the nearest half inch. Is the
key closest to $1\frac{1}{2}$ inches, 2 inches, or $2\frac{1}{2}$ inches?

_____ inches

Name _____

**Measure the length to the nearest fourth inch.**

2. 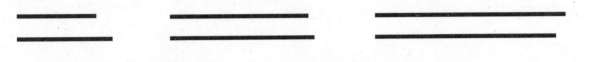 _____ inches

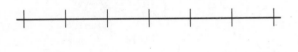

**Use the lines for 3–4.**

3. Measure the length of the lines to the nearest half inch and make a line plot.

+———+———+———+———+———+———+

4. Measure the length of the lines to the nearest fourth inch and make a line plot.

+—+—+—+—+—+—+—+—+—+—+—+

# Problem Solving · Applications

**Use the line plot for 5–7.**

5. GO DEEPER  Tara has a magnet collection from places she visited. She measures the length of the magnets to the nearest half inch and records the data in a line plot. Are more magnets longer than $2\frac{1}{2}$ inches or shorter than $2\frac{1}{2}$ inches? Explain.

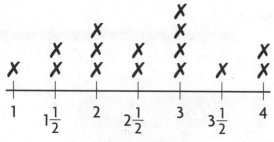

**Length of Magnets**

_____

_____

_____

6. THINK SMARTER  How many magnets measure a whole number of inches? How many magnets have a length between two whole numbers?

_____

_____

7. MATHEMATICAL PRACTICE ⑥ **Explain** why you think the line plot starts at 1 and stops at 4.

_____

_____

_____

8. THINK SMARTER  What is the length of the pencil to the nearest half inch?

_____ inches

Explain how you measured the pencil.

_____

_____

## Measure Length

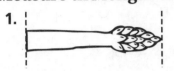

**COMMON CORE STANDARD—3.MD.B.4**
*Represent and interpret data.*

**Measure the length to the nearest half inch.**

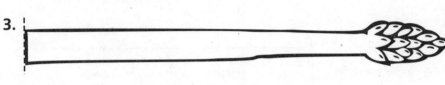

1.

___$1\frac{1}{2}$___ inches

2.

_____ inches

3.

_____ inches

**Measure the length to the nearest fourth inch.**

4.

_____ inches

5.

_____ inches

## Problem Solving (Real World)

**Use a separate sheet of paper for 6.**

6. Draw 8 lines that are between 1 inch and 3 inches long. Measure each line to the nearest fourth inch, and make a line plot.

7. Alex's dog has a tail that is $5\frac{1}{4}$ inches long. On a ruler, what inch marks are closest to $5\frac{1}{4}$ inches? Name two inch marks.

_____          _____

8. **WRITE** *Math* Measure the lengths of 10 color pencils to the nearest fourth inch. Then make a line plot of the data.

_____

_____

## Lesson Check (3.MD.B.4)

1. What is the length of the string to the nearest half inch?

2. What is the length of the leaf to the nearest fourth inch?

## Spiral Review (3.OA.C.7, 3.MD.A.1)

3. Write the equations included in the same set of related facts as $6 \times 8 = 48$.

4. Brooke says there are 49 days until July 4. There are 7 days in a week. In how many weeks will it be July 4?

5. It is 20 minutes before 8:00 in the morning. What time is this? Use A.M. or P.M.

6. Marcy played the piano for 45 minutes. She stopped playing at 4:15 P.M. At what time did she start playing the piano?

FOR MORE PRACTICE
GO TO THE
Personal Math Trainer

Name _____

# Estimate and Measure Liquid Volume

**Essential Question** How can you estimate and measure liquid volume in metric units?

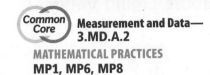

Common Core **Measurement and Data—3.MD.A.2**
**MATHEMATICAL PRACTICES**
**MP1, MP6, MP8**

## Unlock the Problem

**Liquid volume** is the amount of liquid in a container. The **liter (L)** is the basic metric unit for measuring liquid volume.

## Activity 1

**Materials** ■ 1-L beaker ■ 4 containers ■ water ■ tape

**STEP 1**  Fill a 1-liter beaker with water to the 1-liter mark.

**STEP 2**  Pour 1 liter of water into a container. Mark the level of the water with a piece of tape. Draw the container below and name the container.

**STEP 3**  Repeat Steps 1 and 2 with three different-sized containers.

Container 1             Container 2

_____   _____

Container 3             Container 4

_____   _____

 **MATHEMATICAL PRACTICES** ⑧

**Draw Conclusions**
What happens to the liquid volume when you pour the same amount of liquid into different sized containers?

1. How much water did you pour into each container? _____

2. Which containers are mostly full? Describe them.

_____

3. Which containers are mostly empty? Describe them.

_____

## Compare Liquid Volumes

A full glass holds less than 1 liter.

A water bottle holds about 1 liter.

A fish bowl holds more than 1 liter.

 **Activity 2 Materials** ■ 1-L beaker ■ 5 different containers ■ water

**STEP 1** Write the containers in order from the one you think will hold the least water to the one you think will hold the most water.

_____, _____, _____,

_____, _____

**STEP 2** Estimate how much each container will hold. Write *more than 1 liter*, *about 1 liter*, or *less than 1 liter* in the table.

**STEP 3** Pour 1 liter of water into one of the containers. Repeat until the container is full. Record the number of liters you poured. Repeat for each container.

| Container | Estimate | Number of Liters |
|-----------|----------|------------------|
|           |          |                  |
|           |          |                  |
|           |          |                  |
|           |          |                  |
|           |          |                  |

**STEP 4** Write the containers in order from the least to the greatest liquid volume.

_____, _____, _____,

_____, _____

**Math Talk**

MATHEMATICAL PRACTICES ①

**Evaluate** Was the order in Step 1 different than the order in Step 4? Explain why they may be different.

© Houghton Mifflin Harcourt Publishing Company • Image Credits: (tr) ©PhotoDisc/Getty Images

Name _____

1. The beaker is filled with water. Is the amount *more than 1 liter, about 1 liter,* or *less than 1 liter*?

_____

**Estimate how much liquid volume there will be when the container is filled. Write *more than 1 liter, about 1 liter,* or *less than 1 liter*.**

| 2. cup of tea | 3. kitchen sink | 4. teapot |
|---|---|---|
|  |  |  |
| _____ | _____ | _____ |

**On Your Own**

**Estimate how much liquid volume there will be when the container is filled. Write *more than 1 liter, about 1 liter,* or *less than 1 liter*.**

**Math Talk** MATHEMATICAL PRACTICES ⑧

**Generalize** How can you estimate the liquid volume in a container?

| 5. pitcher | 6. juice box | 7. punch bowl |
|---|---|---|
|  |  |  |
| _____ | _____ | _____ |

**Use the pictures for 8–10. Rosario pours juice into four bottles that are the same size.**

8. Did Rosario pour the same amount into each bottle? _____

9. Which bottle has the least amount of juice? _____

10. Which bottle has the most juice? _____

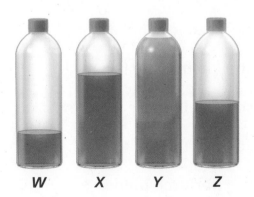

W  X  Y  Z

# Problem Solving • Applications (Real World)

**Use the containers for 11–13. Container A is full when 1 liter of water is poured into it.**

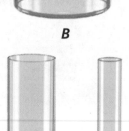

A    D

11. **GO DEEPER** Estimate how many liters will fill Container C and how many liters will fill Container E. Which container will hold more water when filled?

_____

_____

B

12. **MATHEMATICAL PRACTICE 6** Name two containers that will be filled with about the same number of liters of water. **Explain**.

_____

_____

_____

C    E

13. **THINK SMARTER** **What's the Error?** Samuel says that you can pour more liters of water into Container B than into Container D. Is he correct? Explain.

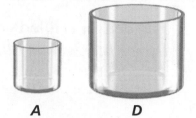

_____

_____

_____

**Personal Math Trainer**

14. **THINK SMARTER +** The bottle of tea holds about 1 liter. For numbers 14a–14e, choose Yes or No to tell whether it will hold more than 1 liter.

14a. teacup            ○ Yes    ○ No

14b. kitchen trash can  ○ Yes    ○ No

14c. small pool         ○ Yes    ○ No

14d. fish tank          ○ Yes    ○ No

14e. perfume bottle     ○ Yes    ○ No

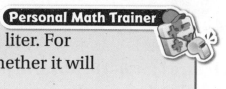

## Problem Solving • Time Intervals

**COMMON CORE STANDARD—3.MD.A.1**
*Solve problems involving measurement and estimation of intervals of time, liquid volumes, and masses of objects.*

**Solve each problem. Show your work.**

1. Hannah wants to meet her friends downtown. Before leaving home, she does chores for 60 minutes and eats lunch for 20 minutes. The walk downtown takes 15 minutes. Hannah starts her chores at 11:45 A.M. At what time does she meet her friends?

_____1:20_ P.M._____

2. Katie practiced the flute for 45 minutes. Then she ate a snack for 15 minutes. Next, she watched television for 30 minutes, until 6:00 P.M. At what time did Katie start practicing the flute?

_____

3. Nick gets out of school at 2:25 P.M. He has a 15-minute ride home on the bus. Next, he goes on a 30-minute bike ride. Then he spends 55 minutes doing homework. At what time does Nick finish his homework?

_____

4. **WRITE** ▸*Math* Write a multistep word problem that has at least two amounts of elapsed time. The problem may require finding a starting time or ending time. Include a solution.

_____

_____

## Lesson Check (3.MD.A.1)

**1.** Gloria went to the mall and spent 50 minutes shopping. Then she had lunch for 30 minutes. If Gloria arrived at the mall at 11:00 A.M., at what time did she finish lunch?

**2.** The ball game begins at 2:00 P.M. It takes Ying 30 minutes to get to the ballpark. At what time should Ying leave home to get to the game 30 minutes before it starts?

## Spiral Review (3.OA.A.2, 3.OA.A.4, 3.NF.A.2, 3.NF.A.3d)

**3.** Write the fractions $\frac{2}{4}$, $\frac{2}{8}$, and $\frac{2}{6}$ in order from least to greatest.

**4.** Find the unknown factor.

$$6 \times \blacksquare = 36$$

**5.** There were 405 books on the library shelf. Some books were checked out. Now there are 215 books left on the shelf. How many books were checked out?

**6.** Savannah has 48 photos. She places 8 photos on each page of her photo album. How many pages in the album does she use?

FOR MORE PRACTICE
GO TO THE
Personal Math Trainer

Name _____

## Estimate and Measure Liquid Volume

 COMMON CORE STANDARD—3.MD.A.2
*Solve problems involving measurement and estimation of intervals of time, liquid measures, and masses of objects.*

**Estimate how much liquid volume there will be when the container is filled. Write** *more than 1 liter, about 1 liter,* **or** *less than 1 liter.*

**1.** large milk container

_____more than 1 liter_____

**2.** small milk container

**3.** water bottle

_____

**4.** spoonful of water

**5.** bathtub

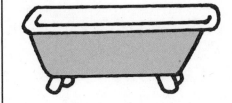

**6.** eyedropper

_____

**Problem Solving** *Real World*

**Use the pictures for 7. Alan pours water into four glasses that are the same size.**

**7.** Which glass has the most amount

of water? _____

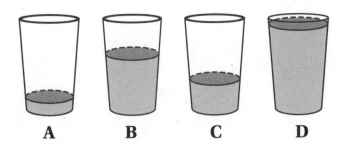

A    B    C    D

**8.** **WRITE** *Math*  Name a container that you see at home that when filled has a liquid volume of about 1 liter.

_____

_____

## Lesson Check (3.MD.A.2)

**1.** Felicia filled the bathroom sink with water. Is the amount more than 1 liter, about 1 liter, or less than 1 liter?

**2.** Kyle needed about 1 liter of water to fill a container. Did Kyle most likely fill a small glass, a spoon, or a vase?

_____

_____

## Spiral Review (3.OA.B.5, 3.NF.A.1, 3.MD.A.1, 3.MD.B.4)

**3.** Cecil had 6 ice cubes. He put 1 ice cube in each glass. In how many glasses did Cecil put ice cubes?

**4.** Juan has 12 muffins. He puts $\frac{1}{4}$ of the muffins in a bag. How many muffins does Juan put in the bag?

_____

_____

**5.** What time is shown on the clock?

**6.** Julianne drew the line segment below. Use your ruler to measure the segment to the nearest fourth inch.

_____

_____

_____

_____

_____

_____

FOR MORE PRACTICE
GO TO THE
**Personal Math Trainer**

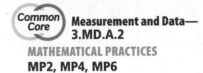

Name _____

# Estimate and Measure Mass

**Essential Question** How can you estimate and measure mass in metric units?

 **Common Core** Measurement and Data—
3.MD.A.2
**MATHEMATICAL PRACTICES**
MP2, MP4, MP6

## Unlock the Problem

Pedro has a dollar bill in his pocket. Should Pedro measure the mass of the dollar bill in grams or kilograms?

The **gram (g)** is the basic metric unit for measuring **mass**, or the amount of matter in an object. Mass can also be measured by using the metric unit **kilogram (kg)**.

| | |
|---|---|
| A small paper clip has a mass of about 1 gram. | A box of 1,000 paper clips has a mass of about 1 kilogram. |

**Think:** The mass of a dollar bill is closer to the mass of a small paper clip than it is to a box of 1,000 paper clips.

So, Pedro should measure the mass of the dollar bill in _____.

## Activity 1

**Materials** ■ pan balance ■ gram and kilogram masses

You can use a pan balance to measure mass.

Do 10 grams have the same mass as 1 kilogram?

- Place 10 gram masses on one side of the balance.

- Place a 1-kilogram mass on the other side of the balance.

**Think:** If it is balanced, then the objects have the same mass. If it is not balanced, the objects do not have the same mass.

- Complete the picture of the balance above by drawing masses to show your balance.

  The pan balance is _____.

So, 10 grams and 1 kilogram _____ the same mass.

**Math Talk** MATHEMATICAL PRACTICES ④

**Use Models** How do you tell from the balance which side has greater mass?

# 🔒 Activity 2

**Materials** ■ pan balance ■ gram and kilogram masses ■ classroom objects

**STEP 1** Use the objects in the table. Decide if the object should be measured in grams or kilograms.

**STEP 2** Estimate the mass of each object. Record your estimates in the table.

**STEP 3** Find the mass of each object to the nearest gram or kilogram. Place the object on one side of the balance. Place gram or kilogram masses on the other side until both sides are balanced.

**STEP 4** Add the measures of the gram or kilogram masses. This is the mass of the object. Record the mass in the table.

▲ 189 marbles have a mass of 1 kilogram.

| Mass | | |
|---|---|---|
| **Object** | **Estimate** | **Mass** |
| crayon | | |
| stapler | | |
| eraser | | |
| marker | | |
| small notepad | | |
| scissors | | |

**Math Talk**

MATHEMATICAL PRACTICES ⑥

**Compare** How did your estimates compare with the actual measurements?

• Write the objects in order from greatest mass to least mass.

_____, _____, _____,

_____, _____, _____

## Share and Show 🖊️ MATH BOARD

1. Five bananas have a mass of about _____.

**Think:** The pan balance is balanced, so the objects on both sides have the same mass.

# Estimate and Measure Mass

**Essential Question** How can you estimate and measure mass in metric units?

 Common Core Measurement and Data—
3.MD.A.2
**MATHEMATICAL PRACTICES**
**MP2, MP4, MP6**

## ⚷ Unlock the Problem

🔓 Pedro has a dollar bill in his pocket. Should Pedro measure the mass of the dollar bill in grams or kilograms?

The **gram (g)** is the basic metric unit for measuring **mass**, or the amount of matter in an object. Mass can also be measured by using the metric unit **kilogram (kg)**.

A small paper clip has a mass of about 1 gram.

A box of 1,000 paper clips has a mass of about 1 kilogram.

**Think:** The mass of a dollar bill is closer to the mass of a small paper clip than it is to a box of 1,000 paper clips.

So, Pedro should measure the mass of the dollar bill in _____.

## 🔓 Activity 1

**Materials** ▪ pan balance ▪ gram and kilogram masses

You can use a pan balance to measure mass.

Do 10 grams have the same mass as 1 kilogram?

• Place 10 gram masses on one side of the balance.

• Place a 1-kilogram mass on the other side of the balance.

**Think:** If it is balanced, then the objects have the same mass. If it is not balanced, the objects do not have the same mass.

• Complete the picture of the balance above by drawing masses to show your balance.

The pan balance is _____.

So, 10 grams and 1 kilogram _____ the same mass.

**Math Talk** MATHEMATICAL PRACTICES ④

**Use Models** How do you tell from the balance which side has greater mass?

# ⬤ Activity 2

**Materials** ■ pan balance ■ gram and kilogram masses ■ classroom objects

**STEP 1** Use the objects in the table. Decide if the object should be measured in grams or kilograms.

**STEP 2** Estimate the mass of each object. Record your estimates in the table.

**STEP 3** Find the mass of each object to the nearest gram or kilogram. Place the object on one side of the balance. Place gram or kilogram masses on the other side until both sides are balanced.

**STEP 4** Add the measures of the gram or kilogram masses. This is the mass of the object. Record the mass in the table.

▲ 189 marbles have a mass of 1 kilogram.

| Mass | | |
|---|---|---|
| **Object** | **Estimate** | **Mass** |
| crayon | | |
| stapler | | |
| eraser | | |
| marker | | |
| small notepad | | |
| scissors | | |

**Math Talk**

MATHEMATICAL PRACTICES ⑥

**Compare** How did your estimates compare with the actual measurements?

• Write the objects in order from greatest mass to least mass.

_____ , _____ , _____ ,

_____ , _____ , _____

**Share and Show** MATH BOARD

1. Five bananas have a mass of about _____.

**Think:** The pan balance is balanced, so the objects on both sides have the same mass.

Name _____

**Choose the unit you would use to measure the mass.**
**Write *gram* or *kilogram*.**

**2.** strawberry

_____

✓**3.** dog

_____

**Compare the masses of the objects. Write**
***is less than, is the same as,*** **or** ***is more than.***

**4.**

The mass of the bowling pin

_____ the mass of
the chess piece.

✓**5.**

The mass of the erasers

_____ the mass of
the clips.

**On Your Own**

**Choose the unit you would use to measure the mass.**
**Write *gram* or *kilogram*.**

**6.** chair

_____

**7.** sunglasses

_____

**8.** watermelon

_____

**Compare the masses of the objects. Write**
***is less than, is the same as,*** **or** ***is more than.***

**9.**

The mass of the pen _____
the mass of the paper clips.

**10.**

The mass of the straws _____
the mass of the blocks.

## Problem Solving • Applications

**Golf ball**

**Table tennis ball**

**Bowling ball**

11. **GO DEEPER** Put the sports balls shown at the right in order from greatest mass to least mass.

_____

_____

12. **MATHEMATICAL PRACTICE ④ Use Diagrams** Choose two objects that have about the same mass. Draw a balance with one of these objects on each side.

13. **MATHEMATICAL PRACTICE ④ Use Diagrams** Choose two objects that have different masses. Draw a balance with one of these objects on each side.

**Baseball**

**Tennis ball**

14. **THINK SMARTER** **Pose a Problem** Write a problem about the objects you chose in Exercise 13. Then solve your problem.

_____

_____

15. **THINK SMARTER** **Sense or Nonsense?** Amber is buying produce at the grocery store. She says that a Fuji apple and a green bell pepper would have the same mass because they are the same size. Does her statement make sense? Explain.

_____

_____

_____

16. **THINK SMARTER** Select the objects with a mass greater than 1 kilogram. Mark all that apply.

(A) skateboard          (D) egg

(B) laptop computer     (E) desk

(C) cell phone          (F) pencil

Name _____

## Estimate and Measure Mass

**Common Core**
**COMMON CORE STANDARD—3.MD.A.2**
*Solve problems involving measurement and intervals of time, liquid volumes, and masses of objects.*

**Choose the unit you would use to measure the mass. Write *gram* or *kilogram*.**

| 1. CD | 2. boy | 3. bag of sugar |
|---|---|---|
|  |  |  |
| gram | | |

**Compare the masses of the objects. Write *is less than*, *is the same as*, or *is more than*.**

4.

The mass of the candle _____ the mass of the light bulb.

5.

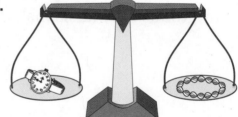

The mass of the watch _____ the mass of the necklace.

## Problem Solving • Real World

6. A red ball has a mass that is less than 1 kilogram. A blue ball has a mass of 1 kilogram. Is the mass of the blue ball more than or less than the mass of the red ball?

_____

7. Brock's dog is a collie. To find the mass of his dog, should Brock use *grams* or *kilograms*?

_____

8. **WRITE** ▸*Math* Name an object in your home  that has a mass of about 1 kg.

_____

_____

## Lesson Check (3.MD.A.2)

1. Which unit of measure would you use to measure the mass of a grape? Write *gram* or *kilogram*.

2. Elsie wants to find the mass of her pony. Which unit should she use? Write *gram* or *kilogram*.

## Spiral Review (3.OA.A.2, 3.OA.D.8, 3.MD.A.2)

3. Marsie blew up 24 balloons. She tied the balloons together in groups of 4. How many groups did Marsie make?

4. Clark used the order of operations to find the unknown number in $15 - 12 \div 3 = n$. What is the value of the unknown number?

**Use the pictures for 5–6. Ralph pours juice into four bottles that are the same size.**

5. Which bottle has the most amount of juice?

6. Which bottle has the least amount of juice?

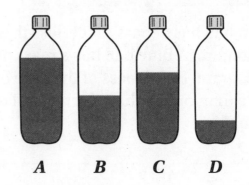

A    B    C    D

FOR MORE PRACTICE
GO TO THE
**Personal Math Trainer**

# Solve Problems About Liquid Volume and Mass

**Essential Question** How can you use models to solve liquid volume and mass problems?

Common Core  **Measurement and Data—3.MD.A.2**
*Also 3.OA.C.7, 3.NBT.A.2*
**MATHEMATICAL PRACTICES**
**MP1, MP2, MP4**

## Unlock the Problem

A restaurant serves iced tea from a large container that can hold 24 liters. Sadie will fill the container with the pitchers of tea shown below. Will Sadie have tea left over after filling the container?

### Example 1 Solve a problem about liquid volume.

_____ L     _____ L     _____ L     _____ L

Since there are _____ equal groups of _____ liters, you can multiply.

_____ ◯ _____ = _____

Circle the correct words to complete the sentences.

_____ liters is *greater than* / *less than* 24 liters.

So, Sadie *will* / *will not* have tea left over.

**Try This!** Use a bar model to solve.

Raul's fish tank contains 32 liters of water. He empties it with a bucket that holds 4 liters of water. How many times will Raul have to fill the bucket?

_____ ◯ _____ = _____

So, Raul will have to fill the bucket _____ times.

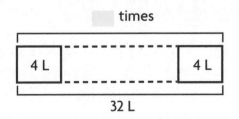

🟦 times

| 4 L | - - - - - - - - | 4 L |
32 L

## 🔑 Activity  Solve a problem about mass.

**Materials** ■ pan balance ■ glue stick ■ gram masses

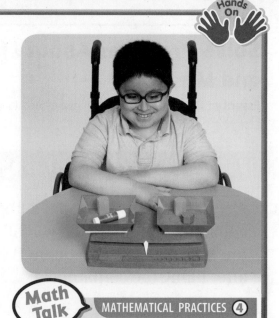

Jeff has a glue stick and a 20-gram mass on one side of a balance and gram masses on the other side. The pan balance is balanced. What is the mass of the glue stick?

**STEP 1**  Place a glue stick and a 20-gram mass on one side of the balance.

**STEP 2**  Place gram masses on the other side until the pans are balanced.

**STEP 3**  To find the mass of the glue stick, remove 20 grams from each side.

> **Think:** I can remove 20 grams from both sides and the pan balance will still be balanced.

**Math Talk**

**MATHEMATICAL PRACTICES ④**

**Write an Equation**
What equation can you write to find the mass of the glue stick?

**STEP 4**  Then add the measures of the gram masses on the balance.

The gram masses have a measure of _____ grams.

So, the glue stick has a mass of _____ .

---

**Try This!**  Use a bar model to solve.

A bag of peas has a mass of 432 grams.
A bag of carrots has a mass of 263 grams.
What is the total mass of both bags?

| _____ g | _____ g |
|---|---|

_____ g

_____ ◯ _____ = _____

So, both bags have a total mass of _____ grams.

---

**Share and Show**

1. Ed's Delivery Service delivered three packages to Ms. Wilson. The packages have masses of 9 kilograms, 12 kilograms, and 5 kilograms. What is the total mass of the three packages? Use the bar model to help you solve.

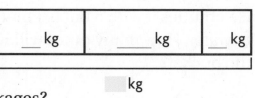

| ___ kg | _____ kg | ___ kg |
|---|---|---|

_____ kg

_____

Name _____

**Write an equation and solve the problem.**

2. Ariel's recipe calls for 64 grams of apples and 86 grams of oranges. How many more grams of oranges than apples does the recipe call for?

_____ ◯ _____ = _____  _____

3. Dan's Clams restaurant sold 45 liters of lemonade. If it sold the same amount each hour for 9 hours, how many liters of lemonade did Dan's Clams sell each hour?

_____ ◯ _____ = _____  _____

**Math Talk** MATHEMATICAL PRACTICES ④
**Use Models** How could you use a model to solve Exercise 2?

## On Your Own

MATHEMATICAL PRACTICE ④ **Write an Equation** Write an equation and solve the problem.

4. Sasha's box holds 4 kilograms of napkins and 29 kilograms of napkin rings. What is the total mass of the napkins and napkin rings?

_____ ◯ _____ = _____  _____

5. Josh has 6 buckets for cleaning a restaurant. He fills each bucket with 4 liters of water. How many liters of water are in the buckets?

_____ ◯ _____ = _____  _____

6. **THINK SMARTER** Ellen will pour water into Pitcher B until it has 1 more liter of water than Pitcher A. How many liters of water will she pour into Pitcher B? Explain how you found your answer.

Pitcher A          Pitcher B

_____

_____

7. **Practice: Copy and Solve** Use the pictures to write two problems. Then solve your problems.

     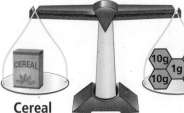 

Grape Juice          Apple Juice          Cereal                    Coffee

© Houghton Mifflin Harcourt Publishing Company

## Unlock the Problem

**8.** Ken's Café serves fruit smoothies. Each smoothie has 9 grams of fresh strawberries. How many grams of strawberries are in 8 smoothies?

**a.** What do you need to find? _____

**b.** What operation will you use to find the answer? _____

**c.** **MATHEMATICAL PRACTICE ④** **Use Diagrams**  Draw a diagram to solve the problem.

**d.** Complete the sentences.

There are _____ smoothies with _____ grams of strawberries in each.

Since each smoothie is an _____ group, you can _____.

_____ ◯ _____ = _____

So, there are _____ grams of strawberries in 8 smoothies.

**9.** **GO DEEPER**  Arturo has two containers, each filled with 12 liters of water. Daniel has two containers, each filled with 16 liters of water. What is the total liquid volume of the boys' containers?

_____

**10.** **THINK SMARTER**  A deli makes its own salad dressing. A small jar has 3 grams of spices. A large jar has 5 grams of spices. Will 25 grams of spices be enough to make 3 small jars and 3 large jars? Show your work.

# Solve Problems About Liquid Volume and Mass

 **COMMON CORE STANDARD—3.MD.A.2**
*Solve problems involving measurement and estimation of intervals of time, liquid volumes, and masses of objects.*

**Write an equation and solve the problem.**

1. Luis was served 145 grams of meat and 217 grams of vegetables at a meal. What was the total mass of the meat and the vegetables?

   **Think:** Add to find how much in all.

   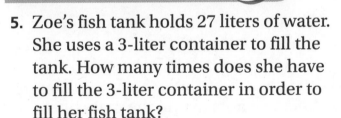

   145 (+) 217 = ____  _____

2. The gas tank of a riding mower holds 5 liters of gas. How many 5-liter gas tanks can you fill from a full 20-liter gas can?

   ____ ◯ ____ = ____  _____

3. To make a lemon-lime drink, Mac mixed 4 liters of lemonade with 2 liters of limeade. How much lemon-lime drink did Mac make?

   ____ ◯ ____ = ____  _____

4. A nickel has a mass of 5 grams. There are 40 nickels in a roll of nickels. What is the mass of a roll of nickels?

   ____ ◯ ____ = ____  _____

## Problem Solving · Real World

5. Zoe's fish tank holds 27 liters of water. She uses a 3-liter container to fill the tank. How many times does she have to fill the 3-liter container in order to fill her fish tank?

   _____

6. Adrian's backpack has a mass of 15 kilograms. Theresa's backpack has a mass of 8 kilograms. What is the total mass of both backpacks?

   _____

7. **WRITE** ▶ *Math* Write a problem that can be solved with a bar model that shows equal groups of liters. Then solve the problem.

   _____

   _____

## Lesson Check (3.MD.A.2)

**1.** Mickey's beagle has a mass of 15 kilograms. His dachshund has a mass of 13 kilograms. What is the combined mass of the two dogs?

_____

**2.** Lois put 8 liters of water in a bucket for her pony. At the end of the day, there were 2 liters of water left. How much water did the pony drink?

_____

## Spiral Review (3.OA.D.8, 3.NF.A.3d, 3.MD.A.1, 3.MD.A.2)

**3.** Josiah has 3 packs of toy animals. Each pack has the same number of animals. Josiah gives 6 animals to his sister Stephanie. Then Josiah has 9 animals left. How many animals were in each pack?

_____

**4.** Tom jogged $\frac{3}{10}$ mile, Betsy jogged $\frac{5}{10}$ mile, and Sue jogged $\frac{2}{10}$ mile. Who jogged a distance longer than $\frac{4}{10}$ mile?

_____

**5.** Bob started mowing at 9:55 A.M. It took him 25 minutes to mow the front yard and 45 minutes to mow the back yard. At what time did Bob finish mowing?

_____

**6.** Juliana wants to find the mass of a watermelon. What unit should she use?

_____

FOR MORE PRACTICE
GO TO THE
**Personal Math Trainer**

## ✓ Chapter 10 Review/Test

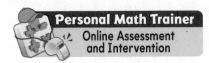

**Personal Math Trainer**
Online Assessment
and Intervention

1. Yul and Sarah's art class started at 11:25 A.M. The class lasted 30 minutes. Yul left when the class was done. Sarah stayed an extra 5 minutes to talk with the teacher and then left.

   Write the time that each student left. Explain how you found each time.

   _____

   _____

2. Julio measured an object that he found. It was about $\frac{3}{4}$ inch wide.

   For numbers 2a–2d, choose Yes or No to tell whether the object could be the one Julio measured.

   2a.        ○ Yes       ○ No

   2b.        ○ Yes       ○ No

   2c.        ○ Yes       ○ No

   2d. 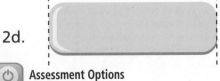       ○ Yes       ○ No

  **Assessment Options**
**Chapter Test**

3. Dina started swimming at 3:38 P.M. She swam until 4:15 P.M. How long did Dina swim?

_____ minutes

4. Rita's class begins social studies at ten minutes before one in the afternoon. At what time does Rita's class begin social studies? Circle a time that makes the sentence true.

Rita's class begins social studies at

| 1:10 A.M. |
| 1:10 P.M. |
| 12:50 A.M. |
| 12:50 P.M. |

5. Select the objects with a mass greater than 1 kilogram. Mark all that apply.

(A) bicycle      (C) eraser

(B) pen      (D) math book

6. A chicken dish needs to bake in the oven for 35 minutes. The dish needs to cool for at least 8 minutes before serving. Scott puts the chicken dish in the oven at 5:14 P.M.

For numbers 6a–6d, select True or False for each statement.

6a. Scott can serve the dish at 5:51 P.M.    ○ True    ○ False

6b. Scott can serve the dish at 5:58 P.M.    ○ True    ○ False

6c. Scott should take the dish out of the oven at 5:51 A.M.    ○ True    ○ False

6d. Scott should take the dish out of the oven at 5:49 P.M.    ○ True    ○ False

**7.** Anthony read a book to his little brother. He started reading at the time shown on the clock. He stopped reading at 5:45 P.M.

**Part A**

How long did Anthony read to his little brother?

_____ minutes

**Part B**

Explain how you found your answer.

_____

_____

_____

_____

**8.** Tran checked the time on his watch after he finished his daily run.

Select the time that Tran finished running. Mark all that apply.

(A) 14 minutes before nine    (C) quarter to nine

(B) eight forty-six          (D) nine forty-six

**9.** Cara uses a balance scale to compare mass.

Circle a symbol that makes the comparison true.

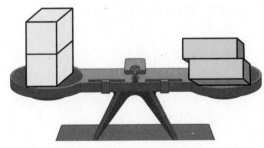

The mass of the blocks
```
<
>
=
```
the mass of the erasers.

**10.** A large bottle of water holds about 2 liters.

For numbers 10a–10e, choose Yes or No to tell whether the container will hold all of the water.

| | | | |
|---|---|---|---|
| 10a. | kitchen sink | ○ Yes | ○ No |
| 10b. | water glass | ○ Yes | ○ No |
| 10c. | ice cube tray | ○ Yes | ○ No |
| 10d. | large soup pot | ○ Yes | ○ No |
| 10e. | lunchbox thermos | ○ Yes | ○ No |

**11.** Select the items that would be best measured in grams. Mark all that apply.

Ⓐ watermelon

Ⓑ lettuce leaf

Ⓒ grape

Ⓓ onion

**12.** Samir made a list of what he did on Tuesday. Write the letter for each activity next to the time he did it.

Ⓐ Get out of bed.  ☐ 8:05 A.M.

Ⓑ Walk to school.  ☐ 6:25 P.M.

Ⓒ Eat lunch.  ☐ 3:50 P.M.

Ⓓ Go to guitar lesson after school.  ☐ 11:48 A.M.

Ⓔ Eat dinner at home.  ☐ 6:25 A.M.

Name _____

13. Amy has 30 grams of flour. She puts 4 grams of flour in each pot of chowder that she makes. She puts 5 grams of flour in each pot of potato soup that she makes. She makes 4 pots of chowder. Does Amy have enough flour left over to make 3 pots of potato soup?

14. **Go DEEPER**  Use an inch ruler to measure.

    **Part A**

    What is the length of the leaf to the nearest fourth inch?

    _____

    **Part B**

    Explain what happens if you line up the left side of the object with the 1 on the ruler.

    _____

    _____

15. Mrs. Park takes the 9:38 A.M. train to the city. The trip takes 3 hours and 20 minutes. What time does Mrs. Park arrive in the city?

    _____

16. Hector buys two bags of gravel for his driveway. He buys a total of 35 kilograms of gravel. Select the bags he buys.

    | 15 kg | 17 kg | 18 kg | 19 kg |
    |-------|-------|-------|-------|
    | ○ | ○ | ○ | ○ |

17. **THINK SMARTER +** Ashley measures the shells she collects.
She records the measurements in a chart.

| Number of Shells | Length in Inches |
|---|---|
| 1 | 1 |
| 2 | $2\frac{1}{2}$ |
| 3 | $1\frac{1}{2}$ |
| 1 | 2 |
| | |

**Part A**

Ashley found a razor clam shell this long.
Use an inch ruler to measure. Record the
measurement in the chart.

_____ inches

**Part B**

Complete the line plot to show the data in the chart. How
many shells are longer than 2 inches? Tell how you know.

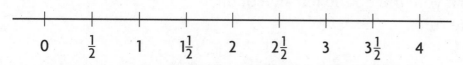

**Length of Shells Measured to the Nearest Half Inch**

_____

_____

18. Lucy fills a bathroom sink with water. Is the amount of
water *more than 1 liter, about 1 liter, or less than 1 liter*?
Explain how you know.

_____

_____

_____

# Chapter 11 Perimeter and Area

 **Show What You Know**

 **Personal Math Trainer**
Online Assessment and Intervention

Check your understanding of important skills.

Name _____

▶ **Use Nonstandard Units to Measure Length**

**Use paper clips to measure the object.** (1.MD.A.2)

1.

   about ____

2.

   about ____

▶ **Add 3 Numbers** **Write the sum.** (1.OA.C.6)

**3.** $2 + 7 + 3 =$ ____     **4.** $3 + 5 + 2 =$ ____     **5.** $6 + 1 + 9 =$ ____

▶ **Model with Arrays** **Use the array. Complete.** (3.OA.A.3)

6.  3 rows of 4

7.  4 rows of 2

____ × ____ = ____     ____ × ____ = ____

**Math in the Real World**

Julia has a picture frame with side lengths of 12 inches and 24 inches. She wants to cut and glue one color of ribbon that will fit exactly around the edge. The green ribbon is 72 inches long. The red ribbon is 48 inches long. Find which ribbon she should use to glue around the picture frame.

## Vocabulary Builder

▶ **Visualize It** •••••••••••••••••••••••••••••••••••••••

**Sort the words with a ✔ into the Venn diagram.**

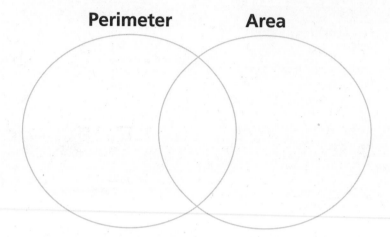

Perimeter          Area

▶ **Understand Vocabulary** ••••••••••••••••••••••••••••

**Complete the sentences by using the review and preview words.**

1. The distance around a figure is the

   _____.

2. The _____ is the measure of the number of unit squares needed to cover a surface.

3. You can count, use _____, or multiply to find the area of a rectangle.

4. A _____ is a square with a side length of 1 unit and is used to measure area.

5. The _____ shows that you can break apart a rectangle into smaller rectangles and add the area of each smaller rectangle to find the total area.

© Houghton Mifflin Harcourt Publishing Company

**Review Words**

addition

array

centimeter (cm)

Distributive Property

foot (ft)

inch (in.)

inverse operations

✓ length

meter (m)

multiplication

pattern

rectangle

repeated addition

✓ unit

✓ width

**Preview Words**

area

perimeter

✓ square unit

✓ unit square

GO DIGITAL
• Interactive Student Edition
• Multimedia eGlossary

# Chapter 11 Vocabulary

**area**

área

3

**centimeter (cm)**

centímetro (cm)

7

**inverse operation**

operaciones inversas

37

**length**

longitud

40

**perimeter**

perímetro

59

**rectangle**

rectángulo

69

**square unit**

unidad cuadrada

75

**unit square**

cuadrado de una unidad

80

A metric unit used to measure length or distance
100 centimeters = 1 meter

The measure of the number of unit squares needed to cover a surface

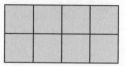

Area = 8 square units

---

The measurement of the distance between two points

Opposite operations, or operations that undo one another, such as addition and subtraction or multiplication and division

Examples: 16 + 8 = 24;  24 − 8 = 16
4 × 3 = 12;  12 ÷ 4 = 3

---

A quadrilateral with two pairs of parallel sides, two pairs of sides of equal length, and four right angles

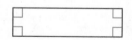

The distance around a figure

Example: The perimeter of this rectangle is 20 inches.

6 in.

4 in.          4 in.

6 in.

---

A square with a side length of 1 unit, used to measure area

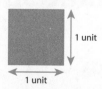

1 unit

1 unit

A unit used to measure area such as square foot, square meter, and so on

# Picture It

| Word Box |
| --- |
| area |
| centimeter (cm) |
| inverse operations |
| length |
| perimeter |
| rectangle |
| square unit |
| unit square |

For 3 to 4 players

## Materials
- timer
- sketch pad

## How to Play

1. Take turns to play.
2. To take a turn, choose a word from the Word Box, but do not say the word aloud.
3. Set the timer for 1 minute.
4. Draw pictures and numbers to give clues about the word.
5. The first player to guess the word before time runs out gets 1 point. If that player can use the word in a sentence, he or she gets 1 more point. Then that player gets a turn choosing a word.
6. The first player to score 10 points wins.

# The Write Way

## Reflect

### Choose one idea. Write about it.

- Define perimeter in your own words.
- Write two things you know about area.
- Explain how two rectangles can have the same area, but different perimeter. Give an example.

# Model Perimeter

**Essential Question** How can you find perimeter?

Common Core  Measurement and Data—
              3.MD.D.8
**MATHEMATICAL PRACTICES**
**MP1, MP3, MP6, MP7**

## Investigate

**Perimeter** is the distance around a figure.

**Materials** ■ geoboard ■ rubber bands

You can find the perimeter of a rectangle on a geoboard or on dot paper by counting the number of units on each side.

**A.** Make a rectangle on the geoboard that is 3 units on two sides and 2 units on the other two sides.

**B.** Draw your rectangle on this dot paper.

←— 1 Unit

**C.** Write the length next to each side of your rectangle.

**D.** Add the number of units on each side.

_____ + _____ + _____ + _____ = _____

**E.** So, the perimeter of the rectangle

is _____ units.

- How would the perimeter of the rectangle change if the length of two of the sides was 4 units instead of 3 units?

_____

_____

## Draw Conclusions

1. Describe how you would find the perimeter of a rectangle that is 5 units wide and 6 units long.

_____

2.  A rectangle has two pairs of sides of equal length. Explain how you can find the unknown length of two sides when the length of one side is 4 units, and the perimeter is 14 units.

_____

_____

_____

3. **MATHEMATICAL PRACTICE ①** **Evaluate** Jill says that finding the perimeter of a figure with all sides of equal length is easier than finding the perimeter of other figures. Do you agree? Explain.

_____

_____

## Make Connections

You can also use grid paper to find the perimeter of figures by counting the number of units on each side.

Start at the arrow and trace the perimeter. Begin counting with 1. Continue counting each unit around the figure until you have counted each unit.

**Math Talk** MATHEMATICAL PRACTICES ③

Apply If a rectangle has a perimeter of 12 units, how many units wide and how many units long could it be?

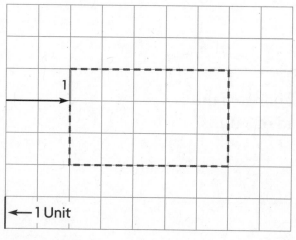

**A**

←1 Unit

Perimeter = _____ units

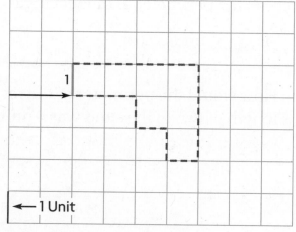

**B**

←1 Unit

Perimeter = _____ units

Name _____

**Find the perimeter of the figure. Each unit is 1 centimeter.**

1.

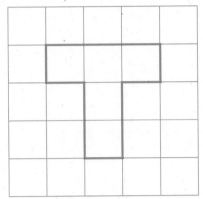

_____ centimeters

 2.

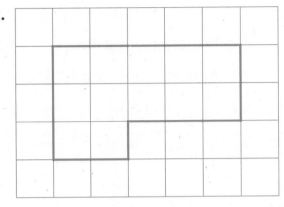

_____ centimeters

3.

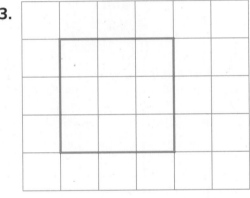

_____ centimeters

4.

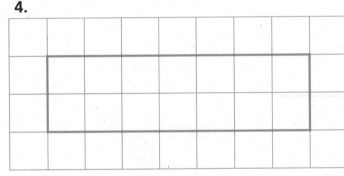

_____ centimeters

**Find the perimeter.**

5. A figure with four sides that measure 4 centimeters, 6 centimeters, 5 centimeters, and 1 centimeter

_____ centimeters

 6. A figure with two sides that measure 10 inches, one side that measures 8 inches, and one side that measures 4 inches

_____ inches

**Problem Solving • Applications** (Real World)

7. **MATHEMATICAL PRACTICE 6** **Explain** how to find the length of each side of a triangle with sides of equal length and a perimeter of 27 inches.

_____

_____

© Houghton Mifflin Harcourt Publishing Company

8. **THINK SMARTER**  Luisa drew a rectangle with a perimeter of 18 centimeters. Select the rectangles that Luisa could have drawn. Mark all that apply. Use the grid to help you.

(A)  9 centimeters long and 2 centimeters wide

(B)  6 centimeters long and 3 centimeters wide

(C)  4 centimeters long and 4 centimeters wide

(D)  5 centimeters long and 4 centimeters wide

(E)  7 centimeters long and 2 centimeters wide

9. **THINK SMARTER**  **What's the Error?**  Kevin is solving perimeter problems. He counts the units and says that the perimeter of this figure is 18 units.

**Look at Kevin's solution.**

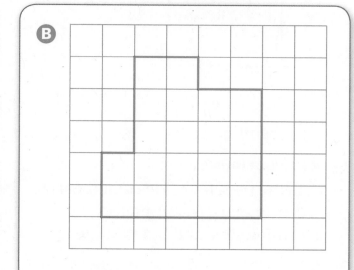

A

| | | 18 | 17 | | | |
| | 1 | | | 16 | 15 | |
| | 2 | | | | | 14 |
| | 3 | | | | | 13 |
| 4 | | | | | | 12 |
| 5 | | | | | | 11 |
| | 6 | 7 | 8 | 9 | 10 | |

Perimeter = _____ units

**Find Kevin's error.**

B

Perimeter = _____ units

• **GO DEEPER**  Describe the error Kevin made. Circle the places in the drawing of Kevin's solution where he made an error.

_____

_____

Name _____

# Model Perimeter

**COMMON CORE STANDARD—3.MD.D.8**
*Geometric measurement: recognize perimeter as an attribute of plane figures and distinguish between linear and area measures.*

## Find the perimeter of the figure. Each unit is 1 centimeter.

**1.**

_____22_____ centimeters

**2.**

_____ centimeters

**Problem Solving** Real World

## Use the drawing for 3–4. Each unit is 1 centimeter.

**3.** What is the perimeter of Patrick's figure?

_____

**4.** How much greater is the perimeter of Jillian's shape than the perimeter of Patrick's figure?

_____

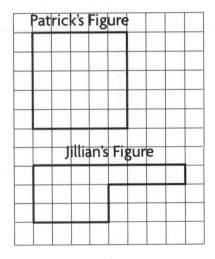

Patrick's Figure

Jillian's Figure

**5.** **WRITE** ▸*Math* Draw a rectangle and another figure that is not a rectangle by tracing lines on grid paper. Describe how to find the perimeter of both figures.

_____

_____

_____

## Lesson Check (3.MD.D.8)

1. Find the perimeter of the figure. Each unit is 1 centimeter.

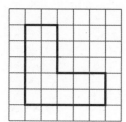

2. Find the perimeter of the figure. Each unit is 1 centimeter.

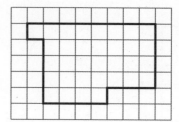

_____

_____

## Spiral Review (3.NF.A.3d, 3.MD.A.1, 3.MD.A.2)

3. Order the fractions from least to greatest.

$$\frac{2}{4}, \frac{2}{3}, \frac{2}{6}$$

4. Kasey's school starts at the time shown on the clock. What time does Kasey's school start?

_____

_____

5. Compare. Write $<$, $>$, or $=$.

$$\frac{4}{8} \bigcirc \frac{3}{8}$$

6. Aiden wants to find the mass of a bowling ball. Which unit should he use?

_____

FOR MORE PRACTICE
GO TO THE
Personal Math Trainer

Name _____

# Find Perimeter

**Essential Question** How can you measure perimeter?

Common Core  Measurement and Data—
3.MD.D.8  Also 3.NBT.A.2, 3.MD.B.4
MATHEMATICAL PRACTICES
MP1, MP2, MP4, MP5

You can estimate and measure perimeter in standard units, such as inches and centimeters.

##  Unlock the Problem

Find the perimeter of the cover of a notebook.

### 🔑 Activity  Materials ▪ inch ruler

**STEP 1** Estimate the perimeter of a notebook in inches. Record your estimate. _____ inches

**STEP 2** Use an inch ruler to measure the length of each side of the notebook to the nearest inch.

**STEP 3** Record and add the lengths of the sides measured to the nearest inch.

_____ + _____ + _____ + _____ = _____

So, the perimeter of the notebook cover measured

to the nearest inch is _____ inches.

**Math Talk**  MATHEMATICAL PRACTICES ①
**Evaluate** How does your estimate compare with your measurement?

## Try This! Find the perimeter.

| Use an inch ruler to find the length of each side. | Use a centimeter ruler to find the length of each side. |
|---|---|
| 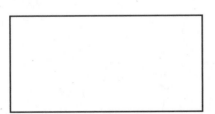 |  |
| Add the lengths of the sides: | Add the lengths of the sides: |
| _____ + _____ + _____ + _____ = _____ | _____ + _____ + _____ + _____ = _____ |
| The perimeter is _____ inches. | The perimeter is _____ centimeters. |

# Share and Show

**1.** Find the perimeter of the triangle in inches.

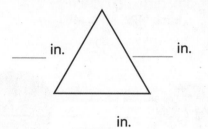

_____ in. _____ in. Think: How long is each side?

_____ in.

_____ inches

Math Talk

MATHEMATICAL PRACTICES ②

**Reason Abstractly** How do you use addition to find the perimeter of a figure?

**Use a centimeter ruler to find the perimeter.**

**2.**

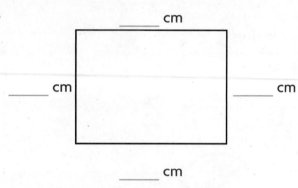

_____ centimeters

**☑3.**

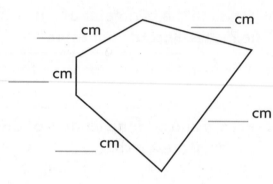

_____ centimeters

**Use an inch ruler to find the perimeter.**

**4.**

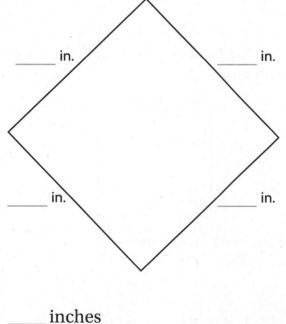

_____ inches

**☑5.**

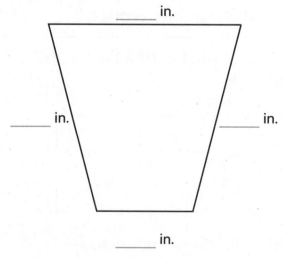

_____ inches

632

Name _____

## Use a ruler to find the perimeter.

**6.**

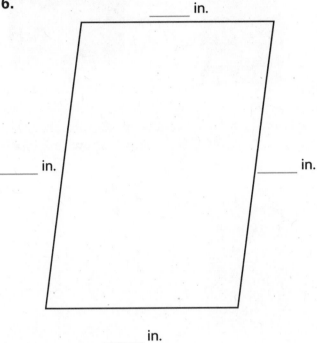

_____ in.

_____ in.        _____ in.

_____ in.

_____ inches

**7.**

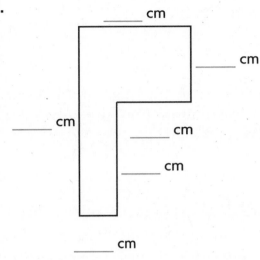

_____ cm

_____ cm

_____ cm

_____ cm

_____ cm

_____ cm

_____ centimeters

**8.** MATHEMATICAL PRACTICE 4 **Model Mathematics** Use the grid paper to draw a figure that has a perimeter of 24 centimeters. Label the length of each side.

← 1 cm

# Problem Solving • Applications Real World

**Use the photos for 9–10.**

5 in.

7 in.

9. Which of the animal photos has a perimeter of 26 inches?

8 in.    8 in.    4 in.    4 in.

5 in.    7 in.

_____

10. **GO DEEPER** How much greater is the perimeter of the bird photo than the perimeter of the cat photo?

_____

| WRITE ▸ *Math* • **Show Your Work**

11. **THINK SMARTER** Erin is putting a fence around her square garden. Each side of her garden is 3 meters long. The fence costs $5 for each meter. How much will the fence cost?

_____

12. **WRITE** ▸ *Math* Gary's garden is shaped like a rectangle with two pairs of sides of equal length, and it has a perimeter of 28 feet. Explain how to find the lengths of the other sides if one side measures 10 feet.

_____

_____

_____

_____

_____

13. **THINK SMARTER** Use an inch ruler to measure this sticker to the nearest inch. Then write an equation you can use to find its perimeter.

# Find Perimeter

Common Core

**COMMON CORE STANDARD—3.MD.D.8**
*Geometric measurement: recognize perimeter
as an attribute of plane figures and distinguish
between linear and area measures.*

## Use a ruler to find the perimeter.

1.

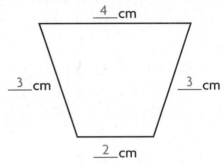

___4___ cm

___3___ cm      ___3___ cm

___2___ cm

___12___ centimeters

2.

____ cm

____ cm

____ cm

____ cm

____ cm

_____ centimeters

**Problem Solving** (Real World)

## Draw a picture to solve 3–4.

3. Evan has a square sticker that measures 5 inches on each side. What is the perimeter of the sticker?

   _____

4. Sophie draws a shape that has 6 sides. Each side is 3 centimeters. What is the perimeter of the shape?

   _____

5. **WRITE** ▸*Math* Draw two different figures that each have a perimeter of 20 units.

   _____

## Lesson Check (3.MD.D.8)

**Use an inch ruler for 1–2.**

1. Ty cut a label the size of the shape shown. What is the perimeter, in inches, of Ty's label?

_____

2. Julie drew the shape shown below. What is the perimeter, in inches, of the shape?

_____

## Spiral Review (3.NF.A.3d, 3.MD.A.1, 3.MD.A.2, 3.MD.D.8)

3. What is the perimeter of the shape below?

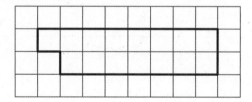

_____

4. Vince arrives for his trumpet lesson after school at the time shown on the clock. What time does Vince arrive for his trumpet lesson?

_____

5. Matthew's small fish tank holds 12 liters. His large fish tank holds 25 liters. How many more liters does his large fish tank hold?

_____

6. Compare. Write $<$, $>$, or $=$.

$$\frac{1}{6} \bigcirc \frac{1}{4}$$

**FOR MORE PRACTICE GO TO THE**
**Personal Math Trainer**

Name _____

# Find Perimeter

Common Core

**COMMON CORE STANDARD—3.MD.D.8**
*Geometric measurement: recognize perimeter as an attribute of plane figures and distinguish between linear and area measures.*

## Use a ruler to find the perimeter.

1.
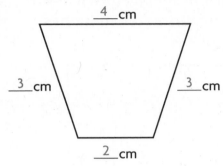

_____12_____ centimeters

2.
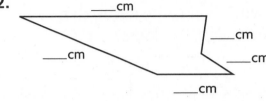

_____ centimeters

## Problem Solving Real World

**Draw a picture to solve 3–4.**

3. Evan has a square sticker that measures 5 inches on each side. What is the perimeter of the sticker?

_____

4. Sophie draws a shape that has 6 sides. Each side is 3 centimeters. What is the perimeter of the shape?

_____

5. **WRITE** ▸*Math* Draw two different figures that each have a perimeter of 20 units.

_____

## Lesson Check (3.MD.D.8)

**Use an inch ruler for 1–2.**

1. Ty cut a label the size of the shape shown. What is the perimeter, in inches, of Ty's label?

_____

2. Julie drew the shape shown below. What is the perimeter, in inches, of the shape?

_____

## Spiral Review (3.NF.A.3d, 3.MD.A.1, 3.MD.A.2, 3.MD.D.8)

3. What is the perimeter of the shape below?

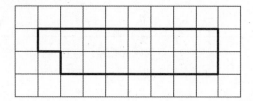

_____

4. Vince arrives for his trumpet lesson after school at the time shown on the clock. What time does Vince arrive for his trumpet lesson?

_____

5. Matthew's small fish tank holds 12 liters. His large fish tank holds 25 liters. How many more liters does his large fish tank hold?

_____

6. Compare. Write <, >, or =.

$$\frac{1}{6} \bigcirc \frac{1}{4}$$

FOR MORE PRACTICE
GO TO THE
**Personal Math Trainer**

Name _____

# Algebra • Find Unknown Side Lengths

**Essential Question** How can you find the unknown length of a side in a plane figure when you know its perimeter?

**Common Core** Measurement and Data—
**3.MD.D.8** *Also 3.NBT.A.2*

**MATHEMATICAL PRACTICES**
**MP3, MP4, MP7**

## Unlock the Problem (Real World)

Chen has 27 feet of fencing to put around his garden. He has already used the lengths of fencing shown. How much fencing does he have left for the last side?

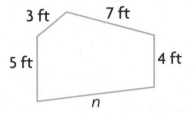

3 ft    7 ft

5 ft    4 ft

$n$

**Find the unknown side length.**

Write an equation for the perimeter.

**Think:** If I knew the length $n$, I would add all the side lengths to find the perimeter.

Add the lengths of the sides you know.

**Think:** Addition and subtraction are inverse operations.

Write a related equation.

So, Chen has _____ feet of fencing left.

$$5 + 3 + \underline{\phantom{x}} + \underline{\phantom{x}} + n = 27$$

$$5 + 3 + 7 + 4 + n = 27$$

$$\underline{\phantom{xxx}} + n = 27$$

$$n = 27 - 19$$

$$\underline{\phantom{xxx}} = 27 - 19$$

### Math Idea
A symbol or letter can stand for an unknown side length.

## Try This!

The perimeter of the figure is 24 meters. Find the unknown side length, $w$.

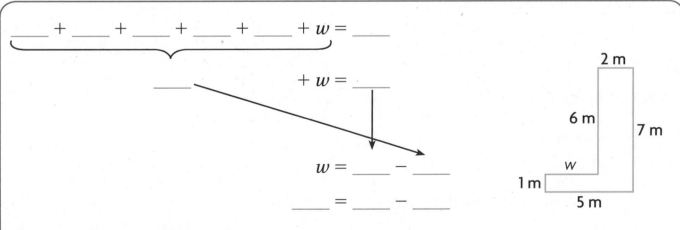

$$\underline{\phantom{x}} + \underline{\phantom{x}} + \underline{\phantom{x}} + \underline{\phantom{x}} + \underline{\phantom{x}} + w = \underline{\phantom{x}}$$

$$\underline{\phantom{x}} + w = \underline{\phantom{x}}$$

$$w = \underline{\phantom{x}} - \underline{\phantom{x}}$$

$$\underline{\phantom{x}} = \underline{\phantom{x}} - \underline{\phantom{x}}$$

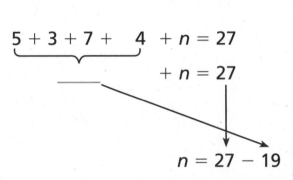

2 m

6 m    7 m

$w$

1 m    5 m

So, the unknown side length, $w$, is _____ meters.

5 ft

## 🔑 Example  Find unknown side lengths of a rectangle.

Lauren has a rectangular blanket. The perimeter is 28 feet. The width of the blanket is 5 feet. What is the length of the blanket?

$l$                    $l$

**Hint:** A rectangle has two pairs of opposite sides that are equal in length.

You can predict the length and add to find the perimeter. If the perimeter is 28 feet, then that is the correct length.

5 ft

| Predict | Check | Does it check? |
|---------|-------|----------------|
| $l = 7$ feet | 5 + ____ + 5 + ____ = ____ | **Think:** Perimeter is not 28 feet, so the length does not check. |
| $l = 8$ feet | 5 + ____ + 5 + ____ = ____ | **Think:** Perimeter is not 28 feet, so the length does not check. |
| $l = 9$ feet | 5 + ____ + 5 + ____ = ____ | **Think:** Perimeter is 28 feet, so the length is correct. ✓ |

So, the length of the blanket is _____ feet.

## Try This!  Find unknown side lengths of a square.

The square has a perimeter of 20 inches. What is the length of each side of the square?

**Think:** A square has four sides that are equal in length.

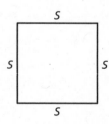

$s$

$s$                    $s$

$s$

You can multiply to find the perimeter.

- Write a multiplication equation for the perimeter.       $4 \times s = 20$
- Use a multiplication fact you know to solve.       $4 \times$ _____ $= 20$

So, the length of each side of the square is _____ inches.

**638**

© Houghton Mifflin Harcourt Publishing Company • Image Credits: ©D. Hurst/Alamy

Name _____

## Share and Show

**Find the unknown side lengths.**

1. Perimeter = 25 centimeters

$$9 + \underline{\hspace{1cm}} + \underline{\hspace{1cm}} + n = 25$$

$$\underline{\hspace{1cm}} + n = 25$$

$$\underline{\hspace{1cm}} = \underline{\hspace{1cm}} - \underline{\hspace{1cm}}$$

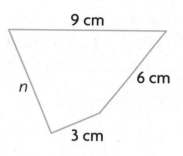

$n = $ _____ centimeters

2. Perimeter = 34 meters

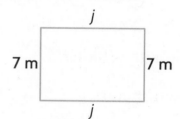

$j = $ _____ meters

3. Perimeter = 12 feet

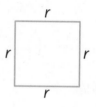

$r = $ _____ feet

## On Your Own

**Find the unknown side lengths.**

4. Perimeter = 32 centimeters

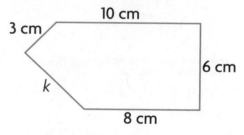

$k = $ _____ centimeters

5. **THINK SMARTER** Perimeter = 42 feet

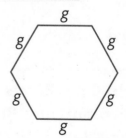

$g = $ _____ feet

6. **MATHEMATICAL PRACTICE ④ Use a Diagram** Eleni wants to put up a fence around her square garden. The garden has a perimeter of 28 meters. How long will each side of the fence be? Explain.

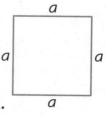

**Math Talk**

MATHEMATICAL PRACTICES ③

**Apply** How can you use division to find the length of a side of a square?

_____

_____

© Houghton Mifflin Harcourt Publishing Company

**Unlock the Problem** Real World

7. **GO DEEPER** Latesha wants to make a border with ribbon around a figure she made and sketched at the right. She will use 44 centimeters of ribbon for the border. What is the unknown side length?

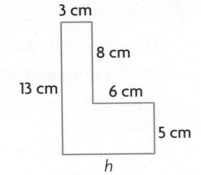

3 cm

8 cm

13 cm    6 cm

5 cm

*h*

a. What do you need to find?

_____

b. How will you use what you know about perimeter to help you solve the problem?

_____

_____

c. Write an equation to solve the problem.

_____

d. So, the length of side *h* is

_____ centimeters.

8. **THINK SMARTER** A rectangle has a perimeter of 34 inches. The left side is 6 inches long. What is the length of the top side?

_____

Math on the Spot

**Personal Math Trainer**

9. **THINK SMARTER +** Michael has 40 feet of fencing to make a rectangular dog run for his dog, Buddy. One side of the run will be 5 feet long. For numbers 9a–9d, choose Yes or No to show what the length of another side will be.

9a. 20 feet        ○ Yes    ○ No

9b. 15 feet        ○ Yes    ○ No

9c. 10 feet        ○ Yes    ○ No

9d. 8 feet         ○ Yes    ○ No

Name _____

# Find Unknown Side Lengths

**COMMON CORE STANDARD—3.MD.D.8**
*Geometric measurement: recognize perimeter as an attribute of plane figures and distinguish between linear and area measures.*

## Find the unknown side lengths.

**1.** Perimeter = 33 centimeters

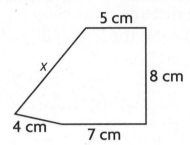

$5 + 8 + 7 + 4 + x = 33$
$24 + x = 33$
$x = 9$

$x =$ _____9_____ centimeters

**2.** Perimeter = 92 inches

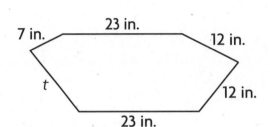

$t =$ _____ inches

## Problem Solving Real World

**3.** Steven has a rectangular rug with a perimeter of 16 feet. The width of the rug is 5 feet. What is the length of the rug?

_____

**4.** Kerstin has a square tile. The perimeter of the tile is 32 inches. What is the length of each side of the tile?

_____

**5.** **WRITE** ▸*Math* Explain how to write and solve an equation to find an unknown side length of a rectangle when given the perimeter.

_____

_____

_____

## Lesson Check (3.MD.D.8)

**1.** Jesse is putting a ribbon around a square frame. He uses 24 inches of ribbon. How long is each side of the frame?

_____

**2.** Davia draws a shape with 5 sides. Two sides are each 5 inches long. Two other sides are each 4 inches long. The perimeter of the shape is 27 inches. What is the length of the fifth side?

_____

## Spiral Review (3.OA.A.1, 3.OA.D.8, 3.NF.A.3c, 3.MD.A.1)

**3.** What multiplication expression represents $7 + 7 + 7 + 7$?

_____

**4.** Bob bought 3 packs of model cars. He gave 4 cars to Ann. Bob has 11 cars left. How many model cars were in each pack?

_____

**5.** Randy read a book in the afternoon. He looked at his watch when he started and finished reading. How long did Randy read?

**Start**          **End**

_____

**6.** What fraction and whole number does the model represent?

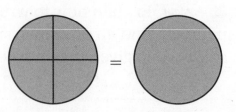

_____ = _____

**FOR MORE PRACTICE GO TO THE Personal Math Trainer**

# Understand Area

**Essential Question** How is finding the area of a figure different from finding the perimeter of a figure?

 Measurement and Data—
**3.MD.C.5, 3.MD.C.5a** *Also*
*3.MD.C.5b, 3.MD.C.6, 3.MD.D.8*
**MATHEMATICAL PRACTICES**
**MP2, MP3, MP5, MP8**

## 🔑 Unlock the Problem (Real World)

**CONNECT** You learned that perimeter is the distance around a figure. It is measured in linear units, or units that are used to measure the distance between two points.

**Area** is the measure of the number of unit squares needed to cover a flat surface. A **unit square** is a square with a side length of 1 unit. It has an area of 1 **square unit**.

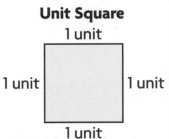

**Unit Square**
1 unit
1 unit          1 unit
1 unit

Perimeter

1 unit + 1 unit + 1 unit +
1 unit = 4 units

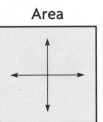

Area

1 square unit

### Math Idea

You can count the number of units on each side of a figure to find its perimeter. You can count the number of unit squares inside a figure to find its area in square units.

## 🔓 Activity  **Materials** ▪ geoboard ▪ rubber bands  (Hands On)

**A** Use your geoboard to form a figure made from 2 unit squares. Record the figure on this dot paper.

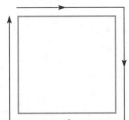

What is the area of this figure?

Area = _____ square units

**B** Change the rubber band so that the figure is made from 3 unit squares. Record the figure on this dot paper.

What is the area of this figure?

Area = _____ square units

(Math Talk)  **MATHEMATICAL PRACTICES ③**

**Compare Representations**
For B, did your figure look like your classmate's figure?

**Try This!** Draw three different figures that are each made from 4 unit squares. Find the area of each figure.

| Figure 1 | Figure 2 | Figure 3 |
|---|---|---|
|  | | |

Area = _____ square units   Area = _____ square units   Area = _____ square units

• How are the figures the same? How are the figures different?

---

**Share and Show**  MATH BOARD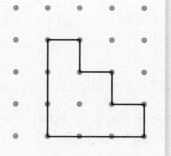

1. Shade each unit square in the figure shown. Count the unit squares to find the area.

   Area = _____ square units

**Count to find the area of the figure.**

2.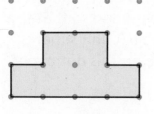

3.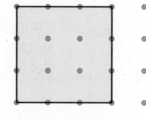

✓4.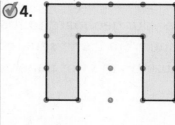

Area = _____ square units   Area = _____ square units   Area = _____ square units

**Write _area_ or _perimeter_ for the situation.**

5. buying a rug for a room

_____

✓6. putting a fence around a garden

_____

 Math Talk   MATHEMATICAL PRACTICES ⑧

Generalize What are other situations where you need to find area?

Name _____

**Count to find the area of the figure.**

7.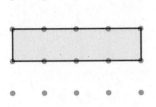

Area = _____ square units

8.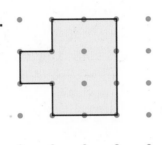

Area = _____ square units

9.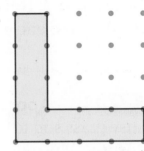

Area = _____ square units

10.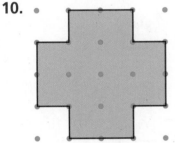

Area = _____ square units

11.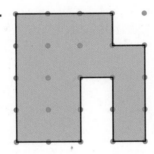

Area = _____ square units

12.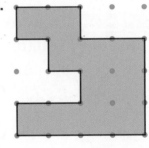

Area = _____ square units

**Write *area* or *perimeter* for the situation.**

13. painting a wall

_____

14. covering a patio with tiles

_____

15. putting a wallpaper border around a room

_____

16. gluing a ribbon around a picture frame

_____

17. **GO DEEPER** Nicole's mother put tiles on a section of their kitchen floor. The section included 5 rows with 4 tiles in each row. Each tile cost $2. How much money did Nicole's mother spend on the tiles?

_____

## Problem Solving · Applications

**Juan is building an enclosure for his small dog, Eli. Use the diagram for 18–19.**

Eli's Enclosure

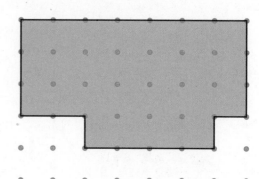

18. Juan will put fencing around the outside of the enclosure. How much fencing does he need for the enclosure?

_____

19. **MATHEMATICAL PRACTICE ⑤ Use Appropriate Tools** Juan will use grass sod to cover the ground in the enclosure. How much grass sod does Juan need?

_____

20. **THINK SMARTER** Draw two different figures, each with an area of 10 square units.

21. **THINK SMARTER** What is the perimeter and area of this figure? Explain how you found the answer.

Perimeter _____ units

Area _____ square units

_____

_____

_____

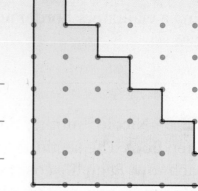

## Understand Area

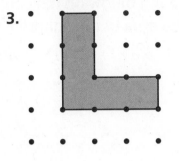

COMMON CORE STANDARDS—3.MD.C.5, 3.MD.C.5a *Geometric measurement: understand concepts of area and relate area to multiplication and to addition.*

**Count to find the area for the shape.**

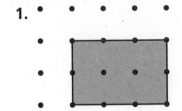

1.

Area = ___6___ square units

2.

Area = _____ square units

3.

Area = _____ square units

**Write *area* or *perimeter* for each situation.**

4. carpeting a floor

5. fencing a garden

_____

_____

## Problem Solving Real World

**Use the diagram for 6–7.**

6. Roberto is building a platform for his model railroad. What is the area of the platform?

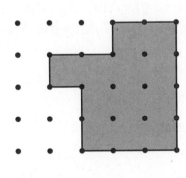

_____

7. Roberto will put a border around the edges of the platform. How much border will he need?

_____

8. **WRITE** ▸*Math* Draw a rectangle using dot paper. Find the area, and explain how you found your answer.

_____

## Lesson Check (3.MD.C.5, 3.MD.C.5a)

1. Josh used rubber bands to make the shape below on his geoboard. What is the area of the shape?

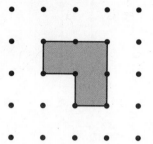

_____

2. Wilma drew the shape below on dot paper. What is the area of the shape she drew?

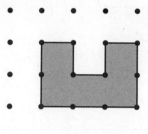

_____

## Spiral Review (3.OA.C.7, 3.NF.A.1, 3.MD.A.1, 3.MD.A.2)

3. Leonardo knows it is 42 days until summer break. How many weeks is it until Leonardo's summer break? (Hint: There are 7 days in a week.)

_____

4. Nan cut a submarine sandwich into 4 equal parts and ate one part. What fraction represents the part of the sandwich Nan ate?

_____

5. Wanda is eating breakfast at fifteen minutes before eight. What time is this? Use A.M. or P.M.

_____

6. Dick has 2 bags of dog food. Each bag contains 5 kilograms of food. How many kilograms of food does Dick have in all?

_____

FOR MORE PRACTICE
GO TO THE
Personal Math Trainer

Name _____

# Measure Area

**Essential Question** How can you find the area of a plane figure?

 **Measurement and Data—**
**3.MD.C.5b, 3.MD.C.6** *Also 3.MD.C.5,*
*3.MD.C.5a, 3.MD.C.7, 3.MD.C.7a*
**MATHEMATICAL PRACTICES**
**MP2, MP4, MP7**

## Unlock the Problem

1 square inch

Jaime is measuring the area of the rectangles with 1-inch square tiles.

**Activity 1** **Materials** ■ 1-inch grid paper ■ scissors
Cut out eight 1-inch squares. Use the dashed lines as guides to place tiles for A–C.

**Rectangle A**

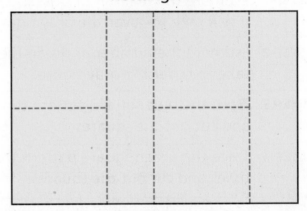

**A** Place 4 tiles on Rectangle A.

• Are there any gaps? _____

• Are there any overlaps? _____

• Jaime says that the area is 4 square inches. Is Jaime's measurement correct? _____

So, when you measure area, there can be no space between the tiles, or no gaps.

**B** Place 8 tiles on Rectangle B.

**Rectangle B**

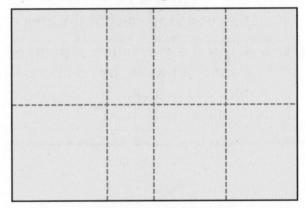

• Are there any gaps? _____

• Are there any overlaps? _____

• Jaime says that the area is 8 square inches. Is Jaime's measurement correct? _____

So, when you measure the area, the tiles cannot overlap.

**C** Place 6 tiles on Rectangle C.

**Rectangle C**

• Are there any gaps? _____

• Are there any overlaps? _____

• Jaime says that the area is 6 square inches. Is Jaime's measurement correct? _____

So, the area of the rectangles is

_____ square inches.

## Activity 2 Materials ■ green and blue paper ■ scissors

**STEP 1**  Estimate the number of blue square tiles it will take to cover the gray figure.

_____ blue square tiles

**STEP 2**  Estimate the number of green tiles it will take to cover the gray figure.

_____ green square tiles

**STEP 3**  Trace the blue square pattern ten times and cut out the squares.

**STEP 4**  Trace the green square pattern thirty-six times and cut out the squares.

**STEP 5**  Cover the gray figure with blue square tiles. Count and write the number of blue square tiles you used. Record the area of the figure.

_____ blue square tiles

Area = _____ blue square units

**STEP 6**  Cover the gray figure with green square tiles. Count and write the number of green square tiles you used. Record the area of the figure.

_____ green square tiles

Area = _____ green square units

**Math Talk**

MATHEMATICAL PRACTICES ⑦

**Identify Relationships** Explain why the number of green square tiles needed to cover the figure is different than the number of blue square tiles needed.

## Try This! Count to find the area of the figure.

☐ is 1 square centimeter.

There are _____ unit squares in the figure.

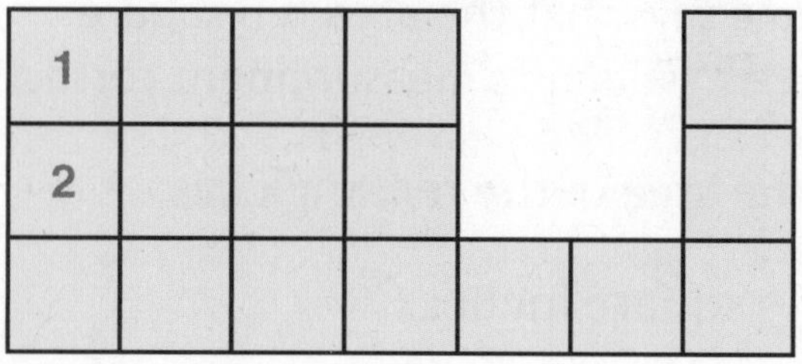

So, the area is _____ square centimeters.

© Houghton Mifflin Harcourt Publishing Company

Name _____

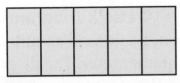

1. Count to find the area of the figure. Each unit square is 1 square centimeter.

   Think: Are there any gaps? Are there any overlaps?

   There are _____ unit squares in the figure.

   So, the area is _____ square centimeters.

**MATHEMATICAL PRACTICES ②**

**Math Talk**

**Use Reasoning** How can you use square centimeters to find the area of different figures?

**Count to find the area of the figure.**
**Each unit square is 1 square centimeter.**

 2.

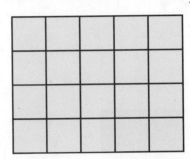

Area = _____ square centimeters

3.

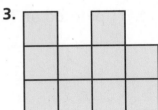

Area = _____ square centimeters

**Count to find the area of the figure.**
**Each unit square is 1 square inch.**

4.

Area = _____ square inches

5.

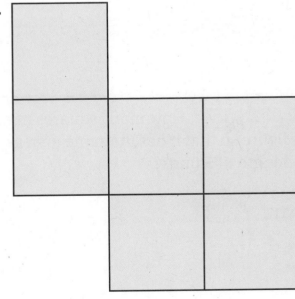

Area = _____ square inches

# Problem Solving · Applications

6. **MATHEMATICAL PRACTICE ④ Use a Diagram** Danny is placing tiles on the floor of an office lobby. Each tile is 1 square meter. The diagram shows the lobby. What is the area of the lobby?

_____

7. **GO DEEPER** Angie is painting a space shuttle mural on a wall. Each section is one square foot. The diagram shows the unfinished mural. How many more square feet has Angie painted than NOT painted on her mural?

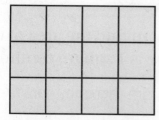

_____

Rectangle A

8. **THINK SMARTER** You measure the area of a table top with blue unit squares and green unit squares. Which unit square will give you a greater number of square units for area? **Explain.**

_____

_____

_____

_____

9. **THINK SMARTER** How many squares need to be added to this figure so that it has the same area as a square with a side length of 5 units?

_____ squares

# Measure Area

 COMMON CORE STANDARDS—
3.MD.C.5b, 3.MD.C.6 *Geometric
measurement: understand concepts of area and
relate area to multiplication and to addition.*

**Count to find the area of the shape.
Each unit square is 1 square centimeter.**

1.

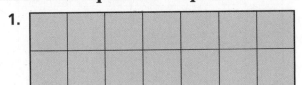

2.

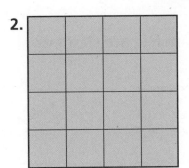

Area = ___14___ square centimeters

Area = _____ square centimeters

3.

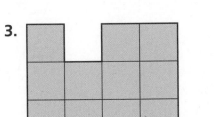

4.

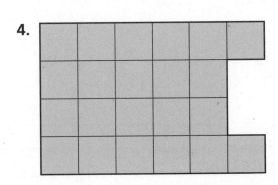

Area = _____ square centimeters

Area = _____ square centimeters

## Problem Solving Real World

**Alan is painting his deck gray. Use the
diagram at the right for 5. Each unit
square is 1 square meter.**

Alan's Deck

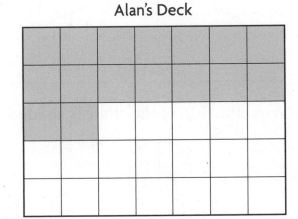

5. What is the area of the deck that Alan
has already painted gray?

_____

6. **WRITE** ▸*Math* Explain how to find the area of a figure
using square tiles.

_____

_____

## Lesson Check (3.MD.C.5b, 3.MD.C.6)

**Each unit square in the diagram is 1 square foot.**

1. How many square feet are shaded?

   _____

2. What is the area that has NOT been shaded?

   _____

## Spiral Review (3.OA.A.3, 3.NF.A.1, 3.NF.A.3b, 3.MD.A.2)

3. Sonya buys 6 packages of rolls. There are 6 rolls in each package. How many rolls does Sonya buy?

   _____

4. Charlie mixed 6 liters of juice with 2 liters of soda to make fruit punch. How many liters of fruit punch did Charlie make?

   _____

5. What fraction of the circle is shaded?

   _____

6. Use the model on the right to name a fraction that is equivalent to $\frac{1}{2}$.

   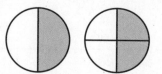

   _____

FOR MORE PRACTICE
GO TO THE
Personal Math Trainer

Name _____

# Use Area Models

**Essential Question** Why can you multiply to find the area of a rectangle?

**Common Core** Measurement and Data—3.MD.C.7, 3.MD.C.7a *Also 3.MD.C.5, 3.MD.C.5a, 3.MD.C.5b, 3.MD.C.6, 3.MD.C.7b, 3.OA.A.3, 3.OA.C.7, 3.NBT.A.2*
MATHEMATICAL PRACTICES
MP1, MP4, MP5, MP6

## Unlock the Problem (Real World)

Cristina has a garden that is shaped like the rectangle below. Each unit square represents 1 square meter. What is the area of her garden?

• Circle the shape of the garden.

### One Way  Count unit squares.

Count the number of unit squares in all.

There are _____ unit squares.

So, the area is _____ square meters.

### Other Ways

**A** Use repeated addition.

Count the number of rows. Count the number of unit squares in each row.

_____ rows of _____ =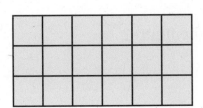

Write an addition equation.

_____ + _____ + _____ = _____

So, the area is _____ square meters.

_____ unit squares

_____ unit squares

_____ unit squares

**B** Use multiplication.

Count the number of rows. Count the number of unit squares in each row.

_____ rows of _____ =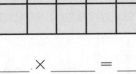

This rectangle is like an array. How do you find the total number of squares in an array?

_____

Write a multiplication equation.

So, the area is _____ square meters.

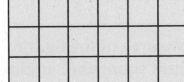

_____ unit squares in each row

_____ rows

_____ × _____ = _____

**Math Talk**

MATHEMATICAL PRACTICES ①

**Analyze** Can you use all 3 methods mentioned to find the area of all figures?

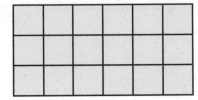

**Try This!**

**Find the area of the figure.**
**Each unit square is 1 square foot.**

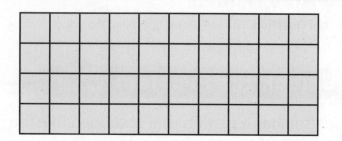

**Think:** There are 4 rows of 10 unit squares.

_____ × _____ = _____

So, the area is _____ square feet.

**Share and Show** MATH BOARD

1. Look at the figure.

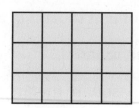

_____ rows of _____ =

Add. _____ + _____ + _____ = _____

Multiply. _____ × _____ = _____

What is the area of the figure?

_____ square units

 **Math Talk** | MATHEMATICAL PRACTICES ⑥

**Compare** Which method do you prefer using?

**Find the area of the figure.**
**Each unit square is 1 square foot.**

2.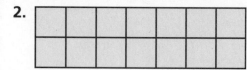

_____

✓ 3.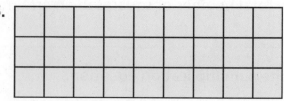

_____

**Find the area of the figure.**
**Each unit square is 1 square meter.**

4.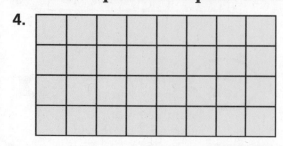

_____

✓ 5.

_____

Name _____

**Find the area of the figure.**
**Each unit square is 1 square foot.**

6.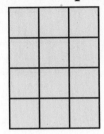

_____

7.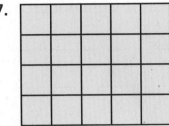

_____

**Find the area of the figure.**
**Each unit square is 1 square meter.**

8.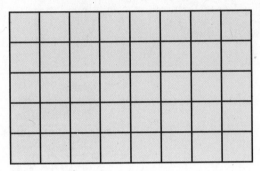

_____

9.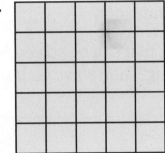

_____

10. **MATHEMATICAL PRACTICE ④ Use Diagrams** Draw and shade three rectangles with an area of 24 square units. Then write an addition or multiplication equation for each.

_____

_____

## Problem Solving • Applications

**11.** **GO DEEPER** Compare the areas of the two rugs at the right. Each unit square represents 1 square foot. Which rug has the greater area? Explain.

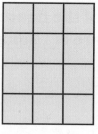

_____

_____

_____

**12.** **THINK SMARTER** A tile company tiled a wall using square tiles. A mural is painted in the center. The drawing shows the design. The area of each tile used is 1 square foot.

Write a problem that can be solved by using the drawing. Then solve your problem.

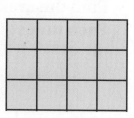

_____

_____

_____

**13.** **THINK SMARTER** Colleen drew this rectangle. Select the equation that can be used to find the area of the rectangle. Mark all that apply.

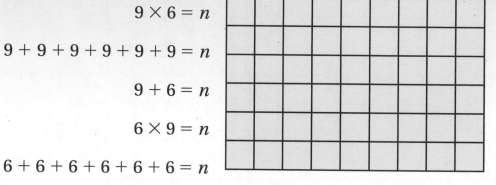

Ⓐ     $9 \times 6 = n$

Ⓑ   $9 + 9 + 9 + 9 + 9 + 9 = n$

Ⓒ     $9 + 6 = n$

Ⓓ     $6 \times 9 = n$

Ⓔ   $6 + 6 + 6 + 6 + 6 + 6 = n$

Name _____

## Use Area Models

Common Core

**COMMON CORE STANDARDS—**
**3.MD.C.7, 3.MD.C.7a** *Geometric*
*measurement: understand concepts of area and*
*relate area to multiplication and to addition.*

**Find the area of each shape. Each unit square is 1 square foot.**

1.
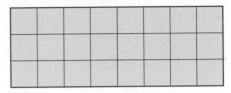

2.
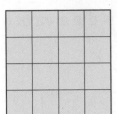

There are 3 rows of 8 unit squares.
$3 \times 8 = 24$

_____ **24 square feet** _____       _____

**Find the area of each shape.**
**Each unit square is 1 square meter.**

3.
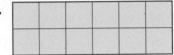

4.
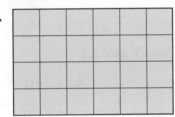

5.
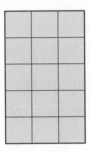

_____       _____       _____

## Problem Solving Real World

6. Landon made a rug for the hallway.
Each unit square is 1 square foot.
What is the area of the rug?

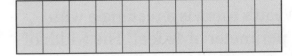

7. Eva makes a border at the top of
a picture frame. Each unit square
is 1 square inch. What is the area
of the border?

_____       _____

8. **WRITE** ▸*Math*  Describe each of the three methods you
can use to find the area of a rectangle.

_____

## Lesson Check (3.MD.C.7, 3.MD.C.7a)

**1.** The entrance to an office has a tiled floor. Each square tile is 1 square meter. What is the area of the floor?

**2.** Ms. Burns buys a new rug. Each unit square is 1 square foot. What is the area of the rug?

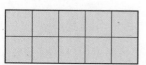

## Spiral Review (3.OA.A.4, 3.NF.A.3d, 3.MD.A.1, 3.MD.D.8)

**3.** Compare the fractions. Write <, >, or =.

$$\frac{1}{3} \bigcirc \frac{2}{3}$$

**4.** Claire bought 6 packs of baseball cards. Each pack had the same number of cards. If Claire bought 48 baseball cards in all, how many cards were in each pack?

**5.** Austin left for school at 7:35 A.M. He arrived at school 15 minutes later. What time did Austin arrive at school?

**6.** Wyatt's room is a rectangle with a perimeter of 40 feet. The width of the room is 8 feet. What is the length of the room?

FOR MORE PRACTICE
GO TO THE
Personal Math Trainer

Name _____

## ✓ Mid-Chapter Checkpoint

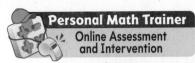

### Vocabulary

**Choose the best term from the box.**

| Vocabulary |
| --- |
| area |
| perimeter |
| square unit |

1. The distance around a figure is the _____. (p. 625)

2. The measure of the number of unit squares needed to cover a figure with no gaps or overlaps is the _____. (p. 643)

### Concepts and Skills

**Find the perimeter of the figure. Each unit is 1 centimeter.** (3.MD.D.8)

3.

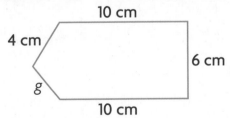

_____ centimeters

4.

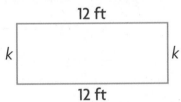

_____ centimeters

**Find the unknown side lengths.** (3.MD.D.8)

5. Perimeter = 33 centimeters

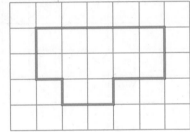

g = _____ centimeters

6. Perimeter = 32 feet

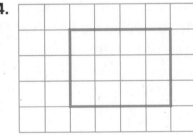

k = _____ feet

**Find the area of the figure. Each unit square is 1 square meter.**

(3.MD.C.5, 3.MD.C.5a, 3.MD.C.5b, 3.MD.C.6, 3.MD.C.7, 3.MD.C.7a)

7.

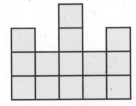

_____ square meters

8.

_____ square meters     **Chapter 11   661**

**9.** Ramona is making a lid for her rectangular jewelry box. The jewelry box has side lengths of 6 centimeters and 4 centimeters. What is the area of the lid Ramona is making? (3.MD.C.7, 3.MD.C.7a)

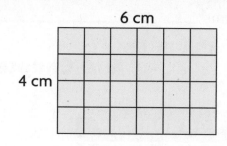

_____

**10.** Adrienne is decorating a square picture frame. She glued 36 inches of ribbon around the edge of the frame. What is the length of each side of the picture frame?(3.MD.D.8)

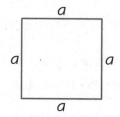

_____

**11.** Margo will sweep a room. A diagram of the floor that she needs to sweep is shown at the right. What is the area of the floor? (3.MD.C.5b, 3.MD.C.6)

_____

**12.** Jeff is making a poster for a car wash for the Campout Club. What is the perimeter of the poster? (3.MD.D.8)

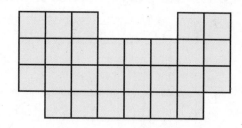

_____

**13.** GO DEEPER  A rectangle has two side lengths of 8 inches and two side lengths of 10 inches. What is the perimeter of the rectangle? What is the area of the rectangle? (3.MD.C.5, 3.MD.C.5a, 3.MD.D.8)

_____

Name _____

# Problem Solving • Area of Rectangles

**Essential Question** How can you use the strategy *find a pattern* to solve area problems?

Common Core  **Measurement and Data—3.MD.C.7b**
*Also 3.OA.A.3, 3.OA.C.7, 3.OA.D.9*
MATHEMATICAL PRACTICES
**MP1, MP2, MP7**

## ? Unlock the Problem

Mr. Koi wants to build storage buildings, so he drew plans for the buildings. He wants to know how the areas of the buildings are related. How does the area change from the area of Building *A* to the area of Building *B*? How does the area change from the area of Building *C* to the area of Building *D*?

Use the graphic organizer to help you solve the problem.

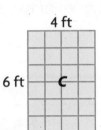
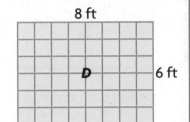

## Read the Problem

| What do I need to find? | What information do I need to use? | How will I use the information? |
|---|---|---|
| I need to find how the areas will change from *A* to *B* and from _____ to _____. | I need to use the _____ and _____ of each building to find its area. | I will record the areas in a table. Then I will look for a pattern to see how the _____ will change. |

## Solve the Problem

I will complete the table to find patterns to solve the problem.

| | Length | Width | Area | | Length | Width | Area |
|---|---|---|---|---|---|---|---|
| Building *A* | 3 ft | | | Building *C* | | 4 ft | |
| Building *B* | 3 ft | | | Building *D* | | 8 ft | |

I see that the lengths will be the same and the widths will be doubled.

The areas will change from _____ to _____ and from _____ to _____.

So, when the lengths are the same and the widths are doubled,

the areas will be _____.

© Houghton Mifflin Harcourt Publishing Company

# 🔑 Try Another Problem

Mr. Koi is building more storage buildings. He wants to know how the areas of the buildings are related. How does the area change from the area of Building *E* to the area of Building *F*? How does the area change from the area of Building *G* to the area of Building *H*?

Use the graphic organizer to help you solve the problem.

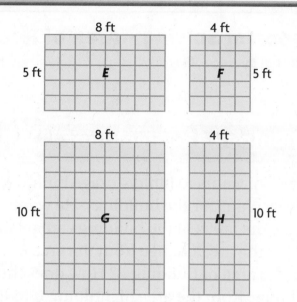

## Read the Problem

| What do I need to find? | What information do I need to use? | How will I use the information? |
|---|---|---|
| | | |

## Solve the Problem

| | Length | Width | Area | | Length | Width | Area |
|---|---|---|---|---|---|---|---|
| Building *E* | | | | Building *G* | | | |
| Building *F* | | | | Building *H* | | | |

- How did your table help you find a pattern?

_____

_____

_____

MATHEMATICAL PRACTICES ②

**Reason Abstractly**
What if the length of both sides is doubled? How would the areas change?

## Share and Show MATH BOARD

**Use the table for 1–2.**

1. Many pools come in rectangular shapes. How do the areas of the swimming pools change when the widths change?

   **First,** complete the table by finding the area of each pool.

   Think: I can find the area by multiplying the length and the width.

| Swimming Pool Sizes | | | |
|---|---|---|---|
| Pool | Length (in feet) | Width (in feet) | Area (in square feet) |
| A | 8 | 20 | |
| B | 8 | 30 | |
| C | 8 | 40 | |
| D | 8 | 50 | |

   **Then,** find a pattern of how the lengths change and how the widths change.

   The _____ stays the same. The widths

   _____.

   **Last,** describe a pattern of how the area changes.

   The areas _____ by ____ square feet.

2. What if the length of each pool was 16 feet? Explain how the areas would change.

   _____

## On Your Own

3. **MATHEMATICAL PRACTICE ⑦** **Look for a Pattern** If the length of each pool in the table is 20 feet, and the widths change from 5, to 6, to 7, and to 8 feet, describe the pattern of the areas.

   _____

   _____

4. **MATHEMATICAL PRACTICE ①** **Analyze Relationships** Jacob has a rectangular garden with an area of 56 square feet. The length of the garden is 8 feet. What is the width of the garden?

_____

5. **GO DEEPER** A diagram of Paula's bedroom is at the right. Her bedroom is in the shape of a rectangle. Write the measurements for the other sides. What is the perimeter of the room? (Hint: The two pairs of opposite sides are equal lengths.)

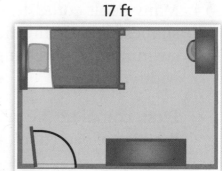

17 ft

12 f

_____

6. **THINK SMARTER** Elizabeth built a sandbox that is 4 feet long and 4 feet wide. She also built a flower garden that is 4 feet long and 6 feet wide and a vegetable garden that is 4 feet long and 8 feet wide. How do the areas change?

_____

_____

_____

_____

7. **THINK SMARTER** Find the pattern and complete the chart.

| Total Area (in square feet) | 50 | 60 | 70 | 80 | |
|---|---|---|---|---|---|
| Length (in feet) | 10 | 10 | | 10 | |
| Width (in feet) | 5 | 6 | 7 | | |

How can you use the chart to find the length and width of a figure with an area of 100 square feet?

_____

_____

Name _____

# Problem Solving • Area of Rectangles

Common Core  **COMMON CORE STANDARD—3.MD.C.7b**
*Geometric measurement: understand concepts of area and relate area to multiplication and to addition.*

**Use the information for 1-3.**

An artist makes rectangular murals in different sizes. Below are the available sizes. Each unit square is 1 square meter.

  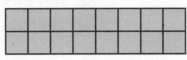

A          B          C                    D

1. Complete the table to find the area of each mural.

| Mural | Length (in meters) | Width (in meters) | Area (in square meters) |
|-------|--------------------|-------------------|-------------------------|
| A | 2 | 1 | 2 |
| B | 2 | 2 | 4 |
| C | 2 | | |
| D | 2 | | |

2. Find and describe a pattern of how the length changes and how the width changes for murals A through D.

_____

_____

3. How do the areas of the murals change when the width changes?

_____

4. **WRITE** ▸*Math* Write and solve an area problem that illustrates the use of the *find a pattern* strategy.

_____

_____

## Lesson Check (3.MD.C.7b)

1. Lauren drew the designs below. Each unit square is 1 square centimeter. If the pattern continues, what will be the area of the fourth figure?

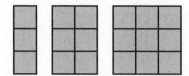

2. Henry built one garden that is 3 feet wide and 3 feet long. He also built a garden that is 3 feet wide and 6 feet long, and a garden that is 3 feet wide and 9 feet long. How do the areas change?

## Spiral Review (3.OA.A.3, 3.NBT.A.3, 3.NF.A.1, 3.MD.C.5b, 3.MD.C.6)

3. Joe, Jim, and Jack share 27 football cards equally. How many cards does each boy get?

4. Nita uses $\frac{1}{3}$ of a carton of 12 eggs. How many eggs does she use?

5. Brenda made 8 necklaces. Each necklace has 10 large beads. How many large beads did Brenda use to make the necklaces?

6. Neal is tiling his kitchen floor. Each square tile is 1 square foot. Neal uses 6 rows of tiles with 9 tiles in each row. What is the area of the floor?

FOR MORE PRACTICE
GO TO THE
Personal Math Trainer

Name _____

# Problem Solving • Area of Rectangles

Common Core  **COMMON CORE STANDARD—3.MD.C.7b**
*Geometric measurement: understand concepts of area and relate area to multiplication and to addition.*

**Use the information for 1–3.**

An artist makes rectangular murals in different sizes. Below are the available sizes. Each unit square is 1 square meter.

  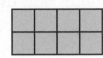  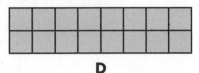

A    B        C              D

1. Complete the table to find the area of each mural.

| Mural | Length (in meters) | Width (in meters) | Area (in square meters) |
|-------|--------------------|-------------------|--------------------------|
| A | 2 | 1 | 2 |
| B | 2 | 2 | 4 |
| C | 2 | | |
| D | 2 | | |

2. Find and describe a pattern of how the length changes and how the width changes for murals A through D.

_____

_____

3. How do the areas of the murals change when the width changes?

_____

4. **WRITE** ▸*Math* Write and solve an area problem that illustrates the use of the *find a pattern* strategy.

_____

_____

## Lesson Check (3.MD.C.7b)

**1.** Lauren drew the designs below. Each unit square is 1 square centimeter. If the pattern continues, what will be the area of the fourth figure?

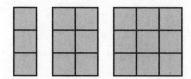

**2.** Henry built one garden that is 3 feet wide and 3 feet long. He also built a garden that is 3 feet wide and 6 feet long, and a garden that is 3 feet wide and 9 feet long. How do the areas change?

## Spiral Review (3.OA.A.3, 3.NBT.A.3, 3.NF.A.1, 3.MD.C.5b, 3.MD.C.6)

**3.** Joe, Jim, and Jack share 27 football cards equally. How many cards does each boy get?

**4.** Nita uses $\frac{1}{3}$ of a carton of 12 eggs. How many eggs does she use?

**5.** Brenda made 8 necklaces. Each necklace has 10 large beads. How many large beads did Brenda use to make the necklaces?

**6.** Neal is tiling his kitchen floor. Each square tile is 1 square foot. Neal uses 6 rows of tiles with 9 tiles in each row. What is the area of the floor?

FOR MORE PRACTICE
GO TO THE
**Personal Math Trainer**

Name _____

# Area of Combined Rectangles

**Essential Question** How can you break apart a figure to find the area?

**Common Core** Measurement and Data—
3.MD.C.7c, 3.MD.C.7d
*Also 3.MD.C.5, 3.MD.C.5a, 3.MD.C.5b, 3.MD.C.7b, 3.OA.A.3, 3.OA.B.5, 3.OA.C.7, 3.NBT.A.2*
MATHEMATICAL PRACTICES
MP1, MP4, MP6

## 🔑 Unlock the Problem

Anna's rug has side lengths of 4 feet and 9 feet. What is the area of Anna's rug?

### 🔒 Activity **Materials** ■ square tiles

**Remember**

You can use the Distributive Property to break apart an array.

$3 \times 3 = 3 \times (2 + 1)$

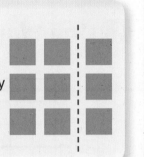

**STEP 1** Use square tiles to model $4 \times 9$.

**STEP 2** Draw a rectangle on the grid paper to show your model.

**STEP 3** Draw a vertical line to break apart the model to make two smaller rectangles.

The side length 9 is broken into _____ plus _____.

**STEP 4** Find the area of each of the two smaller rectangles.

Rectangle 1: _____ × _____ = _____

Rectangle 2: _____ × _____ = _____

**STEP 5** Add the products to find the total area.

_____ + _____ = _____ square feet

**STEP 6** Check your answer by counting the number of square feet.

_____ square feet

So, the area of Anna's rug is _____ square feet.

**Math Talk**

MATHEMATICAL PRACTICES ⑥

**Compare** Did you draw a line in the same place as your classmates? Explain why you found the same total area.

CONNECT Using the Distributive Property, you found that you could break apart a rectangle into smaller rectangles, and add the area of each smaller rectangle to find the total area.

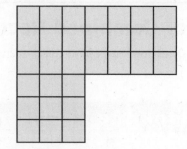

How can you break apart this figure into rectangles to find its area?

**One Way** Use a horizontal line.

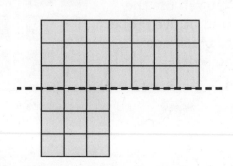

**STEP 1** Write a multiplication equation for each rectangle.

Rectangle 1: ___ × ___ = ___

Rectangle 2: ___ × ___ = ___

**STEP 2** Add the products to find the total area.

___ + ___ = ___ square units

So, the area is _____ square units.

**Another Way** Use a vertical line.

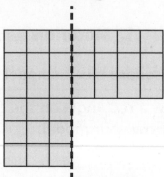

**STEP 1** Write a multiplication equation for each rectangle.

Rectangle 1: ___ × ___ = ___

Rectangle 2: ___ × ___ = ___

**STEP 2** Add the products to find the total area.

___ + ___ = ___ square units

MATHEMATICAL PRACTICES ①

**Evaluate** How can you check your answer?

**Share and Show**

1. Draw a line to break apart the figure into rectangles. Find the total area of the figure.

   **Think:** I can draw vertical or horizontal lines to break apart the figure to make rectangles.

   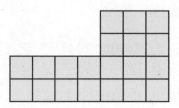

   Rectangle 1: ___ × ___ = ___

   Rectangle 2: ___ × ___ = ___

   ___ + ___ = ___ square units

Name _____

# Area of Combined Rectangles

**Essential Question** How can you break apart a figure to find the area?

**Common Core** Measurement and Data—
3.MD.C.7c, 3.MD.C.7d
*Also 3.MD.C.5, 3.MD.C.5a, 3.MD.C.5b, 3.MD.C.7b, 3.OA.A.3, 3.OA.B.5, 3.OA.C.7, 3.NBT.A.2*
MATHEMATICAL PRACTICES
MP1, MP4, MP6

## 🔑 Unlock the Problem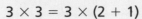

Anna's rug has side lengths of 4 feet and 9 feet. What is the area of Anna's rug?

**🔑 Activity Materials** ■ square tiles

**STEP 1** Use square tiles to model 4 × 9.

**STEP 2** Draw a rectangle on the grid paper to show your model.

**STEP 3** Draw a vertical line to break apart the model to make two smaller rectangles.

The side length 9 is broken into _____ plus _____.

**STEP 4** Find the area of each of the two smaller rectangles.

Rectangle 1: _____ × _____ = _____

Rectangle 2: _____ × _____ = _____

**STEP 5** Add the products to find the total area.

_____ + _____ = _____ square feet

**STEP 6** Check your answer by counting the number of square feet.

_____ square feet

So, the area of Anna's rug is _____ square feet.

**Remember**

You can use the Distributive Property to break apart an array.

3 × 3 = 3 × (2 + 1)

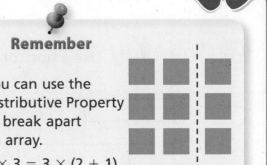

**Math Talk** MATHEMATICAL PRACTICES ⑥

**Compare** Did you draw a line in the same place as your classmates? Explain why you found the same total area.

**CONNECT** Using the Distributive Property, you found that you could break apart a rectangle into smaller rectangles, and add the area of each smaller rectangle to find the total area.

How can you break apart this figure into rectangles to find its area?

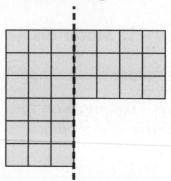

## One Way Use a horizontal line.

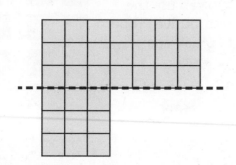

**STEP 1** Write a multiplication equation for each rectangle.

Rectangle 1: ___ × ___ = ___

Rectangle 2: ___ × ___ = ___

---

**STEP 2** Add the products to find the total area.

___ + ___ = ___ square units

So, the area is _____ square units.

## Another Way Use a vertical line.

**STEP 1** Write a multiplication equation for each rectangle.

Rectangle 1: ___ × ___ = ___

Rectangle 2: ___ × ___ = ___

---

**STEP 2** Add the products to find the total area.

___ + ___ = ___ square units

**Math Talk**

**Evaluate** How can you check your answer?

### Share and Show MATH BOARD

1. Draw a line to break apart the figure into rectangles. Find the total area of the figure.

   **Think:** I can draw vertical or horizontal lines to break apart the figure to make rectangles.

   Rectangle 1: ___ × ___ = ___

   Rectangle 2: ___ × ___ = ___

   ___ + ___ = ___ square units

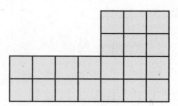

Name _____

**Use the Distributive Property to find the area. Show your multiplication and addition equations.**

2.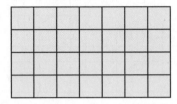

_____

_____ square units

3.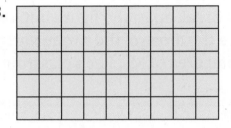

_____

_____ square units

**On Your Own**

**Use the Distributive Property to find the area. Show your multiplication and addition equations.**

4.

_____

_____ square units

5.

_____

_____ square units

**Draw a line to break apart the figure into rectangles. Find the area of the figure.**

6.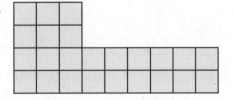

Rectangle 1: ___ × ___ = ___

Rectangle 2: ___ × ___ = ___

___ + ___ = ___ square units

7. GO DEEPER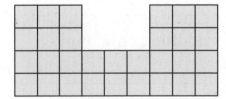

Rectangle 1: ___ × ___ = ___

Rectangle 2: ___ × ___ = ___

Rectangle 3: ___ × ___ = ___

___ + ___ + ___ = ___ square units

© Houghton Mifflin Harcourt Publishing Company

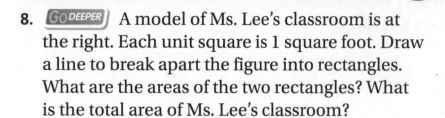
8. **GO DEEPER** A model of Ms. Lee's classroom is at the right. Each unit square is 1 square foot. Draw a line to break apart the figure into rectangles. What are the areas of the two rectangles? What is the total area of Ms. Lee's classroom?

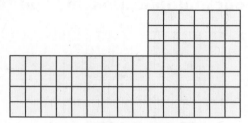

_____

9. David has a rectangular bedroom with a rectangular closet. Each unit square is 1 square foot. Draw a line to break apart the figure into rectangles. What is the total area of David's bedroom?

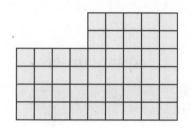

_____

10. **THINK SMARTER** **Explain** how to break apart the figure to find its area.

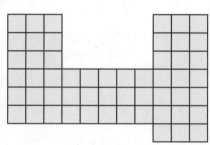

_____

_____

_____

_____

1 unit square = 1 square meter

11. **MATHEMATICAL PRACTICE ④** **Interpret a Result** Use the Distributive Property to find the area of the figure at the right. Write your multiplication and addition equations.

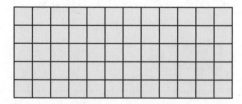

_____

_____

1 unit square = 1 square centimeter

**Personal Math Trainer**

12. **THINK SMARTER +** Pete drew a diagram of his backyard on grid paper. Each unit square is 1 square meter. The area surrounding the patio is grass.

How much more of the backyard is grass than patio? Show your work.

_____ more square meters

Name _____

# Area of Combined Rectangles

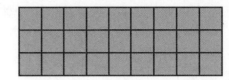

COMMON CORE STANDARDS—3.MD.C.7c, 3.MD.C.7d *Geometric measurement: understand concepts of area and relate area to multiplication and to addition.*

**Use the Distributive Property to find the area. Show your multiplication and addition equations.**

1.

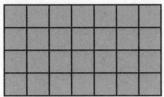

$4 \times 2 = 8$; $4 \times 5 = 20$

$8 + 20 = 28$

___28___ square units

2.

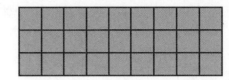

_____

_____

_____ square units

**Draw a line to break apart the shape into rectangles. Find the area of the shape.**

3.

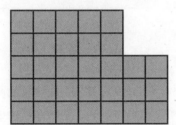

Rectangle 1: _____ × _____ = _____

Rectangle 2: _____ × _____ = _____

_____ + _____ = _____ square units

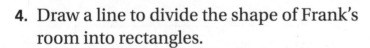

A diagram of Frank's room is at right. Each unit square is 1 square foot.

4. Draw a line to divide the shape of Frank's room into rectangles.

5. What is the total area of Frank's room?

_____ square feet

6. **WRITE** ▸*Math* Draw a figure that is not a rectangle and find its area. Use grid paper and show each step.

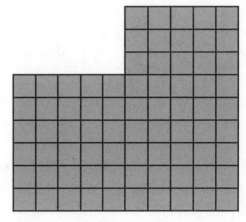

_____

_____

## Lesson Check (3.MD.C.7c, 3.MD.C.7d)

**1.** The diagram shows Ben's backyard. Each unit square is 1 square yard. What is the area of Ben's backyard?

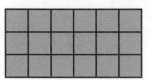

**2.** The diagram shows a room in an art gallery. Each unit square is 1 square meter. What is the area of the room?

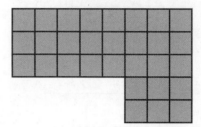

_____

_____

## Spiral Review (3.OA.B.6, 3.NF.A.1, 3.MD.B.4, 3.MD.D.8)

**3.** Naomi needs to solve $28 \div 7 =$ ■. What related multiplication fact can she use to find the unknown number?

**4.** Karen drew a triangle with side lengths 3 centimeters, 4 centimeters, and 5 centimeters. What is the perimeter of the triangle?

_____

_____

_____

_____

**5.** The rectangle is divided into equal parts. What is the name of the equal parts?

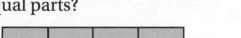

**6.** Use an inch ruler. To the nearest half inch, how long is this line segment?

_____

_____

Name _____

# Same Perimeter, Different Areas

**Essential Question** How can you use area to compare rectangles with the same perimeter?

 Common Core   **Measurement and Data—3.MD.D.8**
Also 3.MD.C.5, 3.MD.C.5a, 3.MD.C.5b,
3.MD.C.7b, 3.OA.A.3, 3.OA.C.7, 3.NBT.A.2
**MATHEMATICAL PRACTICES**
**MP2, MP3, MP4, MP6**

 **Unlock the Problem**

Toby has 12 feet of boards to put around a rectangular sandbox. How long should he make each side so that the area of the sandbox is as large as possible?

> • What is the greatest perimeter Toby can make for his sandbox?
> _____

## Activity

**Materials** ■ square tiles

Use square tiles to make all the rectangles you can that have a perimeter of 12 units. Draw and label the sandboxes. Then find the area of each.

| Sandbox 1 | Sandbox 2 | Sandbox 3 |
|---|---|---|
| <u>1</u> ft | __ ft | __ ft |
| <u>5</u> ft | __ ft | __ ft |

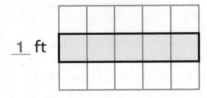

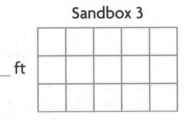

Find the perimeter and area of each rectangle.

| | Perimeter | Area |
|---|---|---|
| Sandbox 1 | <u>5</u> + <u>1</u> + <u>5</u> + <u>1</u> = <u>12</u> feet | <u>1</u> × <u>5</u> = ___ square feet |
| Sandbox 2 | __ + __ + __ + __ = ___ feet | __ × __ = ___ square feet |
| Sandbox 3 | __ + __ + __ + __ = ___ feet | __ × __ = ___ square feet |

The area of Sandbox ____ is the greatest.

So, Toby should build a sandbox that is

____ feet wide and ____ feet long.

 **Math Talk**   MATHEMATICAL PRACTICES ⑥

**Compare** How are the sandboxes alike? How are the sandboxes different?

## 🔑 Examples Draw rectangles with the same perimeter and different areas.

**Ⓐ** Draw a rectangle that has a perimeter of 20 units and an area of 24 square units.

The sides of the rectangle measure

_____ units and _____ units.

**Ⓑ** Draw a rectangle that has a perimeter of 20 units and an area of 25 square units.

The sides of the rectangle measure

_____ units and _____ units.

**Math Talk**   MATHEMATICAL PRACTICES ③

**Compare Representations**
Explain how the perimeters of Example *A* and Example *B* are related. Explain how the areas are related.

## Share and Show 📝 MATH BOARD

1. The perimeter of the rectangle at the right is

_____ units. The area is _____ square units.

2. Draw a rectangle that has the same perimeter as the rectangle in Exercise 1 but with a different area.

3. The area of the rectangle in Exercise 2 is

_____ square units.

✓ 4. Which rectangle has the greater area?

_____

5. If you were given a rectangle with a certain perimeter, how would you draw it so that it has the greatest area?

_____

**Math Talk**   MATHEMATICAL PRACTICES ⑥

**Explain** how you knew what the rectangle for Exercise 5 would look like.

Name _____

**Find the perimeter and the area. Tell which rectangle has a greater area.**

6.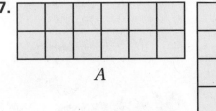

*A*: Perimeter = _____ ; Area = _____

*B*: Perimeter = _____ ; Area = _____

Rectangle _____ has a greater area.

**On Your Own**

**Find the perimeter and the area. Tell which rectangle has a greater area.**

7.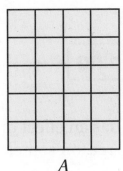

8.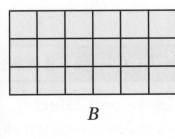

*A*: Perimeter = _____ ;

    Area = _____

*B*: Perimeter = _____ ;

    Area = _____

Rectangle ___ has a greater area.

*A*: Perimeter = _____ ;

    Area = _____

*B*: Perimeter = _____ ;

    Area = _____

Rectangle ___ has a greater area.

9. **MATHEMATICAL PRACTICE 6** **Use Math Vocabulary** Todd's flower garden is 4 feet wide and 8 feet long. If the answer is 32 square feet, what is the question?

_____

## Problem Solving • Applications

**10.** **THINK SMARTER** Draw a rectangle with the same perimeter as Rectangle *C*, but with a smaller area. What is the area?

Area = _____

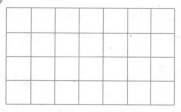

*C*

**11.** **THINK SMARTER** Which figure has a perimeter of 20 units and an area of 16 square units?

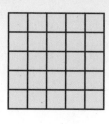    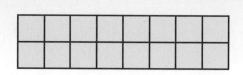    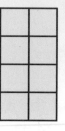    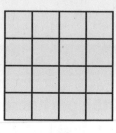

Ⓐ                          Ⓑ                    Ⓒ              Ⓓ

## Connect to Reading

### Cause and Effect

Sometimes one action has an effect on another action. The *cause* is the reason something happens. The *effect* is the result.

**12.** **GO DEEPER** Sam wanted to print a digital photo that is 3 inches wide and 5 inches long. What if Sam accidentally printed a photo that is 4 inches wide and 6 inches long?

Sam can make a table to understand cause and effect.

| Cause | Effect |
|---|---|
| The wrong size photo was printed. | Each side of the photo is a greater length. |

**Use the information and the strategy to solve the problems.**

**a.** What effect did the mistake have on the perimeter of the photo?

_____

_____

**b.** What effect did the mistake have on the area of the photo?

_____

_____

# Same Perimeter, Different Areas

**COMMON CORE STANDARD—3.MD.D.8**
*Geometric measurement: recognize perimeter as an attribute of plane figures and distinguish between linear and area measures.*

**Find the perimeter and the area.**
**Tell which rectangle has a greater area.**

1.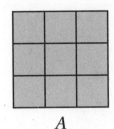

   *A*: Perimeter = ____**12 units**____ ;

   Area = ____**9 square units**____

   *B*: Perimeter = _____ ;

   Area = _____

   Rectangle _____ has a greater area.

2.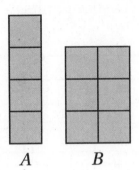

   *A*: Perimeter = _____ ;

   Area = _____

   *B*: Perimeter = _____ ;

   Area = _____

   Rectangle _____ has a greater area.

## Problem Solving (Real World)

3. Tara's and Jody's bedrooms are shaped like rectangles. Tara's bedroom is 9 feet long and 8 feet wide. Jody's bedroom is 7 feet long and 10 feet wide. Whose bedroom has the greater area? **Explain**.

   _____

   _____

4. **WRITE** ▸*Math* Draw three examples of rectangles that have the same perimeter, but different areas. Note which of the areas is greatest and which is the least.

   _____

   _____

## Lesson Check (3.MD.D.8)

1. Draw a rectangle that has a perimeter of 12 units and an area of 8 square units.

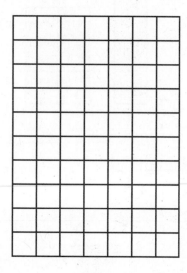

2. Find the perimeter and the area. Tell which rectangle has the greater area.

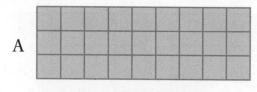

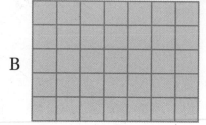

A: Perimeter = _____ units

Area = _____ square units

B: Perimeter = _____ units

Area = _____ square units

Rectangle _____ has a greater area.

## Spiral Review (3.MD.C.7, 3.MD.C.7a, 3.MD.D.8)

3. Kerrie covers a table with 8 rows of square tiles. There are 7 tiles in each row. What is the area that Kerrie covers in square units?

4. Von has a rectangular workroom with a perimeter of 26 feet. The length of the workroom is 6 feet. What is the width of Von's workroom?

FOR MORE PRACTICE
GO TO THE
Personal Math Trainer

Name _____

# Same Area, Different Perimeters

**Essential Question** How can you use perimeter to compare rectangles with the same area?

Common Core) Measurement and Data—3.MD.D.8
Also 3.MD.C.5, 3.MD.C.5a, 3.MD.C.5b, 3.MD.C.7b, 3.OA.A.3, 3.OA.C.7, 3.NBT.A.2
MATHEMATICAL PRACTICES
MP2, MP3, MP4, MP6

## ⚷ Unlock the Problem

Marcy is making a rectangular pen to hold her rabbits. The area of the pen should be 16 square meters with side lengths that are whole numbers. What is the least amount of fencing she needs?

- What does the least amount of fencing represent?

_____

### 🔑 Activity  **Materials** ■ square tiles

Use 16 square tiles to make rectangles. Make as many different rectangles as you can with 16 tiles. Record the rectangles on the grid, write the multiplication equation for the area shown by the rectangle, and find the perimeter of each rectangle.

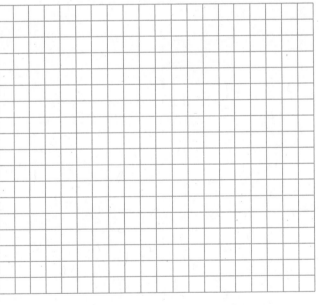

**Math Talk**  MATHEMATICAL PRACTICES ④

**Model Mathematics** How did you determine what rectangles to draw?

Area: _____ × _____ = 16 square meters     Perimeter: _____ meters

Area: _____ × _____ = 16 square meters     Perimeter: _____ meters

Area: _____ × _____ = 16 square meters     Perimeter: _____ meters

To use the least amount of fencing, Marcy should make a rectangular

pen with side lengths of _____ meters and _____ meters.

So, _____ meters is the least amount of fencing Marcy needs.

**Try This!**

Draw three rectangles that have an area of 18 square units on the grid. Find the perimeter of each rectangle. Shade the rectangle that has the greatest perimeter.

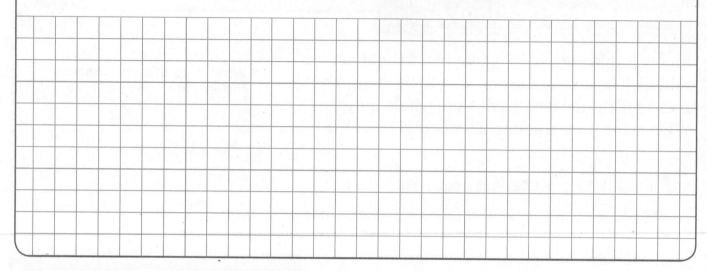

**Share and Show**

1. The area of the rectangle at the right is

   _____ square units. The perimeter is _____ units.

2. Draw a rectangle that has the same area as the rectangle in Exercise 1 but with a different perimeter.

3. The perimeter of the rectangle in Exercise 2 is

   _____ units.

4. Which rectangle has the greater perimeter?

   _____

5. If you were given a rectangle with a certain area, how would you draw it so that it had the greatest perimeter?

   _____

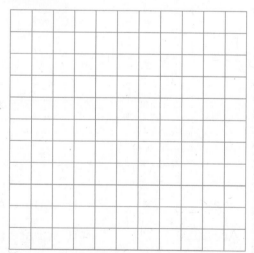

**Math Talk**

MATHEMATICAL PRACTICES ③

**Compare Representations**
Did you and your classmate draw the same rectangle for Exercise 2?

Name _____

**Find the perimeter and the area. Tell which rectangle has a greater perimeter.**

6.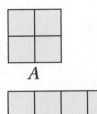

*A*: Area = _____ ; Perimeter = _____

*B*: Area = _____ ; Perimeter = _____

Rectangle _____ has a greater perimeter.

## On Your Own

**Find the perimeter and the area. Tell which rectangle has a greater perimeter.**

7.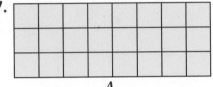

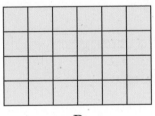

*A*: Area = _____ ;

Perimeter = _____

*B*: Area = _____ ;

Perimeter = _____

Rectangle _____ has a greater perimeter.

8.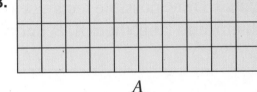

*A*: Area = _____ ;

Perimeter = _____

*B*: Area = _____ ;

Perimeter = _____

Rectangle _____ has a greater perimeter.

9. **THINK SMARTER** **Sense or Nonsense?** Dora says that of all the possible rectangles with the same area, the rectangle with the largest perimeter will have two side lengths that are 1 unit. Does her statement make sense? Explain.

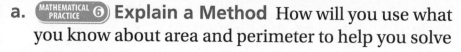

## Unlock the Problem (Real World)

**10.** Roberto has 12 tiles. Each tile is 1 square inch. He will arrange them into a rectangle and glue 1-inch stones around the edge. How can Roberto arrange the tiles so that he uses the least number of stones?

**a.** **MATHEMATICAL PRACTICE 6** **Explain a Method** How will you use what you know about area and perimeter to help you solve

the problem? _____

_____

_____

**b.** **GO DEEPER** Draw possible rectangles to solve the problem, and label them *A*, *B*, and *C*.

_____

_____

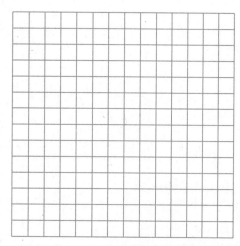

**c.** So, Roberto should arrange

the tiles like Rectangle _____.

**11.** **THINK SMARTER** Draw 2 different rectangles with an area of 20 square units. What is the perimeter of each rectangle you drew?

Area = 20 square units

Perimeter = _____ units

Perimeter = _____ units

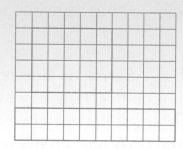

# Same Area, Different Perimeters

Common Core

**COMMON CORE STANDARD—3.MD.D.8**
*Geometric measurement: recognize perimeter as an attribute of plane figures and distinguish between linear and area measures.*

**Find the perimeter and the area. Tell which rectangle has a greater perimeter.**

1.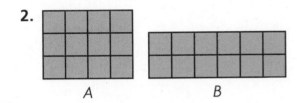

*A*: Area = ____8 square units____ ;

Perimeter = ____18 units____

*B*: Area = _____ ;

Perimeter = _____

Rectangle _____ has a greater perimeter.

2.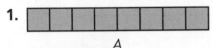

*A*: Area = _____ ;

Perimeter = _____

*B*: Area = _____ ;

Perimeter = _____

Rectangle _____ has a greater perimeter.

## Problem Solving Real World

**Use the tile designs for 3–4.**

3. Compare the areas of Design A and Design B.

_____

_____

Beth's Tile Designs

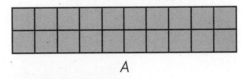

*A*

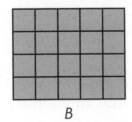

*B*

4. Compare the perimeters. Which design has the greater perimeter?

_____

5. **WRITE** ▸*Math* Draw two rectangles with different perimeters but the same area.

_____

_____

## Lesson Check (3.MD.D.8)

1. Jake drew two rectangles. Which rectangle has the greater perimeter?

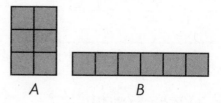

2. Alyssa drew two rectangles. Which rectangle has the greater perimeter?

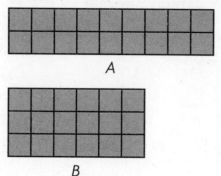

_____

_____

## Spiral Review (3.OA.D.8, 3.NF.A.2a, 3.NF.A.2b, 3.NF.A.3b)

3. Marsha was asked to find the value of $8 - 3 \times 2$. She wrote a wrong answer. What is the correct answer?

4. What fraction names the point on the number line?

$$\xleftarrow{\quad}\overset{\underset{\textstyle\frac{0}{4}}{\big|}}{\quad}\overset{\big|}{\quad}\overset{\big|}{\quad}\overset{\bullet}{\quad}\overset{\underset{\textstyle\frac{4}{4}}{\big|}}{\quad}\xrightarrow{\quad}$$

_____

_____

5. Kyle drew three line segments with these lengths: $\frac{2}{4}$ inch, $\frac{2}{3}$ inch, and $\frac{2}{6}$ inch. List the fractions in order from least to greatest.

6. On Monday, $\frac{3}{8}$ inch of snow fell. On Tuesday, $\frac{5}{8}$ inch of snow fell. Write a statement that correctly compares the snow amounts.

_____

_____

## ✓ Chapter 11 Review/Test

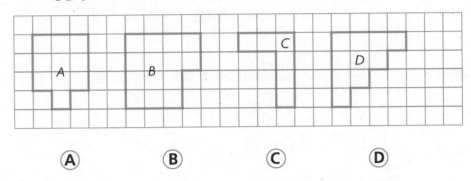

**Personal Math Trainer**
Online Assessment
and Intervention

1. Find the perimeter of each figure on the grid. Identify the figures that have a perimeter of 14 units. Mark all that apply.

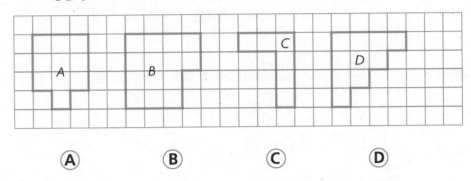

Ⓐ   Ⓑ   Ⓒ   Ⓓ

2. Kim wants to put trim around a picture she drew. How many centimeters of trim does Kim need for the perimeter of the picture?

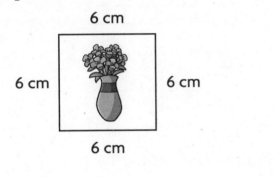

6 cm

6 cm       6 cm

6 cm

_____ centimeters

3. Sophia drew this rectangle on dot paper. What is the area of the rectangle?

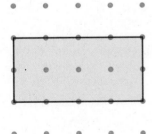

_____ square units

**GO DIGITAL**   **Assessment Options**
**Chapter Test**

4. The drawing shows Seth's plan for a fort in his backyard.
   Each unit square is 1 square foot.

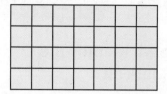

Which equations can Seth use to find the area of the fort?
Mark all that apply.

Ⓐ  $4 + 4 + 4 + 4 = 16$

Ⓑ  $7 + 4 + 7 + 4 = 22$

Ⓒ  $7 + 7 + 7 + 7 = 28$

Ⓓ  $4 \times 4 = 16$

Ⓔ  $7 \times 7 = 49$

Ⓕ  $4 \times 7 = 28$

5. Which rectangle has a number of square units for its area
   equal to the number of units of its perimeter?

Ⓐ

Ⓒ

Ⓑ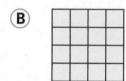

Ⓓ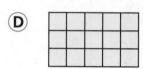

6. Vanessa uses a ruler to draw a square. The perimeter
   of the square is 12 centimeters. Select a number to
   complete the sentence.

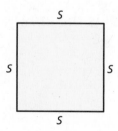

The square has a side length of | 3 4 5 6 | centimeters.

Name _____

**7.** Tomas drew two rectangles on grid paper.

Circle the words that make the sentence true.

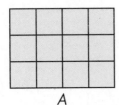
A

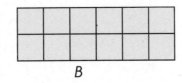
B

Rectangle *A* has an area that is

> less than
>
> the same as
>
> greater than

the area of Rectangle *B*, and a perimeter that is

> less than
>
> the same as
>
> greater than

the perimeter of Rectangle *B*.

**8.** Yuji drew this figure on grid paper. What is the perimeter of the figure?

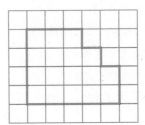

_____ units

**9.** What is the area of the figure shown? Each unit square is 1 square meter.

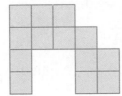

_____ square meters

**10.** Shawn drew a rectangle that was 2 units wide and 6 units long. Draw a different rectangle that has the same perimeter but a different area.

**11.** Mrs. Rios put a wallpaper border around the room shown below. She used 72 feet of wallpaper border.

What is the unknown side length? Show your work.

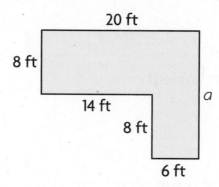

_____ feet

**12.** Elizabeth has two gardens in her yard. The first garden is 6 feet long and 4 feet wide. The second garden is double the width of the first garden. The area of the second garden is double the area of the first garden. For numbers 12a–12d, select True or False.

| | | | |
|---|---|---|---|
| 12a. | The area of the first garden is 24 square feet. | ○ True | ○ False |
| 12b. | The area of the second garden is 48 square feet. | ○ True | ○ False |
| 12c. | The length of the second garden is 12 feet. | ○ True | ○ False |
| 12d. | The length of the second garden is 6 feet. | ○ True | ○ False |

**13.** Marcus bought some postcards. Each postcard had a perimeter of 16 inches. Which could be one of the postcards Marcus bought? Mark all that apply.

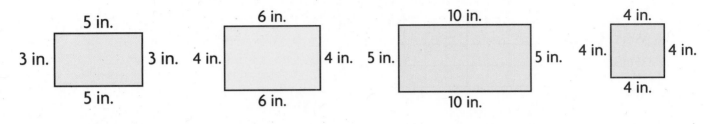

    Ⓐ                 Ⓑ                 Ⓒ                 Ⓓ

**Personal Math Trainer**

**14.** *THINK SMARTER* ✚   Anthony wants to make two different rectangular flowerbeds, each with an area of 24 square feet. He will build a wooden frame around each flowerbed. The flowerbeds will have side lengths that are whole numbers.

**Part A**

Each unit square on the grid below is 1 square foot. Draw two possible flowerbeds. Label each with a letter.

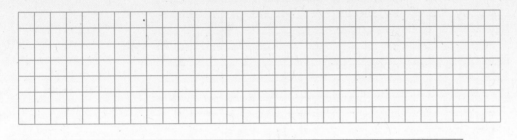

**Part B**

Which of the flowerbeds will take more wood to frame? Explain how you know.

_____

_____

_____

**15.** Keisha draws a sketch of her living room on grid paper. Each unit square is 1 square meter. Write and solve a multiplication equation that can be used to find the area of the living room in square meters.

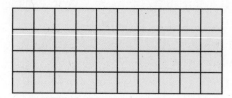

_____

_____ square meters

**16.** 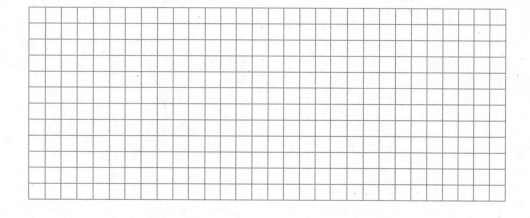 Mr. Wicks designs houses. He uses grid paper to plan a new house design. The kitchen will have an area between 70 square feet and 85 square feet. The pantry will have an area between 4 square feet and 15 square feet. Draw and label a diagram to show what Mr. Wicks could design. Explain how to find the total area.

_____

_____

# Geometry

Common Core

CRITICAL AREA Describing and analyzing two-dimensional shapes

Students at Dommerich Elementary helped design and construct a mosaic to show parts of their community and local plants and animals.

# Make a Mosaic

Have you ever worked to put puzzle pieces together to make a picture or design? Pieces of paper can be put together to make a colorful work of art called a mosaic.

## Get Started    WRITE ▸Math

**Materials** ■ construction paper ■ glue ■ ruler ■ scissors

Work with a partner to make a paper mosaic. Use the Important Facts to help you.

- Draw a simple pattern on a piece of paper.

- Cut out shapes, such as rectangles, squares, and triangles of the colors you need from construction paper. The shapes should be about 1 inch on each side.

- Glue the shapes into the pattern. Leave a little space between each shape to make the mosaic effect.

Describe and compare the shapes you used to make your mosaic.

### Important Facts

- Mosaics is the art of using small pieces of materials, such as tiles or glass, to make a colorful picture or design.
- Mosaic pieces can be small plane shapes, such as rectangles, squares, and triangles.
- Mosaic designs and patterns can be anything from simple flower shapes to common objects found in your home or patterns in nature.

_____

_____

_____

_____

_____

Completed by _____

# Two-Dimensional Shapes

## ✓ Show What You Know

Personal Math Trainer
Online Assessment
and Intervention

Check your understanding of important skills.

Name _____

▶ **Plane Shapes** (2.G.A.1)

**1.** Color the triangles blue.

**2.** Color the rectangles red.

▶ **Number of Sides**   **Write the number of sides.** (2.G.A.1)

**3.**

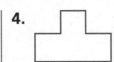

____ sides

**4.**

____ sides

**5.** Circle the shapes that have 4 or more sides.

     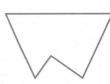

Whitney found this drawing that shows 9 small
squares. Find larger squares in the drawing.
How many squares are there in all? Explain.

## Vocabulary Builder

▶ **Visualize It** •••••••••••••••••••••••••••••••••••••••••••••

**Complete the tree map by using the words with a ✓.**

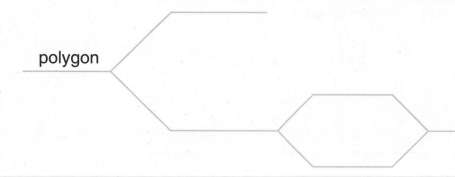

polygon

▶ **Understand Vocabulary** •••••••••••••••••••••••••••••

**Draw a line to match the word with its definition.**

1. closed shape •

2. line segment •

3. right angle •

4. hexagon •

5. angle •

6. polygon •

• A part of a line that includes two endpoints and all the points between them

• A shape formed by two rays that share an endpoint

• A shape that starts and ends at the same point

• An angle that forms a square corner

• A closed plane shape made up of line segments

• A polygon with 6 sides and 6 angles

### Preview Words

angle

closed shape

hexagon

intersecting lines

line

line segment

open shape

parallel lines

perpendicular lines

point

polygon

✓ quadrilateral

ray

✓ rectangle

✓ rhombus

right angle

✓ square

trapezoid

✓ triangle

Venn diagram

vertex

 **GO DIGITAL**
• **Interactive Student Edition**
• **Multimedia eGlossary**

# Chapter 12 Vocabulary

**angle**

ángulo

2

**endpoint**

extremo

19

**intersecting lines**

líneas secantes

36

**line**

línea

42

**line segment**

segmento

44

**octagon**

octágono

54

**parallel lines**

líneas paralelas

56

**pentagon**

pentágono

58

The point at either end of a line segment

endpoints

A shape formed by two rays that share an endpoint

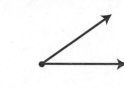 

A straight path extending in both directions with no endpoints

Lines that meet or cross

A polygon with eight sides and eight angles

A part of a line that includes two points, called endpoints, and all of the points between them

A polygon with five sides and five angles

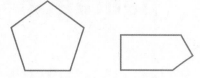

Lines in the same plane that never cross and are always the same distance apart

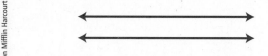

**perpendicular lines**

líneas perpendiculares

60

**polygon**

polígono

64

**quadrilateral**

cuadrilátero

66

**ray**

semirrecta

68

**rhombus**

rombo

71

**trapezoid**

trapecio

78

**Venn diagram**

diagrama de Venn

81

**vertex**

vértice

82

A closed plane shape with straight sides that are line segments

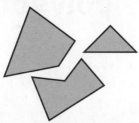

Lines that intersect to form right angles

A part of a line, with one endpoint, that is straight and continues in one direction

A polygon with four sides and four angles

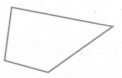

A quadrilateral with at least one pair of parallel sides

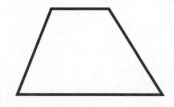

A quadrilateral with two pairs of parallel sides and four sides of equal length

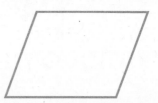

The point at which two rays of an angle or two (or more) line segments meet in a plane shape or where three or more edges meet in a solid shape

Examples:

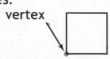
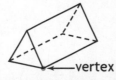

A diagram that shows relationships among sets of things

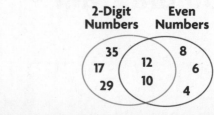

# Going to an Art Museum

**For 2 players**

## Materials

- 1 red playing piece
- 1 blue playing piece
- 1 number cube
- Clue Cards

## How to Play

1. Choose a playing piece and put it on START.
2. Toss the number cube to take a turn. Move your playing piece that many spaces.
3. If you land on one of these spaces, follow the instructions.

   **Blue Space** Follow the directions printed in the space.

   **Red Space** Take a Clue Card from the pile. If you answer the question correctly, keep the Clue Card. If you do not, return the Clue Card to the bottom of the pile.
4. Collect at least 5 Clue Cards. Move around the track as many times as necessary.
5. Only when you have 5 Clue Cards, follow the closest center path to reach FINISH.
6. The first player to reach FINISH wins.

| Word Box |
| --- |
| angle |
| endpoints |
| intersecting lines |
| line |
| line segment |
| octagon |
| parallel lines |
| pentagon |
| perpendicular lines |
| polygon |
| quadrilateral |
| ray |
| rhombus |
| trapezoid |
| Venn diagram |
| vertex |

Game

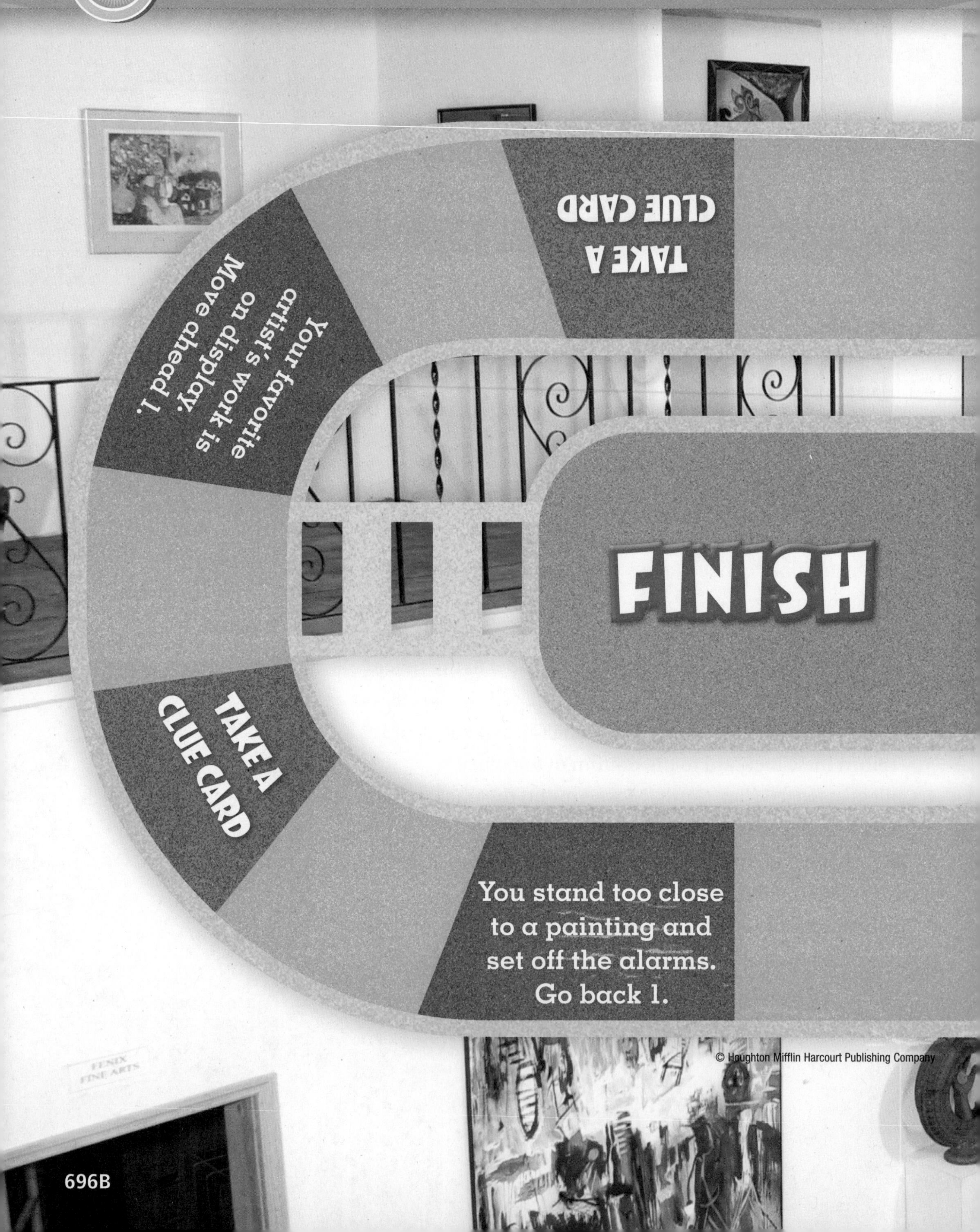
TAKE A CLUE CARD
Your favorite artist's work is on display. Move ahead 1.
FINISH
TAKE A CLUE CARD
You stand too close to a painting and set off the alarms. Go back 1.
FENIX FINE ARTS

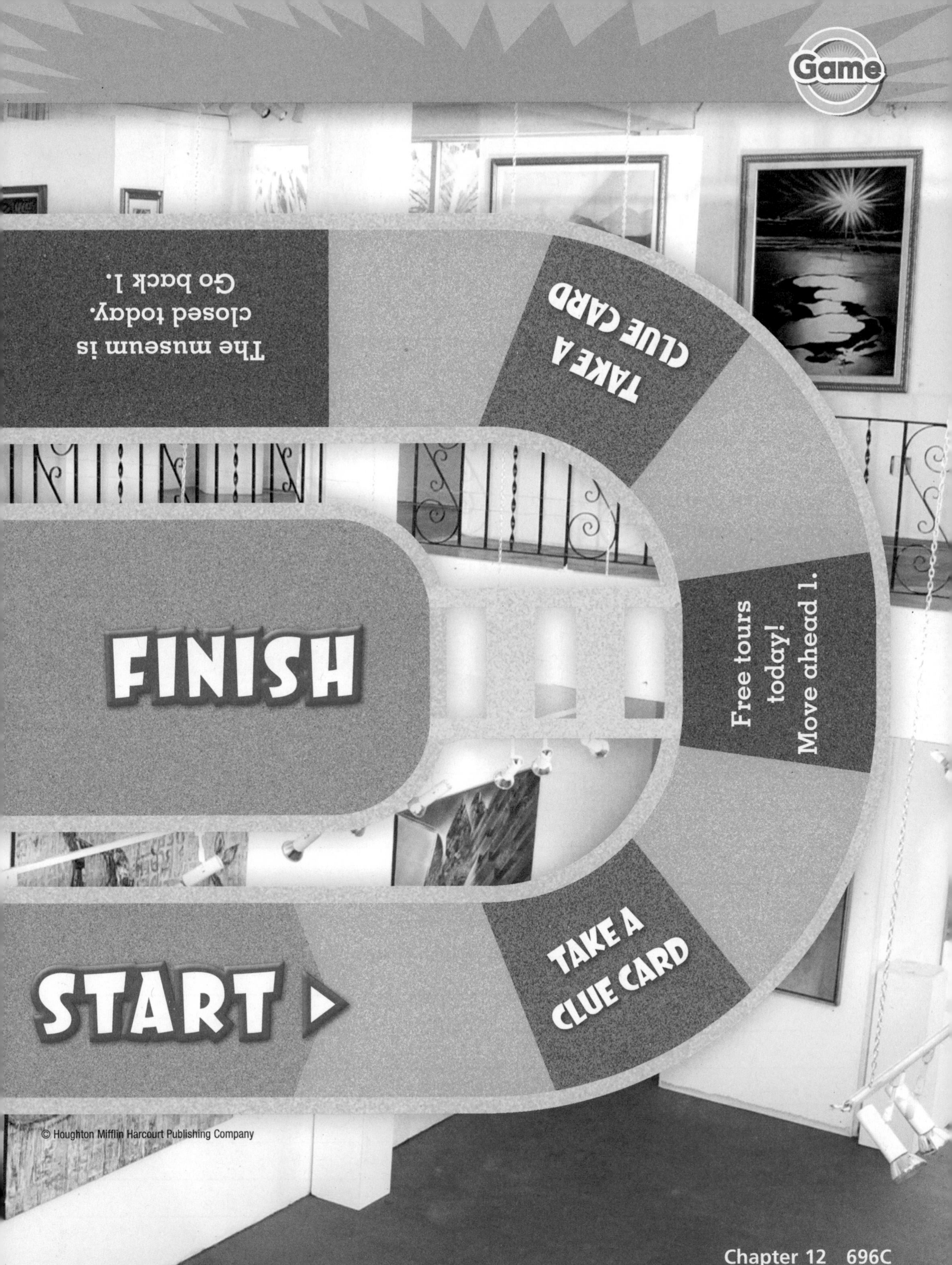
Game
The museum is
closed today.
Go back 1.
TAKE A
CLUE CARD
Free tours
today!
Move ahead 1.
FINISH
START
TAKE A
CLUE CARD

# The Write Way

## Reflect

### Choose one idea. Write about it.

- In two minutes, draw and label as many examples of polygons that you can. Use a separate piece of paper for your drawing.

- Work with a partner to explain and illustrate parallel, intersecting, and perpendicular lines. Use a separate piece of paper for your drawing.

- A reader of your math advice column writes, "I confuse rhombuses, squares, rectangles, and trapezoids. How can I tell the difference between these quadrilaterals?" Write a letter to your reader offering step-by-step advice.

# Describe Plane Shapes

**Essential Question** What are some ways to describe two-dimensional shapes?

Common Core  Geometry—3.G.A.1

MATHEMATICAL PRACTICES
MP1, MP3, MP6

## ? Unlock the Problem

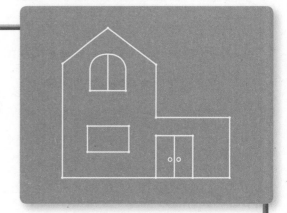

An architect draws plans for houses, stores, offices, and other buildings. Look at the shapes in the drawing at the right.

A **plane shape** is a shape on a flat surface. It is formed by points that make curved paths, line segments, or both.

| **point** | | **line** | |
|---|---|---|---|
| • is an exact position or location | point | • is a straight path<br>• continues in both directions<br>• does not end | |

| **endpoints** | | **line segment** | |
|---|---|---|---|
| • points that are used to show segments of lines | endpoints | • is straight<br>• is part of a line<br>• has 2 endpoints | |

**ray**
• is straight    • is part of a line    • has 1 endpoint    • continues in one direction

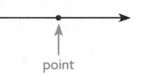

Some plane shapes are made by connecting line segments at their endpoints. One example is a square. Describe a square using math words.

**Think:** How many line segments and endpoints does a square have?

A square has ____ line segments. The line

segments meet only at their _____.

Math Talk

MATHEMATICAL PRACTICES ❸

**Apply** Why can you not measure the length of a line?

Plane shapes have length and width but no thickness, so they are also called **two-dimensional shapes**.

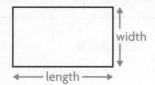

width

←—— length ——→

**Try This!** Draw plane shapes.

Plane shapes can be open or closed.

A **closed shape** starts and ends at the same point.

In the space below, draw more examples of closed shapes.

An **open shape** does not start and end at the same point.

In the space below, draw more examples of open shapes.

Math Talk

MATHEMATICAL PRACTICES ⑥

**Explain** whether a shape with a curved path must be a closed shape, an open shape, or can be either.

• Is the plane shape at the right a closed shape or an open shape? Explain how you know.

_____

_____

**698**

Name _____

1. Write how many line segments the shape has. _____

**Circle all the words that describe the shape.**

2.

ray

point

3.

open shape

closed shape

4.

open shape

closed shape

5.

line

line segment

**Write whether the shape is *open* or *closed*.**

6.

_____

7.

_____

8.

_____

9.

_____

> **Math Talk**
>
> MATHEMATICAL PRACTICES ①
>
> **Describe** How do you know whether a shape is open or closed?

**Write how many line segments the shape has.**

10.

_____

line segments

11.

_____

line segments

12.

_____

line segments

13.

_____

line segments

**Write whether the shape is *open* or *closed*.**

14.

_____

15.

_____

16.
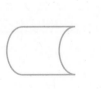

_____

17.

_____

## Problem Solving • Applications (Real World)

**18. What's the Error?** Brittany says there are two endpoints in the shape shown at the right. Is she correct? Explain.

_____

_____

**19.** MATHEMATICAL PRACTICE ⑥ **Explain** how you can make the shape at the right a closed shape. Change the shape so it is a closed shape.

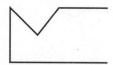

_____

_____

**20.** GO DEEPER  Look at Carly's drawing at the right. What did she draw? How is it like a line? How is it different? Change the drawing so that it is a line.

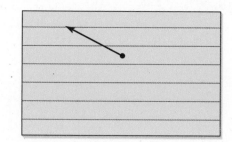

_____

_____

_____

**21.** THINK SMARTER  Draw a closed shape in the workspace by connecting 5 line segments at their endpoints.

**22.** THINK SMARTER  Draw each shape where it belongs in the table.

| Closed Shape | Open Shape |
| --- | --- |
|  |  |
|  |  |

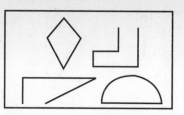

# Describe Plane Shapes

**COMMON CORE STANDARD—3.G.A.1**
*Reason with shapes and their attributes.*

**Write how many line segments the shape has.**

1.

___4___ line segments

2.

_____ line segments

**Write whether the shape is *open* or *closed*.**

3.

_____

4.

_____

## Problem Solving Real World

5. Carl wants to show a closed shape in his drawing. Show and explain how to make the drawing a closed shape.

_____

_____

6. The shape of a fish pond at a park is shown below. Is the shape open or closed?

_____

7. **WRITE** ▸*Math* Draw an open shape and a closed shape. Label your shapes.

_____

_____

## Lesson Check (3.G.A.1)

1. How many line segments does this shape have?

_____

2. What is part of a line, has one endpoint, and continues in one direction?

_____

## Spiral Review (3.OA.A.3, 3.OA.C.7, 3.NF.A.3a)

3. What multiplication sentence does the array show?

_____

_____

4. What is the unknown factor and quotient?

$9 \times \boxed{\phantom{0}} = 27$

$27 \div 9 = \boxed{\phantom{0}}$

_____

_____

5. What fraction is equivalent to $\frac{4}{8}$?

$\frac{1}{8}$ $\frac{1}{8}$ $\frac{1}{8}$ $\frac{1}{8}$ $\frac{1}{8}$ $\frac{1}{8}$ $\frac{1}{8}$ $\frac{1}{8}$

_____

6. Mr. MacTavish has 30 students from his class going on a field trip to the zoo. He puts 6 students in each group. How many groups of students will he make?

_____

FOR MORE PRACTICE
GO TO THE
**Personal Math Trainer**

Name _____

# Describe Angles in Plane Shapes

**Essential Question** How can you describe angles in plane shapes?

 **Common Core** Geometry—3.G.A.1

**MATHEMATICAL PRACTICES**
MP1, MP2

## 🖐 Unlock the Problem

An **angle** is formed by two rays that share an endpoint. Plane shapes have angles formed by two line segments that share an endpoint. The shared endpoint is called a **vertex**. The plural of *vertex* is *vertices*.

vertex ⟶

Jason drew this shape on dot paper.

• How many angles are in Jason's shape?

_____

Look at the angles in the shape that Jason drew.

How can you describe the angles?

### 🔑 Describe angles.

This mark means *right angle.* ⟶

A **right angle** is an angle that forms a square corner.

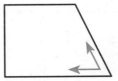

Some angles are less than a right angle.

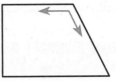

Some angles are greater than a right angle.

Look at Jason's shape.

Two angles are _____ angles, _____ angle

is _____ a right angle, and _____ angle

is _____ a right angle.

 **Math Talk**

**MATHEMATICAL PRACTICES ①**

**Analyze** What are some examples of these types of angles that you see in everyday life? Describe where you see them and what types of angles you see.

# 1 Activity  Model angles.

 **Hands On**

**Materials** ■ bendable straws ■ scissors ■ paper ■ pencil

- Cut a small slit in the shorter section of a bendable straw. Cut off the shorter section of a second straw and the bendable part. Insert the slit end of the first straw into the second straw.

cut slit    cut off                insert

straw 1   straw 2

straw 1      straw 2

- Make an angle with the straws you put together. Compare the angle you made to a corner of the sheet of paper.

- Open and close the straws to make other types of angles.

In the space below, trace the angles you made with the straws. Label each *right angle, less than a right angle,* or *greater than a right angle.*

---

**Share and Show**  **MATH BOARD**

1. How many angles are in the triangle at the right?

   _____

**Math Talk**  MATHEMATICAL PRACTICES ②

**Use Reasoning** How do you know an angle is greater than or less than a right angle?

**Use the corner of a sheet of paper to tell whether the angle is a *right angle, less than a right angle,* or *greater than a right angle.***

2.

   _____

3.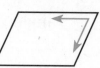

   _____

✓4.

   _____

Name _____

**Write how many of each type of angle the shape has.**

**5.**

_____ right

_____ less than a right

_____ greater than
a right

**6.**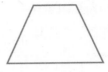

_____ right

_____ less than a right

_____ greater than
a right

✓**7.**

_____ right

_____ less than a right

_____ greater than
a right

**On Your Own**

**Use the corner of a sheet of paper to tell whether the angle is a
*right angle, less than a right angle,* or *greater than a right angle.***

**8.**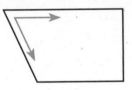

_____

**9.**

_____

**10.**

_____

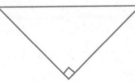 **MATHEMATICAL PRACTICE ❶ Analyze Relationships** **Write how many of each type of angle the shape has.**

**11.**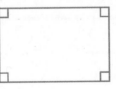

_____ right

_____ less than a right

_____ greater than
a right

**12.**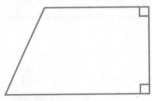

_____ right

_____ less than a right

_____ greater than
a right

**13.**

_____ right

_____ less than a right

_____ greater than a right

**14.** **THINK SMARTER** Describe the types of angles formed when you
divide a circle into 4 equal parts.

_____

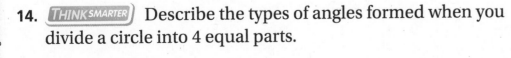

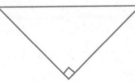

## Unlock the Problem

15. GO DEEPER  Holly drew the four shapes below.
Which shape does NOT have a right angle?

       Q           R         S         T

a. What do you need to know? _____

b. Tell how you might use a sheet of paper to solve the problem.

_____

_____

c. Shape _Q_ has _____ right angle(s), _____ angle(s) greater than
a right angle, and _____ angle(s) less than a right angle.

Shape _R_ has _____ right angle(s), _____ angle(s) greater than
a right angle, and _____ angle(s) less than a right angle.

Shape _S_ has _____ right angle(s), _____ angle(s) greater than
a right angle, and _____ angle(s) less than a right angle.

Shape _T_ has _____ right angle(s), _____ angle(s) greater than
a right angle, and _____ angle(s) less than a right angle.

So, shape _____ does not have a right angle.

16. THINK SMARTER  Circle a number or word
from each box to complete the sentence
to describe all of the angles in this shape.

There are
| 2 |
| 3 |
| 4 |
right angles and
| 2 |
| 3 |
| 4 |
angles
| less |
| greater |
than a right angle.

Name _____

# Describe Angles in Plane Shapes

 COMMON CORE STANDARD—3.G.A.1
*Reason with shapes and their attributes.*

**Use the corner of a sheet of paper to tell whether the angle is a**
*right angle, less than a right angle,* **or** *greater than a right angle.*

1.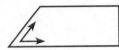

**less than a right
angle**
_____

2.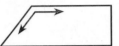

_____

3.

_____

**Write how many of each type of angle the shape has.**

4.

_____ right

_____ less than a right

_____ greater than
a right

5.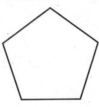

_____ right

_____ less than a right

_____ greater than
a right

6.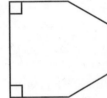

_____ right

_____ less than a right

_____ greater than
a right

## Problem Solving Real World

7. Jeff has a square piece of art paper. He cuts across it from one corner to the opposite corner to make two pieces. What is the total number of sides and angles in both of the new shapes?

_____
_____
_____

8. **WRITE** ▸*Math* Draw an example of a shape that has at least one right angle, one angle less than a right angle, and one angle greater than a right angle. Label the angles.

_____
_____
_____

## Lesson Check (3.G.A.1)

1. What describes this angle?
Write *right angle, less than a right angle,* or *greater than a right angle.*

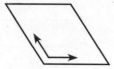

_____

_____

2. How many right angles does this shape have?

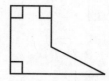

_____

_____

## Spiral Review (3.NF.A.1, 3.NF.A.3d, 3.G.A.1)

3. What fraction of the group is shaded?

_____

4. Compare.

$\frac{4}{8} \bigcirc \frac{3}{8}$

5. What is straight, continues in both directions, and does not end?

_____

6. How many line segments does this shape have?

_____

FOR MORE PRACTICE
GO TO THE
**Personal Math Trainer**

Name _____

# Identify Polygons

**Essential Question** How can you use line segments and angles to make polygons?

 Geometry—3.G.A.1

**MATHEMATICAL PRACTICES**
MP2, MP3, MP8

CONNECT  In earlier lessons, you learned about line segments and angles. In this lesson, you will see how line segments and angles make polygons.

A **polygon** is a closed plane shape that is made up of line segments that meet only at their endpoints. Each line segment in a polygon is a **side**.

**Math Idea**
All polygons are closed shapes. Not all closed shapes are polygons.

## ⚷ Unlock the Problem (Real World)

Circle all the words that describe the shape.

| **A**  | **B**  | **C**  | **D**  |
|---|---|---|---|
| plane shape | plane shape | plane shape | plane shape |
| open shape | open shape | open shape | open shape |
| closed shape | closed shape | closed shape | closed shape |
| curved paths | curved paths | curved paths | curved paths |
| line segments | line segments | line segments | line segments |
| polygon | polygon | polygon | polygon |

## Try This!

**Fill in the blanks with *sometimes*, *always*, or *never*.**

Polygons are _____ plane shapes.

Polygons are _____ closed shapes.

Polygons are _____ open shapes.

Plane shapes are _____ polygons.

**Math Talk**  MATHEMATICAL PRACTICES ②
**Reason Abstractly**
Why are not all closed shapes polygons?

**Name Polygons** Polygons are named by the number of sides and angles they have.

Some traffic signs are in the shape of polygons. A stop sign is in the shape of which polygon?

angle

side →

**Count the number of sides and angles.**

**triangle**

3 sides

3 angles

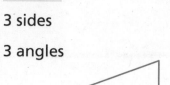

**quadrilateral**

4 sides

_____ angles

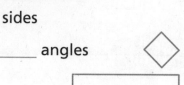

**pentagon**

_____ sides

5 angles

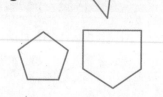

**hexagon**

_____ sides

6 angles

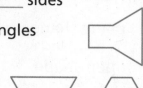

**octagon**

8 sides

_____ angles

**decagon**

_____ sides

10 angles

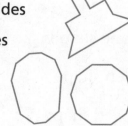

How many sides does the stop sign have? _____

How many angles? _____

So, a stop sign is in the shape of an _____.

**Math Talk**

**MATHEMATICAL PRACTICES ⑧**

Generalize Compare the number of sides and angles. What is a true statement about all polygons?

**Share and Show** MATH BOARD

1. The shape at the right is a polygon. Circle all the words that describe the shape.

plane shape     open shape     closed shape     pentagon

curved paths     line segments     hexagon     quadrilateral

Name _____

**Is the shape a polygon? Write *yes* or *no*.**

2.

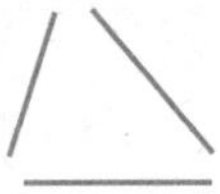

_____

3.

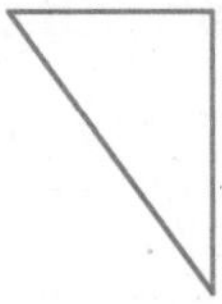

_____

4.

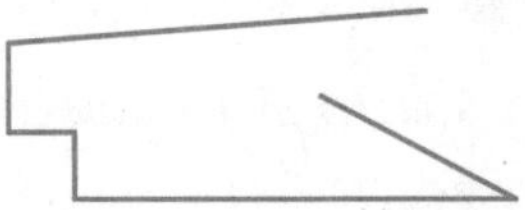

_____

**Write the number of sides and the number of angles. Then name the polygon.**

**Math Talk**

MATHEMATICAL PRACTICES ③

Apply How can you change the shape in Exercise 4 to make it a polygon?

5.

YIELD

_____ sides

_____ angles

_____

6.

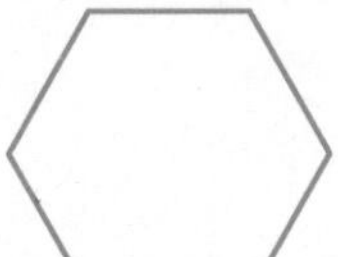

_____ sides

_____ angles

_____

7.

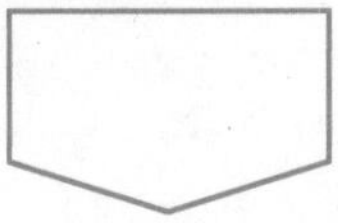

_____ sides

_____ angles

_____

**On Your Own**

**Is the shape a polygon? Write *yes* or *no*.**

8.

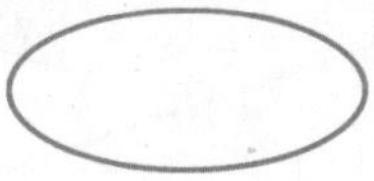

_____

9.

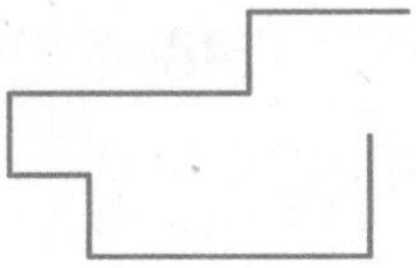

_____

10.

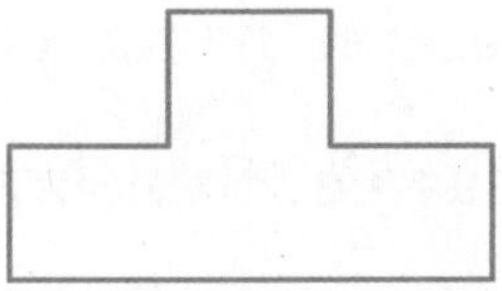

_____

**Write the number of sides and the number of angles. Then name the polygon.**

11.

_____ sides

_____ angles

_____

12.

_____ sides

_____ angles

_____

13.

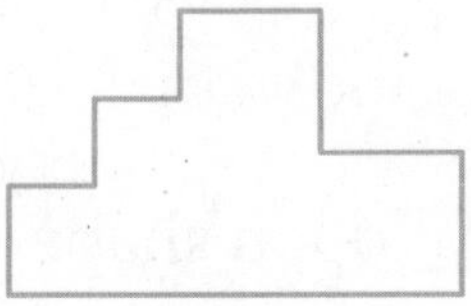

_____ sides

_____ angles

_____

**Chapter 12 • Lesson 3   711**

## Problem Solving · Applications

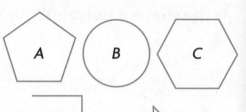
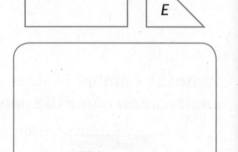

14. **WRITE** ▸*Math* Jake said Shapes *A—E* are all polygons. Does this statement make sense? Explain your answer.

_____

_____

15. **GO DEEPER** I am a closed shape made of 6 line segments. I have 2 angles less than a right angle and no right angles. What shape am I? Draw an example in the workspace.

_____

16. **THINK SMARTER** Is every closed shape a polygon? Use a drawing to help explain your answer.

_____

_____

_____

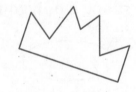

17. **MATHEMATICAL PRACTICE 3** **Make Arguments** Ivan says that the shape at the right is an octagon. Do you agree or disagree? Explain. _____

_____

18. **THINK SMARTER** For numbers 18a–18d, select True or False for each description of this shape.

18a. polygon    ○ True    ○ False

18b. open shape    ○ True    ○ False

18c. hexagon    ○ True    ○ False

18d. pentagon    ○ True    ○ False

# Identify Polygons

Common Core  **COMMON CORE STANDARD—3.G.A.1**
*Reason with shapes and their attributes.*

**Is the shape a polygon? Write *yes* or *no*.**

1.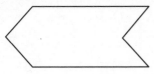

___no___

2.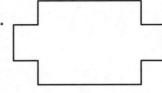

_____

**Write the number of sides and the number of angles. Then name the polygon.**

3.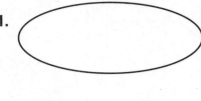

_____ sides

_____ angles

_____

4.

_____ sides

_____ angles

_____

## Problem Solving Real World

5. Mr. Murphy has an old coin that has ten sides. If its shape is a polygon, how many angles does the old coin have?

_____

6. Lin says that an octagon has six sides. Chris says that it has eight sides. Whose statement is correct?

_____

7. **WRITE** ▸ *Math*  Draw a pentagon. Explain how you knew the number of sides and angles to draw.

_____

_____

## Lesson Check (3.G.A.1)

1. What is a name for this polygon?

_____

2. How many sides does this polygon have?

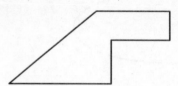

_____

## Spiral Review (3.NF.A.1, 3.G.A.1)

3. How many right angles does this shape have?

_____

4. Erica has 8 necklaces. One fourth of the necklaces are blue. How many necklaces are blue?

_____

5. What is straight, is part of a line, and has 2 endpoints?

_____

6. What describes this angle? Write *right angle*, *less than a right angle*, or *greater than a right angle*.

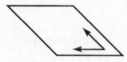

_____

FOR MORE PRACTICE
GO TO THE
Personal Math Trainer

Name _____

# Describe Sides of Polygons

**Essential Question** How can you describe line segments that are sides of polygons?

Common Core    Geometry—3.G.A.1

**MATHEMATICAL PRACTICES**
MP2, MP3, MP6

## Unlock the Problem

Look at the polygon. How many pairs of sides are parallel?

• How do you know the shape is a polygon?

_____

_____

| TYPES OF LINES | TYPES OF LINE SEGMENTS |
|---|---|
| Lines that cross or meet are **intersecting lines**. Intersecting lines form angles.  |  The orange and blue line segments meet and form an angle. So, they are _____. |
| Intersecting lines that cross or meet to form right angles are **perpendicular lines**.  | The red and blue line segments meet to form a right angle. So, they are _____. |
| Lines that never cross or meet and are always the same distance apart are **parallel lines**. They do not form any angles. 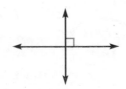 | The green and blue line segments would never cross or meet. They are always the same distance apart. So, they appear to be _____. |

So, the polygon above has _____ pair of parallel sides.

**Math Talk**

MATHEMATICAL PRACTICES ②

Use Reasoning  Why can't parallel lines ever cross?

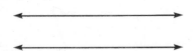

**Try This!** Draw a polygon with only 1 pair of parallel sides. Then draw a polygon with 2 pairs of parallel sides. Outline each pair of parallel sides with a different color.

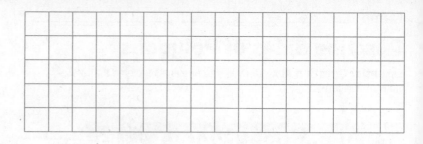

1. Which sides appear to be parallel?

_____

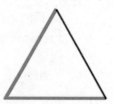

**Think:** Which pairs of sides appear to be the same distance apart?

Look at the green sides of the polygon. Tell if they appear to be *intersecting*, *perpendicular*, or *parallel*. Write all the words that describe the sides.

2.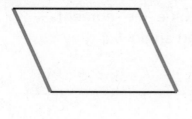

_____

☑ 3. 

_____

☑ 4.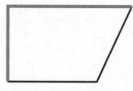

_____

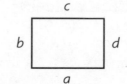

MATHEMATICAL PRACTICES ⑥

**Compare** How are intersecting and perpendicular lines alike and how are they different?

**On Your Own**

Look at the green sides of the polygon. Tell if they appear to be *intersecting*, *perpendicular*, or *parallel*. Write all the words that describe the sides.

5.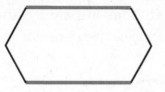

_____

6.

_____

7.

_____

Name _____

**Use pattern blocks *A–E* for 8–11.**

Chelsea wants to sort pattern blocks by
the types of sides.

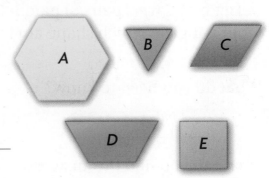

8. Which blocks have intersecting sides?

_____

9. Which blocks have parallel sides?

_____

10. Which blocks have perpendicular sides?

_____

11. Which blocks have neither parallel nor
    perpendicular sides?

_____

12. *GO DEEPER*  On the box at the right, how many
    pairs of edges are perpendicular line segments?

_____

▲ The red line segments show
some pairs of perpendicular
line segments.

13. *THINK SMARTER*  Can the same two lines
    be parallel, perpendicular, and intersecting?
    Explain your answer.

_____

_____

_____

## Unlock the Problem

14. **MATHEMATICAL PRACTICE ③** **Compare Representations** I am a pattern block that has 2 fewer sides than a hexagon. I have 2 pairs of parallel sides and 4 right angles. Which shape am I?

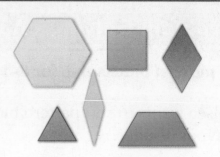

a. What do you need to know? _____

_____

b. How can you find the answer to the riddle? _____

_____

c. Write *yes* or *no* in the table to solve the riddle.

|  | | | | | | |
|---|---|---|---|---|---|---|
| 2 fewer sides than a hexagon | | | | | | |
| exactly 2 pairs of parallel sides | | | | | | |
| 4 right angles | | | | | | |

So, the _____ is the shape.

15. *THINK SMARTER* Select the shapes that have at least one pair of parallel sides. Mark all that apply.

Ⓐ

Ⓑ

Ⓒ

Ⓓ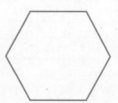

## Describe Sides of Polygons

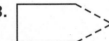 COMMON CORE STANDARD—3.G.A.1
*Reason with shapes and their attributes.*

**Look at the dashed sides of the polygon. Tell if they appear to be *intersecting, perpendicular,* or *parallel.* Write all the words that describe the sides.**

**1.**

_____**parallel**_____

**2.**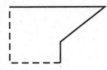

_____

**3.**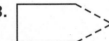

_____

**4.**

_____

**5.**

_____

**6.**

_____

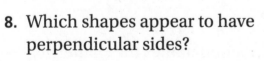

**Use shapes *A–D* for 7–8.**

**7.** Which shapes appear to have parallel sides?

_____

**8.** Which shapes appear to have perpendicular sides?

_____

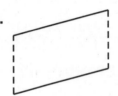

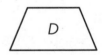

**9.** ▌WRITE ▸*Math*  Give some examples of perpendicular lines inside or outside your classroom.

_____

_____

## Lesson Check (3.G.A.1)

1. How many pairs of parallel sides does the quadrilateral appear to have?

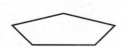

2. Which sides appear to be parallel?

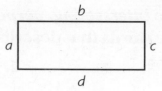

## Spiral Review (3.NF.A.1, 3.G.A.1)

3. Mr. Lance designed a class banner shaped like the polygon shown. What is the name of the polygon?

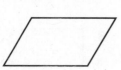

4. How many angles greater than a right angle does this shape have?

5. How many line segments does this shape have?

6. What fraction names the shaded part?

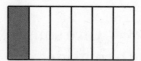

FOR MORE PRACTICE
GO TO THE
Personal Math Trainer

**Mid-Chapter Checkpoint**

**Personal Math Trainer**
Online Assessment
and Intervention

## Vocabulary

Choose the best term from the box to complete
the sentence.

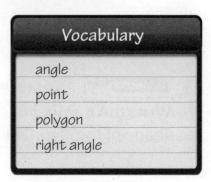
| Vocabulary |
| --- |
| angle |
| point |
| polygon |
| right angle |

1. An _____ is formed by two rays that
   share an endpoint. (p. 703)

2. A _____ is a closed plane shape made up
   of line segments. (p. 709)

3. A _____ forms a square corner. (p. 703)

## Concepts and Skills

Use the corner of a sheet of paper to tell whether the angle is a
*right angle, less than a right angle,* or *greater than a right angle.* (3.G.A.1)

4.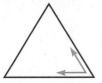

   _____

5.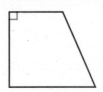

   _____

6.

   _____

Write the number of sides and the number of angles.
Then name the polygon. (3.G.A.1)

7.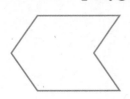

   ____ sides

   ____ angles

   _____

8.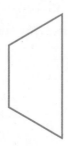

   ____ sides

   ____ angles

   _____

9.

   ____ sides

   ____ angles

   _____

**10.** Anne drew the shape at the right. Is her shape an open shape or a closed shape? (3.G.A.1)

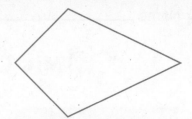

_____

**11.** GO DEEPER This sign tells drivers there is a steep hill ahead. Write the number of sides and the number of angles in the shape of the sign. Then name the shape. (3.G.A.1)

_____

**12.** Why is this closed plane shape NOT a polygon? (3.G.A.1)

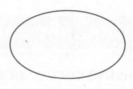

_____

_____

**13.** Sean drew a shape with 2 fewer sides than an octagon. Which shape did he draw? (3.G.A.1)

_____

**14.** John drew a polygon with two line segments that meet to form a right angle. Circle the words that describe the line segments. (3.G.A.1)

| intersecting |
| curved |
| parallel |
| perpendicular |

Name _____

# Classify Quadrilaterals

**Essential Question** How can you use sides and angles to help you describe quadrilaterals?

 Geometry—3.G.A.1

**MATHEMATICAL PRACTICES**
MP1, MP6, MP8

## ⚷ Unlock the Problem

Quadrilaterals are named by their sides and their angles.

🔑 **Describe quadrilaterals.**

**quadrilateral**

_____ sides

_____ angles

**! ERROR Alert**

Some quadrilaterals cannot be classified as a trapezoid, rectangle, square, or rhombus.

---

**trapezoid**

at least _____ pair of opposite sides that are parallel
lengths of sides could be the same

---

**rectangle**

_____ pairs of opposite sides that are parallel

_____ pairs of sides that are of equal length

_____ right angles

**square**

_____ pairs of opposite sides that are parallel

_____ sides that are of equal length

_____ right angles

**rhombus**

_____ pairs of opposite sides that are parallel

_____ sides that are of equal length

**Math Talk** MATHEMATICAL PRACTICES ⑧

Generalize Why can a square also be named a rectangle or a rhombus?

**Look at the quadrilateral at the right.**

1. Outline each pair of opposite sides that are parallel with a different color. How many pairs of opposite sides

   appear to be parallel? _____

2. Look at the parallel sides you colored.

   The sides in each pair are of _____ length.

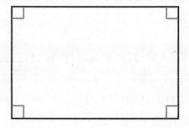

**Think:** All the angles are right angles.

3. Name the quadrilateral in as many ways as you can.

   _____

**Circle all the words that describe the quadrilateral.**

4.

   rectangle

   rhombus

   square

   trapezoid

5.

   rhombus

   quadrilateral

   square

   rectangle

6.

   rectangle

   rhombus

   trapezoid

   quadrilateral

**Math Talk**

MATHEMATICAL PRACTICES ①

**Analyze** How can you have a rhombus that is not a square?

**Circle all the words that describe the quadrilateral.**

7.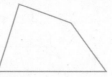

   rectangle

   trapezoid

   quadrilateral

   rhombus

8.

   rectangle

   rhombus

   trapezoid

   square

9.

   quadrilateral

   square

   rectangle

   rhombus

Name _____

**Use the quadrilaterals at the right for 10–12.**

10. Which quadrilaterals appear to have 4 right angles?

    _____

11. Which quadrilaterals appear to have 2 pairs of opposite sides that are parallel?

    _____

12. Which quadrilaterals appear to have no right angles?

    _____

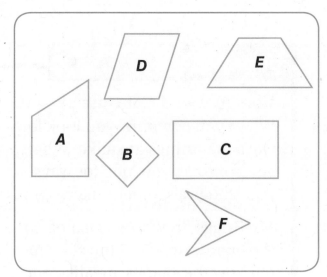

**Write *all* or *some* to complete the sentence for 13–18.**

13. The opposite sides of _____ rectangles are parallel.

14. _____ sides of a rhombus are the same length.

15. _____ squares are rectangles.

16. _____ rhombuses are squares.

17. _____ quadrilaterals are polygons.

18. _____ polygons are quadrilaterals.

19. **MATHEMATICAL PRACTICE ❻** Circle the shape at the right that is not a quadrilateral. **Explain** your choice.

    _____

    _____

    _____

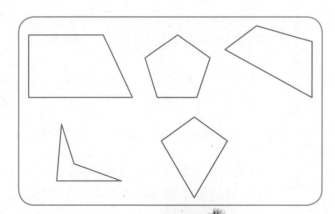

20. **THINK SMARTER** I am a polygon that has 4 sides and 4 angles. At least one of my angles is less than a right angle. Circle all the shapes that I could be.

    quadrilateral    rectangle    square    rhombus    trapezoid

**21.** THINK SMARTER  Identify the quadrilateral that can have two pairs of parallel sides and no right angles.

(A) rhombus          (B) square          (C) rectangle

## Connect to Reading

**Compare and Contrast**

When you *compare*, you look for ways that things are alike. When you *contrast*, you look for ways that things are different.

Mr. Briggs drew some shapes on the board. He asked the class to tell how the shapes are alike and how they are different.

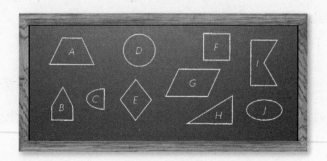

GO DEEPER  **Complete the sentences.**

- Shapes _____, _____, _____, _____, _____, _____, and _____ are polygons.

- Shapes _____, _____, and _____ are not polygons.

- Shapes _____, _____, _____, and _____ are quadrilaterals.

- Shapes _____, _____, and _____ appear to have only 1 pair of opposite sides that are parallel.

- Shapes _____, _____, and _____ appear to have 2 pairs of opposite sides that are parallel.

- All 4 sides of shapes _____ and _____ appear to be the same length.

- In these polygons, all sides do not appear to be the same length. _____

- These shapes can be called rhombuses. _____

- Shapes _____ and _____ are quadrilaterals but cannot be called rhombuses.

- Shape _____ is a rhombus and can be called a square.

## Classify Quadrilaterals

Common Core **COMMON CORE STANDARD—3.G.A.1**
*Reason with shapes and their attributes.*

**Circle all the words that describe the quadrilateral.**

1.

   (square)

   (rectangle)

   (rhombus)

   (trapezoid)

2.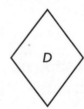

   square

   rectangle

   rhombus

   trapezoid

3. 

   square

   rectangle

   rhombus

   trapezoid

**Use the quadrilaterals below for 4–6.**

A     B     C     D     E

4. Which quadrilaterals appear to have no right angles?

   _____

5. Which quadrilaterals appear to have 4 right angles?

   _____

6. Which quadrilaterals appear to have 4 sides of equal length?

   _____

 **Problem Solving** Real World

7. A picture on the wall in Jeremy's classroom has 4 right angles, 4 sides of equal length, and 2 pairs of opposite sides that are parallel. What quadrilateral best describes the picture?

   _____

8. **WRITE** ▸*Math* Explain how a trapezoid and a rectangle are different.

   _____

   _____

   _____

## Lesson Check (3.G.A.1)

**1.** What word describes the quadrilateral?

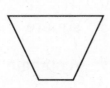

**2.** Which quadrilaterals appear to have 2 pairs of opposite sides that are parallel?

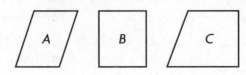

_____

## Spiral Review (3.G.A.1)

**3.** Aiden drew the the polygon shown. What is the name of the polygon he drew?

**4.** How many pairs of parallel sides does this shape appear to have?

_____

**5.** What word describes the dashed sides of the shape shown? Write _intersecting_, _perpendicular_, or _parallel_.

**6.** How many right angles does this shape have?

_____

FOR MORE PRACTICE
GO TO THE
**Personal Math Trainer**

# Draw Quadrilaterals

**Essential Question** How can you draw quadrilaterals?

Common Core  Geometry—3.G.A.1

**MATHEMATICAL PRACTICES**
**MP3, MP6, MP7, MP8**

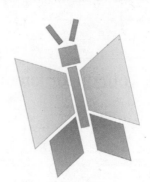

## 🔑 Unlock the Problem

**CONNECT**  You have learned to classify quadrilaterals by the number of pairs of opposite sides that are parallel, by the number of pairs of sides of equal length, and by the number of right angles.

How can you draw quadrilaterals?

### 🔓 Activity 1  Use grid paper to draw quadrilaterals.

**Materials** ■ ruler

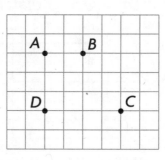

- Use a ruler to draw line segments from points *A* to *B*, from *B* to *C*, from *C* to *D*, and from *D* to *A*.

- Write the name of your quadrilateral.

_____

### 🔓 Activity 2  Draw a shape that does not belong.

**Materials** ■ ruler

Ⓐ Here are three examples of a quadrilateral. Draw an example of a polygon that is not a quadrilateral.

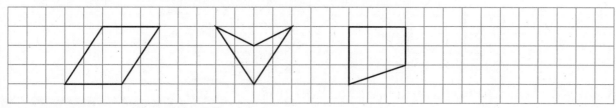

- Explain why your polygon is not a quadrilateral.

_____

_____

**B** **Here are three examples of a square.**
**Draw a quadrilateral that is not a square.**

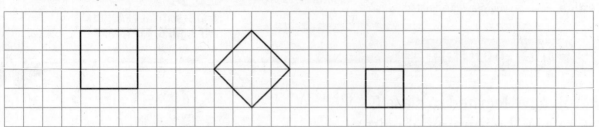

- Explain why your quadrilateral is not a square.

_____

_____

**C** **Here are three examples of a rectangle.**
**Draw a quadrilateral that is not a rectangle.**

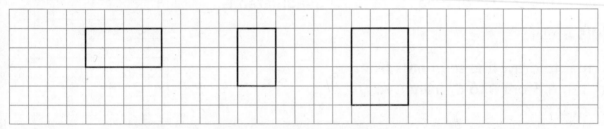

- Explain why your quadrilateral is not a rectangle.

_____

_____

**D** **Here are three examples of a rhombus.**
**Draw a quadrilateral that is not a rhombus.**

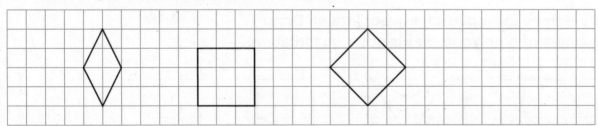

- Explain why your quadrilateral is not a rhombus.

Math Talk

MATHEMATICAL PRACTICES ❸

**Compare Representations** Compare your drawings with your classmates. Explain how your drawings are alike and how they are different.

_____

_____

© Houghton Mifflin Harcourt Publishing Company

Name _____

1. Choose four endpoints, and connect them to make a rectangle.

   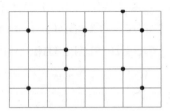

   **Think:** A rectangle has 2 pairs of opposite sides that are parallel, 2 pairs of sides of equal length, and 4 right angles.

**Draw a quadrilateral that is described.**
**Name the quadrilateral you drew.**

2. 2 pairs of sides of equal length

   Name _____

3. 4 sides of equal length

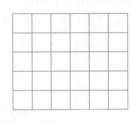

   Name _____

**Math Talk** MATHEMATICAL PRACTICES ⑥

Compare Explain one way the quadrilaterals you drew are alike and one way they are different.

**On Your Own**

**Practice: Copy and Solve** Use grid paper to draw a quadrilateral that is described. Name the quadrilateral you drew.

4. exactly 1 pair of opposite sides that are parallel

5. 4 right angles

6. 2 pairs of sides of equal length

**Draw a quadrilateral that does not belong. Then explain why.**

7.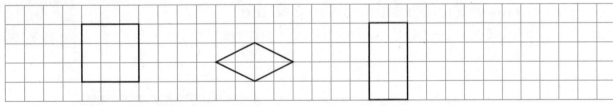

_____

8.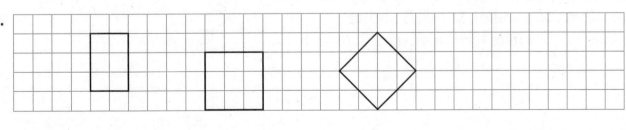

_____

## Problem Solving • Applications Real World

9. **MATHEMATICAL PRACTICE 3 Make Arguments** Jacki drew the shape at the right. She said it is a rectangle because it has 2 pairs of opposite sides that are parallel. Describe her error.

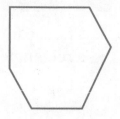

_____

_____

10. **GO DEEPER** Adam drew three quadrilaterals. One quadrilateral has no pairs of parallel sides, one quadrilateral has exactly 1 pair of opposite sides that are parallel, and the last quadrilateral has 2 pairs of opposite sides that are parallel. Draw the three quadrilaterals that Adam could have drawn. Name them.

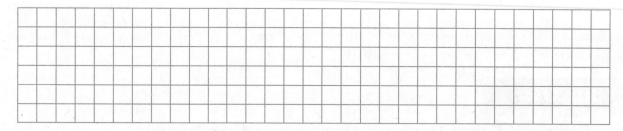

_____    _____    _____

11. **THINK SMARTER** Amy has 4 straws of equal length. Name all the quadrilaterals that can be made using these 4 straws.

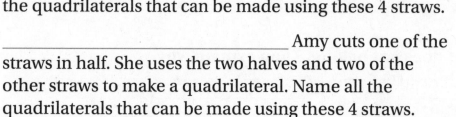

_____ Amy cuts one of the straws in half. She uses the two halves and two of the other straws to make a quadrilateral. Name all the quadrilaterals that can be made using these 4 straws.

_____

**Personal Math Trainer**

12. **THINK SMARTER +** Jordan drew one side of a quadrilateral with 2 pairs of opposite sides that are parallel. Draw the other 3 sides to complete Jordan's quadrilateral.

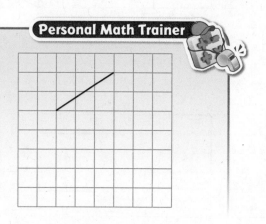

# Draw Quadrilaterals

Common Core  **COMMON CORE STANDARD—3.G.A.1**
*Reason with shapes and their attributes.*

**Draw a quadrilateral that is described.**
**Name the quadrilateral you drew.**

1. always has 4 sides of equal length

2. only 1 pair of opposite sides that are parallel

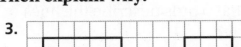
square or rhombus

_____        _____

**Draw a quadrilateral that does not belong.**
**Then explain why.**

3.

_____

_____

_____

## Problem Solving Real World

4. Layla drew a quadrilateral with 4 right angles and 2 pairs of opposite sides that are parallel. What quadrilateral best describes her drawing?

5. **WRITE** ▸*Math* Draw a quadrilateral that is NOT a rectangle. Describe your shape, and explain why it is not a rectangle.

_____        _____

_____        _____

## Lesson Check (3.G.A.1)

1. Chloe drew a quadrilateral with 2 pairs of opposite sides that are parallel. Name all the shapes that could be Chloe's quadrilateral.

_____

_____

2. Mike drew a quadrilateral with four right angles. Name all the shapes he could have drawn.

_____

_____

## Spiral Review (3.MD.C.7a, 3.MD.D.8, 3.G.A.1)

3. What is the name of the quadrilateral that always has 4 right angles and 4 sides of equal length?

_____

4. Mark drew two lines that form a right angle. What words describe the lines Mark drew?

_____

5. Dennis drew the rectangle on grid paper. What is the perimeter of the rectangle Dennis drew?

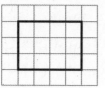

6. Jill drew the rectangle on grid paper. What is the area of the rectangle Jill drew?

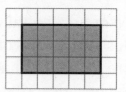

_____

FOR MORE PRACTICE
GO TO THE
**Personal Math Trainer**

Name _____

# Describe Triangles

**Essential Question** How can you use sides and angles to help you describe triangles?

Common Core  Geometry—3.G.A.1

MATHEMATICAL PRACTICES
MP1, MP2, MP6

## Unlock the Problem (Real World)

How can you use straws of different lengths to make triangles?

### Activity  Materials ■ straws ■ scissors ■ MathBoard

**STEP 1** Cut straws into different lengths.

**STEP 2** Find straw pieces that you can put together to make a triangle. Draw your triangle on the MathBoard.

**STEP 3** Find straw pieces that you cannot put together to make a triangle.

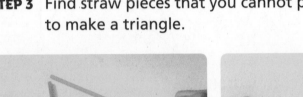

1. Compare the lengths of the sides. Describe when you can make a triangle.

_____

_____

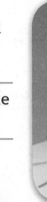
**Math Talk**

**MATHEMATICAL PRACTICES ②**

**Reason Abstractly**
What if you have three straws of equal length? Can you make a triangle?

2. **MATHEMATICAL PRACTICE ①** Describe when you cannot make a triangle.

_____

_____

_____

3. Explain how you can change the straw pieces in

Step 3 to make a triangle. _____

_____

## Ways to Describe Triangles

What are two ways triangles can be described?

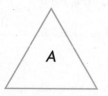    

## 🔑 One Way

Triangles can be described by the number of sides that are of equal length.

**Draw a line to match the description of the triangle(s).**

 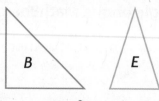 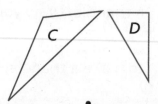

No sides are equal in length.

Two sides are equal in length.

Three sides are equal in length.

## 🔑 Another Way

Triangles can be described by the types of angles they have.

**Draw a line to match the description of the triangle(s).**

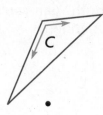   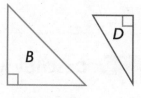

One angle is a right angle.

One angle is greater than a right angle.

Three angles are less than a right angle.

**Math Talk**

MATHEMATICAL PRACTICES ②

Use Reasoning Can a triangle have two right angles?

736

© Houghton Mifflin Harcourt Publishing Company

Name _____

1. Write the number of sides of equal length the triangle appears to have.

   _____

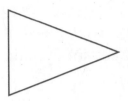

**Use the triangles for 2–4. Write F, G, or H.**

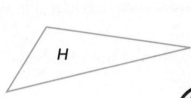

2. Triangle _____ has 1 right angle.

3. Triangle _____ has 1 angle greater than a right angle.

4. Triangle _____ has 3 angles less than a right angle.

Math Talk

MATHEMATICAL PRACTICES ⑧

Generalize Explain the ways you can describe a triangle.

**On Your Own**

**Use the triangles for 5–7. Write K, L, or M.**
**Then complete the sentences.**

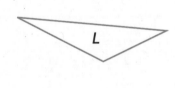
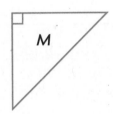

5. Triangle _____ has 1 right angle and appears to have

   _____ sides of equal length.

6. Triangle _____ has 3 angles less than a right angle and

   appears to have _____ sides of equal length.

7. Triangle _____ has 1 angle greater than a right angle and

   appears to have _____ sides of equal length.

## Problem Solving • Applications

8. **MATHEMATICAL PRACTICE ① Make Sense of Problems** Martin said a triangle can have two sides that are parallel. Does his statement make sense? Explain.

_____

_____

9. **GO DEEPER** Compare Triangles *R* and *S*. How are they alike? How are they different?

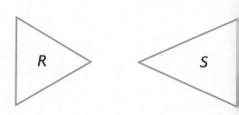

_____

_____

_____

10. **THINK SMARTER** Use a ruler to draw a straight line from one corner of this rectangle to the opposite corner. What shapes did you make? What do you notice about the shapes?

_____

_____

11. **THINK SMARTER** Write the name of each triangle where it belongs in the table. Some triangles might belong in both parts of the table. Some triangles might not belong in either part.

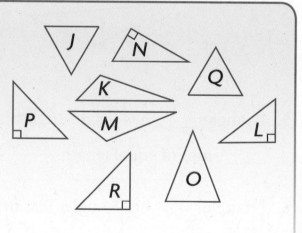

| Has 1 Right Angle | Has at Least 2 Sides of Equal Length |
|---|---|
|  |  |
|  |  |
|  |  |

# Describe Triangles

 COMMON CORE STANDARD—3.G.A.1
*Reason with shapes and their attributes.*

**Use the triangles for 1–3. Write *A*, *B*, or *C*.**
**Then complete the sentences.**

  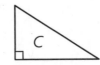  

1. Triangle __*B*__ has 3 angles less than a right angle and

   appears to have __3__ sides of equal length.

2. Triangle _____ has 1 right angle and appears to have

   _____ sides of equal length.

3. Triangle _____ has 1 angle greater than a right angle

   and appears to have _____ sides of equal length.

## Problem Solving Real World

4. Matthew drew the back of his tent.
   How many sides appear to be of
   equal length?

5. Sierra made the triangular picture
   frame shown. How many angles are
   greater than a right angle?

_____          _____

6. **WRITE** *Math* Draw a triangle that has two sides of
   equal length and one right angle.

_____

_____

## Lesson Check (3.G.A.1)

1. How many angles less than a right angle does this triangle have?

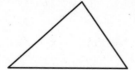

2. How many sides of equal length does this triangle appear to have?

_____

## Spiral Review (3.NF.A.1, 3.MD.D.8, 3.G.A.1)

3. A quadrilateral has 4 right angles, 2 pairs of sides of equal length, and 2 pairs of opposite sides that are parallel. The pairs of opposite sides are not the same length. What quadrilateral could it be?

_____

_____

4. Mason drew a quadrilateral with only one pair of opposite sides that are parallel. What quadrilateral did Mason draw?

_____

_____

5. Draw a rectangle that has an area of 8 square units and a perimeter of 12 units. What are the side lengths of the rectangle?

_____

_____

6. What fraction of the square is shaded?

_____

_____

FOR MORE PRACTICE
GO TO THE
Personal Math Trainer

Name _____

# Problem Solving • Classify Plane Shapes

**Essential Question** How can you use the strategy *draw a diagram* to classify plane shapes?

Common Core  Geometry—3.G.A.1

MATHEMATICAL PRACTICES
MP1, MP2, MP4, MP7

## Unlock the Problem

A **Venn diagram** shows how sets of things are related. In the Venn diagram at the right, one circle has shapes that are rectangles. Shapes that are rhombuses are in the other circle. The shapes in the section where the circles overlap are both rectangles and rhombuses.

What type of quadrilateral is in both circles?

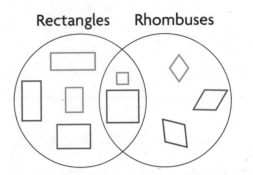
Rectangles    Rhombuses

| Read the Problem | Solve the Problem |
|---|---|
| **What do I need to find?** <br><br> _____ <br><br> _____ | What is true about all quadrilaterals? <br><br> _____ <br><br> Which quadrilaterals always have 2 pairs of opposite sides that are parallel? <br><br> _____ |
| **What information do I need to use?** <br><br> the circles labeled _____ and <br><br> _____ | Which quadrilaterals always have 4 sides of equal length? _____ <br><br> Which quadrilaterals always have 4 right angles? _____ |
| **How will I use the information?** <br><br> _____ <br><br> _____ <br><br> _____ | The quadrilaterals in the section where the circles overlap always have ____ pairs of opposite sides that are parallel, ____ sides of equal length, and ____ right angles. <br><br> So, _____ are in both circles. |

**Math Talk**

MATHEMATICAL PRACTICES ❶

**Make Sense of Problems** Does a ▱ fit in the Venn diagram? Explain.

## 🔒 Try Another Problem

The Venn diagram shows the shapes Andrea used to make a picture. Where would the shape shown below be placed in the Venn diagram?

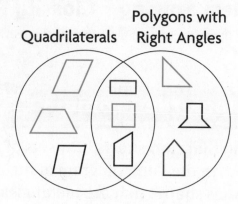

Quadrilaterals      Polygons with Right Angles

---

| Read the Problem | Solve the Problem |
|---|---|
| **What do I need to find?** | **Record the steps you used to solve the problem.** |
| **What information do I need to use?** | |
| **How will I use the information?** | |

**1.** How many shapes do not have right angles?

_____

**2.** How many red shapes have right angles but are

not quadrilaterals? _____

**3.**  **Reason Abstractly** What is a different way to sort the shapes?

_____

_____

 Math Talk     MATHEMATICAL PRACTICES ①

**Make Sense of Problems** What name can be used to describe all the shapes in the Venn diagram? Explain how you know.

Name _____

**Use the Venn diagram for 1–3.**

1. Jordan is sorting the shapes at the right in a Venn diagram. Where does a 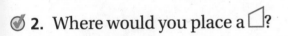 go?

   **First,** look at the sides and angles of the polygons.

   **Next,** draw the polygons in the Venn diagram.

   The shape has _____ sides of equal length

   and _____ right angles.

   So, the shape goes in the

   _____.

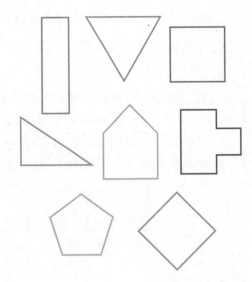

2. Where would you place a 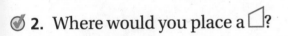?

   _____

3. What if Jordan sorted the shapes by Polygons with Right Angles and Polygons with Angles Less Than a Right Angle? Would the circles still overlap? Explain.

   _____

   _____

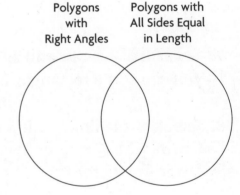

Polygons with Right Angles    Polygons with All Sides Equal in Length

4. GO DEEPER   Eva drew the Venn diagram below. Write labels she could have used for the diagram.

   _____        _____

   _____        _____

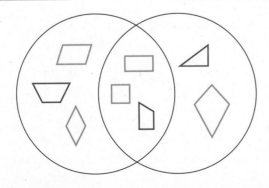

© Houghton Mifflin Harcourt Publishing Company

## On Your Own

**5.** Ben and Marta are both reading the same book. Ben has read $\frac{1}{3}$ of the book. Marta has read $\frac{1}{4}$ of the book. Who has read more? _____

**6.** **MATHEMATICAL PRACTICE ②** **Represent a Problem** There are 42 students from 6 different classes in the school spelling bee. Each class has the same number of students in the spelling bee. Use the bar model to find how many students are from each class.

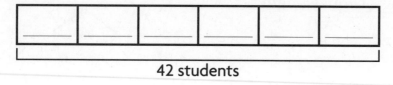

42 students

_____ ÷ _____ = _____

**7.** THINK SMARTER   Draw and label a Venn diagram to show one way you can sort a rectangle, a square, a trapezoid, and a rhombus.

**8.** Ashley is making a quilt with squares of fabric. There are 9 rows with 8 squares in each row. How many squares of fabric are there?

_____

**9.** THINK SMARTER ➕    Personal Math Trainer   Sketch where to place these shapes in the Venn diagram. △ ▢

Polygons with All Sides    Quadrilaterals with
of Equal Length            Right Angles

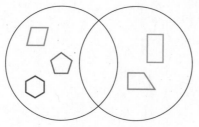

# Problem Solving • Classify Plane Shapes

Common Core  **COMMON CORE STANDARD—3.G.A.1**
*Reason with shapes and their attributes.*

**Solve each problem.**

1. Steve drew the shapes below. Write the letter of each shape where it belongs in the Venn diagram.

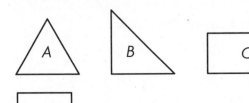

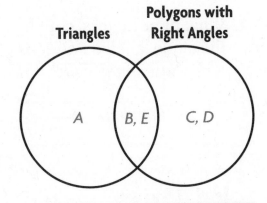

2. Janice drew the shapes below. Write the letter of each shape where it belongs in the Venn diagram.

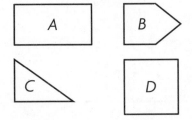

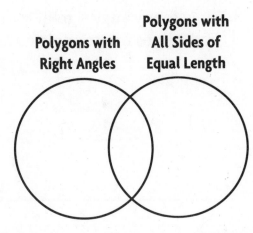

3. **WRITE** ▸*Math* Draw a Venn diagram with one circle labeled *Quadrilaterals* and the other circle labeled *Polygons with at Least 1 Right Angle*. Draw at least two shapes in each section of the diagram. Explain why you drew the shapes you chose in the overlapping section

## Lesson Check (3.G.A.1)

**1.** What shape could go in the section where the two circles overlap?

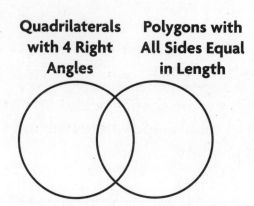

Quadrilaterals with 4 Right Angles    Polygons with All Sides Equal in Length

_____

**2.** What quadrilateral could NOT go in the circle labeled *Polygons with All Sides Equal in Length*?

_____

## Spiral Review (3.NF.A.1, 3.G.A.1)

**3.** How many angles greater than a right angle does this triangle have?

_____

**4.** How many sides of equal length does this triangle appear to have?

_____

**5.** Madison drew this shape. How many angles less than a right angle does it have?

_____

**6.** How many dots are in $\frac{1}{2}$ of this group?

· · · · · ·
· · · · · ·
· · · · · ·

_____

FOR MORE PRACTICE GO TO THE
**Personal Math Trainer**

# Relate Shapes, Fractions, and Area

**Essential Question** How can you divide shapes into parts with equal areas and write the area as a unit fraction of the whole?

Common Core  Geometry—3.G.A.2
*Also 3.NF.A.1, 3.NF.A.3d, 3.MD.C.5*
**MATHEMATICAL PRACTICES**
MP2, MP3, MP4

## Investigate

Hands On

**Materials** ■ pattern blocks ■ color pencils ■ ruler

**CONNECT** You can use what you know about combining and separating plane shapes to explore the relationship between fractions and area.

**A.** Trace a hexagon pattern block.

**B.** Divide your hexagon into two parts with equal area.

**C.** Write the names of the new shapes. _____

**D.** Write the fraction that names each part of the whole

you divided. _____
Each part is $\frac{1}{2}$ of the whole shape's area.

**E.** Write the fraction that names the whole area. _____

### Math Idea

Equal parts of a whole have equal area.

## Draw Conclusions

1. Explain how you know the two shapes have the same area.

_____

_____

2. Predict what would happen if you divide the hexagon into three shapes with equal area. What fraction names the area of each part of the divided hexagon? What fraction names the whole area?

_____

3. **THINK SMARTER** Show how you can divide the hexagon into four shapes with equal area.

Each part is _____ of the whole shape's area.

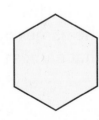

The rectangle at the right is divided into four parts with equal area.

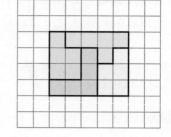

- Write the unit fraction that names each part of the divided whole. _____

- What is the area of each part? _____

- How many $\frac{1}{4}$ parts does it take to make one whole? _____

- Is the shape of each of the $\frac{1}{4}$ parts the same? _____

- Is the area of each of the $\frac{1}{4}$ parts the same? Explain how you know.

_____

_____

**Divide the shape into equal parts.**

Draw lines to divide the rectangle below into six parts with equal area.

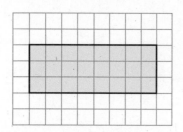

Math Talk

MATHEMATICAL PRACTICES ③

Apply How do you know the areas of all the parts are equal?

- Write the fraction that names each part of the divided whole. _____

- Write the area of each part. _____

- Each part is _____ of the whole shape's area.

1. Divide the trapezoid into 3 parts with equal area. Write the names of the new shapes. Then write the fraction that names the area of each part of the whole.

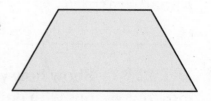

_____

Name _____

**Draw lines to divide the shape into equal parts that show the fraction given.**

2.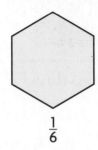

$\frac{1}{6}$

3.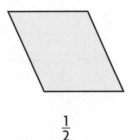

$\frac{1}{2}$

4.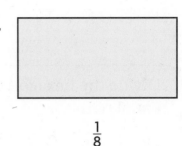

$\frac{1}{8}$

**Draw lines to divide the shape into parts with equal area. Write the area of each part as a unit fraction.**

5.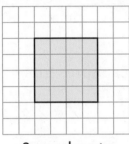

8 equal parts

6.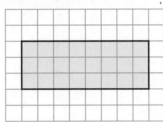

6 equal parts

7.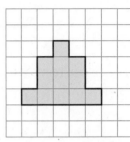

4 equal parts

## Problem Solving • Applications Real World

8. **MATHEMATICAL PRACTICE ②** Use Reasoning  If the area of three ◇ is equal to the area of one ⬡, the area of how many ◇ equals four ⬡? Explain your answer.

_____

9. *THINK SMARTER*  Divide each shape into the number of equal parts shown. Then write the fraction that describes each part of the whole.

2 equal parts        4 equal parts        6 equal parts

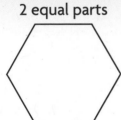        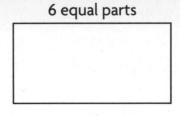

_____        _____        _____

© Houghton Mifflin Harcourt Publishing Company

10. **THINK SMARTER**   **Sense or Nonsense?**

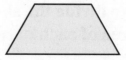

Divide the hexagon into six equal parts.

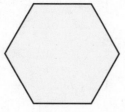

Which pattern block represents $\frac{1}{6}$ of the whole area?

_____

Divide the trapezoid into three equal parts.

Which pattern block represents $\frac{1}{3}$ of the whole area?

_____

Alexis said the area of $\frac{1}{3}$ of the trapezoid is greater than the area of $\frac{1}{6}$ of the hexagon because $\frac{1}{3} > \frac{1}{6}$. Does her statement make sense? Explain your answer.

_____

_____

_____

_____

- Write a statement that makes sense.

_____

_____

- **GO DEEPER**   What if you divide the hexagon into 3 equal parts? Write a sentence that compares the area of each equal part of the hexagon to each equal part of the trapezoid.

_____

_____

# Relate Shapes, Fractions, and Area

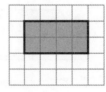

COMMON CORE STANDARD—3.G.A.2
*Reason with shapes and their attributes.*

**Draw lines to divide the shape into equal parts that show the fraction given.**

**1.**

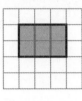

$\frac{1}{3}$

**2.**

$\frac{1}{8}$

**3.**

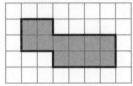

$\frac{1}{2}$

**Draw lines to divide the shape into parts with equal area. Write the area of each part as a unit fraction.**

**4.**

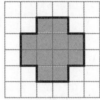

4 equal parts

_____

**5.**

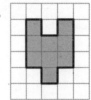

6 equal parts

_____

**6.**

3 equal parts

_____

 **Problem Solving** Real World

**7.** Robert divided a hexagon into 3 equal parts. Show how he might have divided the hexagon. Write the fraction that names each part of the whole you divided.

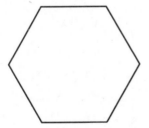

_____

**8.** **WRITE** ▸*Math* Trace a pattern block. Divide it into two equal parts, and write a unit fraction to describe the area of each part. Explain your work.

_____

## Lesson Check (3.G.A.1)

1. What fraction names each part of the divided whole?

_____

2. What fraction names the whole area that was divided?

_____

## Spiral Review (3.G.A.1)

3. Lil drew the figure below. Is the shape open or closed?

_____

4. How many line segments does this shape have?

_____

**Use the Venn diagram for 5–6.**

5. Where would a square be placed in the Venn diagram?

_____

_____

6. Where would a rectangle be placed in the Venn diagram?

_____

_____

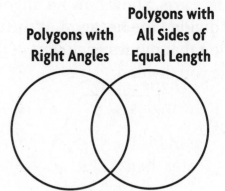

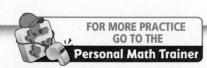

FOR MORE PRACTICE
GO TO THE
Personal Math Trainer

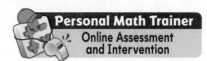

✅ **Chapter 12 Review/Test**

**Personal Math Trainer**
Online Assessment
and Intervention

1. Which words describe this shape? Mark all that apply.

Ⓐ  polygon

Ⓑ  open shape

Ⓒ  pentagon

Ⓓ  quadrilateral

2. Umberto drew one side of a quadrilateral with 4 equal sides and no right angles. Draw the other 3 sides to complete Umberto's shape.

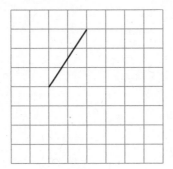

3. Mikael saw a painting that included this shape.

For numbers 3a–3d, select True or False for each statement about the shape.

3a.  The shape has no right angles.                        ○ True        ○ False

3b.  The shape has 2 angles greater than a right angle.    ○ True        ○ False

3c.  The shape has 2 right angles.                         ○ True        ○ False

3d.  The shape has 1 angle greater than a right angle.     ○ True        ○ False

**GO DIGITAL**  Assessment Options
Chapter Test

**4.** **GO DEEPER** Fran used a Venn Diagram to sort shapes.

**Polygons with Right Angles**    **Quadrilaterals**

**Part A**

Draw another plane shape that belongs inside the left circle of the diagram but NOT in the section where the circles overlap.

**Part B**

How can you describe the shapes in the section where the circles overlap?

_____

_____

**5.** Match each object in the left column with its name in the right column.

⟷  •                    • point

•————•                 • line

•———→  •               • ray

• •                     • line segment

**6.** Describe the angles and sides of this triangle.

_____

Name _____

**7.** Which words describe this shape. Mark all that apply.

rectangle      rhombus      quadrilateral      square

  Ⓐ         Ⓑ           Ⓒ          Ⓓ

**8.** Divide each shape into the number of equal parts shown. Then write the fraction that describes each part of the whole.

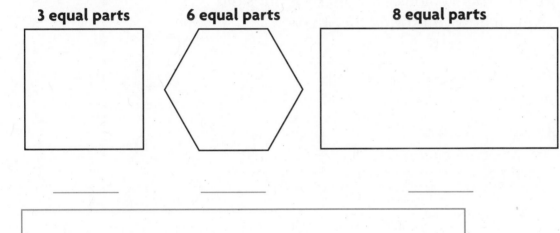

**3 equal parts**      **6 equal parts**      **8 equal parts**

_____      _____      _____

**9.** Han drew a triangle with 1 angle greater than a right angle.

For numbers 9a–9d, choose Yes or No to tell whether the triangle could be the triangle Han drew.

9a.        ○ Yes      ○ No

9b.  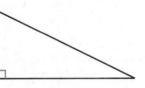      ○ Yes      ○ No

9c.  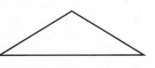      ○ Yes      ○ No

9d.  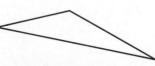      ○ Yes      ○ No

10. THINK SMARTER + Look at this group of pattern blocks.

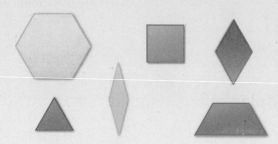

**Part A**

Sort the pattern blocks by sides. How many groups did you make? Explain how you sorted the shapes.

_____

_____

_____

_____

**Part B**

Sort the pattern blocks by angles. How many groups did you make? Explain how you sorted the shapes.

_____

_____

_____

_____

11. Teresa drew a quadrilateral that had 4 sides of equal length and no right angles. What quadrilateral did she draw?

_____

**12.** Rhea used a Venn diagram to sort shapes. What label could she use for circle *A*?

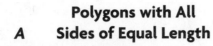
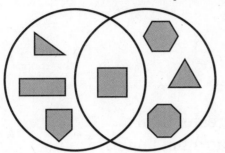

**13.** Colette drew lines to divide a rectangle into equal parts that each represent $\frac{1}{6}$ of the whole area. Her first line is shown. Draw lines to complete Colette's model.

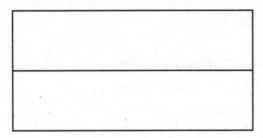

**14.** Brad drew a quadrilateral. Select the pairs of sides that appear to be parallel. Mark all that apply.

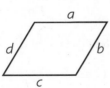

(A)  *a* and *b*       (C)  *c* and *a*

(B)  *b* and *d*       (D)  *d* and *c*

**15.** Give two reasons that this shape is **not** a polygon.

_____

**16.** The triangle at the right has one angle greater than a right angle. What statements describe the other angles? Mark all that apply.

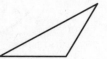

Ⓐ   At least one is less than a right angle.

Ⓑ   One is a right angle.

Ⓒ   Both are less than a right angle.

Ⓓ   One is greater than a right angle.

**17.** Ava drew a quadrilateral with 2 pairs of opposite sides that are parallel. The shape has at least 2 right angles. Draw a shape that Ava could have drawn.

**18.** For 18a–18d, select True or False for each description of a ray.

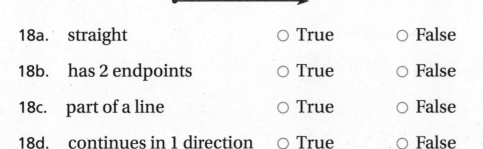

| | | True | False |
|---|---|---|---|
| 18a. | straight | ○ True | ○ False |
| 18b. | has 2 endpoints | ○ True | ○ False |
| 18c. | part of a line | ○ True | ○ False |
| 18d. | continues in 1 direction | ○ True | ○ False |

# Glossary

| | | | | | | | | | |
|---|---|---|---|---|---|---|---|---|---|
| a | add, map | f | fit, half | n | nice, tin | p | pit, stop | û(r) | burn, term |
| ā | ace, rate | g | go, log | ng | ring, song | r | run, poor | yōō | fuse, few |
| â(r) | care, air | h | hope, hate | o | odd, hot | s | see, pass | v | vain, eve |
| ä | palm, father | i | it, give | ō | open, so | sh | sure, rush | w | win, away |
| b | bat, rub | ī | ice, write | ô | order, jaw | t | talk, sit | y | yet, yearn |
| ch | check, catch | j | joy, ledge | oi | oil, boy | th | thin, both | z | zest, muse |
| d | dog, rod | k | cool, take | ou | pout, now | th | this, bathe | zh | vision, pleasure |
| e | end, pet | l | look, rule | ōō | took, full | u | up, done | | |
| ē | equal, tree | m | move, seem | ōō | pool, food | u̇ | pull, book | | |

ə the schwa, an unstressed vowel representing the sound spelled *a* in *above*, e in *sicken*, i in *possible*, o in *melon*, u in *circus*

Other symbols:
* • separates words into syllables
* ' indicates stress on a syllable

## A

**addend** [a'dend] **sumando** Any of the numbers that are added in addition
*Examples:* 2 + 3 = 5
　　　　　↑　　↑
　　　addend　addend

**addition** [ə•dish'ən] **suma** The process of finding the total number of items when two or more groups of items are joined; the opposite operation of subtraction

**A.M.** [ā•em] **a.m.** The time after midnight and before noon

**analog clock** [an'ə•log kläk] **reloj analógico** A tool for measuring time, in which hands move around a circle to show hours and minutes
*Example:*

**angle** [ang'gəl] **ángulo** A shape formed by two rays that share an endpoint
*Example:*

### Word History

When the letter *g* is replaced with the letter *k* in the word **angle**, the word becomes *ankle*. Both words come from the same Latin root, *angulus*, which means "a sharp bend."

**area** [âr'ē•ə] **área** The measure of the number of unit squares needed to cover a surface
*Example:*

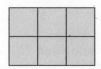

Area = 6 square units

**array** [ə·rā'] **matriz** A set of objects arranged in rows and columns
*Example:*

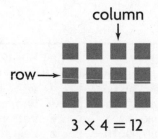

column

row →

$3 \times 4 = 12$

**Associative Property of Addition** [ə·sō'shē·āt·iv präp'ər·tē əv ə·dish'ən] **propiedad asociativa de la suma** The property that states that you can group addends in different ways and still get the same sum
*Example:*
$4 + (2 + 5) = 11$
$(4 + 2) + 5 = 11$

**Associative Property of Multiplication** [ə·sō'shē·āt·iv präp'ər·tē əv mul·tə·pli·kā'shən] **propiedad asociativa de la multiplicación** The property that states that when the grouping of factors is changed, the product remains the same
*Example:*
$(3 \times 2) \times 4 = 24$
$3 \times (2 \times 4) = 24$

**bar graph** [bär graf] **gráfica de barras** A graph that uses bars to show data
*Example:*

**Favorite Food**

Number of Votes

Tacos  Pizza  Chili  Pasta

Food

**capacity** [kə·pas'i·tē] **capacidad** The amount a container can hold
*Example:*
1 liter = 1,000 milliliters

**cent sign (¢)** [sent sīn] **símbolo de centavo** A symbol that stands for *cent* or *cents*
*Example:* 53¢

**centimeter (cm)** [sen'tə·mēt·ər] **centímetro (cm)** A metric unit that is used to measure length or distance
*Example:*

1 cm

**circle** [sûr'kəl] **círculo** A round closed plane shape
*Example:*

**closed shape** [klōzd shāp] **figura cerrada** A shape that begins and ends at the same point
*Examples:*

**Commutative Property of Addition** [kə·myōōt'ə·tiv präp'ər·tē əv ə·dish'ən] **propiedad conmutativa de la suma** The property that states that you can add two or more numbers in any order and get the same sum
*Example:*     $6 + 7 = 13$
$7 + 6 = 13$

**Commutative Property of Multiplication** [kə·myōōt'ə·tiv präp'ər·tē əv mul·tə·pli·kā'shən] **propiedad conmutativa de la multiplicación** The property that states that you can multiply two factors in any order and get the same product
*Example:*     $2 \times 4 = 8$
$4 \times 2 = 8$

**compare** [kəm·pâr'] **comparar** To describe whether numbers are equal to, less than, or greater than each other

**compatible numbers** [kəm·pat'ə·bəl num'bərz] **números compatibles** Numbers that are easy to compute with mentally

**cone** [kōn] **cono** A three-dimensional, pointed shape that has a flat, round base
*Example:*

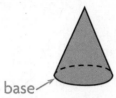
base

**counting number** [kount'ing num'bər] **número natural** A whole number that can be used to count a set of objects (1, 2, 3, 4 . . .)

**cube** [kyōōb] **cubo** A three-dimensional shape with six square faces of the same size
*Example:*

**cylinder** [sil'ən•dər] **cilindro** A three-dimensional object that is shaped like a can
*Example:*

 **D**

**data** [dāt'ə] **datos** Information collected about people or things

**decagon** [dek'ə•gän] **decágono** A polygon with ten sides and ten angles
*Example:*

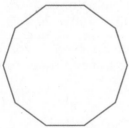

**decimal point** [des'ə•məl point] **punto decimal** A symbol used to separate dollars from cents in money
*Example:* $4.52
↑ decimal point

**denominator** [dē•näm'ə•nāt•ər] **denominador** The part of a fraction below the line, which tells how many equal parts there are in the whole or in the group
*Example:* $\frac{3}{4}$ ← denominator

**difference** [dif'ər•əns] **diferencia** The answer to a subtraction problem
*Example:* 6 − 4 = 2
↑ difference

**digital clock** [dij'i•təl kläk] **reloj digital** A clock that shows time to the minute, using digits
*Example:*

**digits** [dij'its] **dígitos** The symbols 0, 1, 2, 3, 4, 5, 6, 7, 8, and 9

**dime** [dīm] **moneda de 10¢** A coin worth 10 cents and with a value equal to that of 10 pennies; 10¢
*Example:*

**Distributive Property** [di•strib'yōō•tiv präp'ər•tē] **propiedad distributiva** The property that states that multiplying a sum by a number is the same as multiplying each addend by the number and then adding the products
*Example:*   5 × 8 = 5 × (4 + 4)
          5 × 8 = (5 × 4) + (5 × 4)
          5 × 8 = 20 + 20
          5 × 8 = 40

**divide** [də•vīd'] **dividir** To separate into equal groups; the opposite operation of multiplication

**dividend** [div'ə•dend] **dividendo** The number that is to be divided in a division problem
*Example:* 35 ÷ 5 = 7
          ↑ dividend

**division** [də•vizh′ən] **división** The process of sharing a number of items to find how many groups can be made or how many items will be in a group; the opposite operation of multiplication

**divisor** [de•vī′zər] **divisor** The number that divides the dividend
*Example:* 35 ÷ 5 = 7

divisor

**dollar** [däl′ər] **dólar** Paper money worth 100 cents and equal to 100 pennies; $1.00
*Example:*

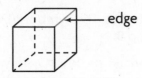

**edge** [ej] **arista** A line segment formed where two faces meet

edge

**eighths** [ātths] **octavos**

These are eighths

**elapsed time** [ē•lapst′ tīm] **tiempo transcurrido** The time that passes from the start of an activity to the end of that activity

**endpoint** [end′point] **extremo** The point at either end of a line segment

**equal groups** [ē′kwəl groōpz] **grupos iguales** Groups that have the same number of objects

**equal parts** [ē′kwəl pärts] **partes iguales** Parts that are exactly the same size

**equal sign (=)** [ē′kwəl sīn] **signo de igualdad** A symbol used to show that two numbers have the same value
*Example:* 384 = 384

**equal to (=)** [ē′kwəl too] **igual a** Having the same value
*Example:* 4 + 4 is equal to 3 + 5.

**equation** [ē•kwā′zhən] **ecuación** A number sentence that uses the equal sign to show that two amounts are equal
*Examples:*
  3 + 7 = 10
  4 − 1 = 3
  6 × 7 = 42
  8 ÷ 2 = 4

**equivalent** [ē•kwiv′ə•lənt] **equivalente** Two or more sets that name the same amount

**equivalent fractions** [ē•kwiv′ə•lənt frak′shənz] **fracciones equivalentes** Two or more fractions that name the same amount
*Example:*

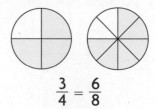

$$\frac{3}{4} = \frac{6}{8}$$

**estimate** [es′tə•māt] *verb* **estimar** To find about how many or how much

**estimate** [es′tə•mit] *noun* **estimación** A number close to an exact amount

**even** [ē′vən] **par** A whole number that has a 0, 2, 4, 6, or 8 in the ones place

**expanded form** [ek•span′did fôrm] **forma desarrollada** A way to write numbers by showing the value of each digit
*Example:* 721 = 700 + 20 + 1

**experiment** [ek•sper′ə•mənt] **experimento** A test that is done in order to find out something

**face** [fās] **cara** A polygon that is a flat surface of a solid shape

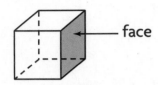

**factor** [fak'tər] **factor** A number that is multiplied by another number to find a product
*Examples:* $3 \times 8 = 24$

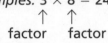

factor    factor

**foot (ft)** [foŏt] **pie** A customary unit used to measure length or distance;
1 foot = 12 inches

**fourths** [fôrths] **cuartos**

These are fourths

**fraction** [frak'shən] **fracción** A number that names part of a whole or part of a group
*Examples:*

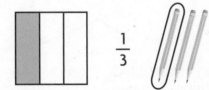

$\frac{1}{3}$

**Word History**

Often, a ***fraction*** is a part of a whole that is broken into pieces. *Fraction* comes from the Latin word *frangere*, which means "to break."

**fraction greater than 1** [frak'shən grāt'ər than wun] **fracción mayor que 1** A number which has a numerator that is greater than its denominator
*Examples:*

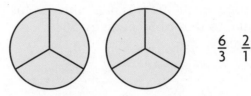

$\frac{6}{3}$  $\frac{2}{1}$

**frequency table** [frē'kwən•sē tā'bəl] **tabla de frecuencia** A table that uses numbers to record data
*Example:*

| Favorite Color | |
|---|---|
| **Color** | **Number** |
| Blue | 10 |
| Green | 8 |
| Red | 7 |
| Yellow | 4 |

**G**

**gram (g)** [gram] **gramo (g)** A metric unit that is used to measure mass;
1 kilogram = 1,000 grams

**greater than (>)** [grāt'ər than] **mayor que** A symbol used to compare two numbers when the greater number is given first
*Example:*
Read 6 > 4 as "six is greater than four."

**Grouping Property of Addition** [groōp'ing präp'ər•tē əv ə•dish'ən] **propiedad de agrupación de la suma** *See* Associative Property of Addition.

**Grouping Property of Multiplication** [groōp'ing präp'ər•tē əv mul•tə•pli•kā'shən] **propiedad de agrupación de la multiplicación** *See* Associative Property of Multiplication.

**half dollar** [haf dol'ər] **moneda de 50¢**
A coin worth 50 cents and with a value
equal to that of 50 pennies; 50¢
*Example:*

**half hour** [haf our] **media hora** 30 minutes
*Example:* Between 4:00 and 4:30 is one
half hour.

**halves** [havz] **mitades**

These are halves

**hexagon** [hek'sə•gän] **hexágono** A polygon
with six sides and six angles
*Examples:*

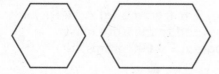

**horizontal bar graph** [hôr•i•zänt'l bär graf]
**gráfica de barras horizontales** A bar graph
in which the bars go from left to right
*Examples:*

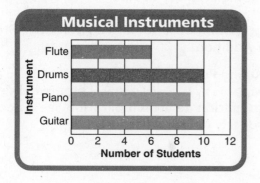

**hour (hr)** [our] **hora (h)** A unit used to measure
time; in one hour, the hour hand on an analog
clock moves from one number to the next;
1 hour = 60 minutes

**hour hand** [our hand] **horario** The short hand on
an analog clock

**Identity Property of Addition** [ī•den'tə•tē
präp'ər•tē əv ə•dish'ən] **propiedad de
identidad de la suma** The property that
states that when you add zero to a number,
the result is that number
*Example:* 24 + 0 = 24

**Identity Property of Multiplication** [ī•den'tə•tē
präp'ər•tē əv mul•tə•pli•kā'shən] **propiedad de
identidad de la multiplicación** The property
that states that the product of any number
and 1 is that number
*Examples:* 5 × 1 = 5
1 × 8 = 8

**inch (in.)** [inch] **pulgada (pulg.)** A customary
unit used to measure length or distance
*Example:*

**intersecting lines** [in•tər•sekt'ing līnz] **líneas
secantes** Lines that meet or cross
*Example:*

**inverse operations** [in'vûrs äp•ə•rā'shənz]
**operaciones inversas** Opposite operations,
or operations that undo one another, such
as addition and subtraction or multiplication
and division

**key** [kē] **clave** The part of a map or graph
that explains the symbols

**kilogram (kg)** [kil'ō•gram] **kilogramo (kg)**
A metric unit used to measure mass;
1 kilogram = 1,000 grams

**length** [lengkth] **longitud** The measurement of the distance between two points

**less than (<)** [les than] **menor que** A symbol used to compare two numbers when the lesser number is given first
*Example:*
Read 3 < 7 as "three is less than seven."

**line** [līn] **línea** A straight path extending in both directions with no endpoints
*Example:*

<---------->

---

**Word History**

The word *line* comes from *linen*, a thread spun from the fibers of the flax plant. In early times, thread was held tight to mark a straight line between two points.

---

**line plot** [līn plät] **diagrama de puntos** A graph that records each piece of data on a number line
*Example:*

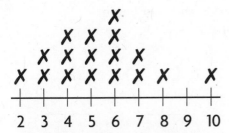

**Height of Bean Seedlings
to the Nearest Centimeter**

**line segment** [līn seg'mənt] **segmento** A part of a line that includes two points, called endpoints, and all of the points between them
*Example:*

**liquid volume** [lik'wid väl'yōōm] **volumen de un líquido** The amount of liquid in a container

**liter (L)** [lēt'ər] **litro (L)** A metric unit used to measure capacity and liquid volume;
1 liter = 1,000 milliliters

---

**mass** [mas] **masa** The amount of matter in an object

**meter (m)** [mēt'ər] **metro (m)** A metric unit used to measure length or distance;
1 meter = 100 centimeters

**midnight** [mid'nīt] **medianoche** 12:00 at night

**milliliter (mL)** [mil'i•lēt•ər] **mililitro (mL)** A metric unit used to measure capacity and liquid volume

**minute (min)** [min'it] **minuto (min)** A unit used to measure short amounts of time; in one minute, the minute hand on an analog clock moves from one mark to the next

**minute hand** [min'it hand] **minutero** The long hand on an analog clock

**multiple** [mul'tə•pəl] **múltiplo** A number that is the product of two counting numbers
*Examples:*

| 6 | 6 | 6 | 6 | counting |
|---|---|---|---|---|
| × 1 | × 2 | × 3 | × 4 | ← numbers |
| 6 | 12 | 18 | 24 | ← multiples of 6 |

**multiplication** [mul•tə•pli•kā'shən] **multiplicación** The process of finding the total number of items in two or more equal groups; the opposite operation of division

**multiply** [mul'tə•plī] **multiplicar** To combine equal groups to find how many in all; the opposite operation of division

---

**nickel** [nik'əl] **moneda de 5¢** A coin worth 5 cents and with a value equal to that of 5 pennies; 5¢
*Example:*

**noon** [nōōn] **mediodía** 12:00 in the day

**number line** [num′bər līn] **recta numérica**
A line on which numbers can be located
*Example:*

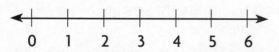

**number sentence** [num′bər sent′ns] **enunciado numérico** A sentence that includes numbers, operation symbols, and a greater than symbol, a less than symbol, or an equal sign
*Example:* 5 + 3 = 8

**numerator** [nōō′mər•āt•ər] **numerador** The part of a fraction above the line, which tells how many parts are being counted
*Example:* $\frac{3}{4}$ ← numerator

 **O**

**octagon** [ăk′tə•gän] **octágono** A polygon with eight sides and eight angles
*Examples:*

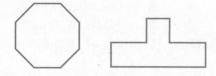

**odd** [od] **impar** A whole number that has a 1, 3, 5, 7, or 9 in the ones place

**open shape** [ō′pən shāp] **figura abierta** A shape that does not begin and end at the same point
*Examples:*

**order** [ôr′dər] **orden** A particular arrangement or placement of numbers or things, one after another

**order of operations** [ôr′dər əv äp•ə•rā′shənz] **orden de las operaciones** A special set of rules that gives the order in which calculations are done

**Order Property of Addition** [ôr′dər präp′ər•tē əv ə•dish′ən] **propiedad de orden de la suma** *See* Commutative Property of Addition.

**Order Property of Multiplication** [ôr′dər präp′ər•tē əv mul•tə•pli•kā′shən] **propiedad de orden de la multiplicación** *See* Commutative Property of Multiplication.

 **P**

**parallel lines** [pâr′ə•lel līnz] **líneas paralelas** Lines in the same plane that never cross and are always the same distance apart
*Example:*

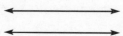

**pattern** [pat′ərn] **patrón** An ordered set of numbers or objects in which the order helps you predict what will come next
*Examples:*
2, 4, 6, 8, 10

**pentagon** [pen′tə•gän] **pentágono** A polygon with five sides and five angles
*Examples:*

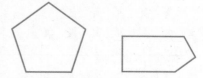

**perimeter** [pə•rim′ə•tər] **perímetro** The distance around a figure
*Example:*

**perpendicular lines** [pər•pən•dik′yōō•lər līnz] **líneas perpendiculares** Lines that intersect to form right angles
*Example:*

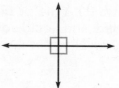

**picture graph** [pik'chər graf] **gráfica con dibujos** A graph that uses pictures to show and compare information
*Example:*

| How We Get to School | |
|---|---|
| Walk | 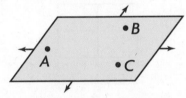 |
| Ride a Bike | |
| Ride a Bus | |
| Ride in a Car | |
| Key: Each ✳ = 10 students. | |

**place value** [plās val'yoo] **valor posicional** The value of each digit in a number, based on the location of the digit

**plane** [plān] **plano** A flat surface that extends without end in all directions
*Example:*

**plane shape** [plān shāp] **figura plana** A shape in a plane that is formed by curves, line segments, or both
*Example:*

**P.M.** [pē•em] **p.m.** The time after noon and before midnight

**point** [point] **punto** An exact position or location

**polygon** [päl'i•gän] **polígono** A closed plane shape with straight sides that are line segments
*Examples:*

polygons          not polygons

© Houghton Mifflin Harcourt Publishing Company

**Word History**

Did you ever think that a *polygon* looks like a bunch of knees that are bent? This is how the term got its name. *Poly-* is from the Greek word *polys*, which means "many." The ending *-gon* is from the Greek word *gony*, which means "knee."

**product** [präd'əkt] **producto** The answer in a multiplication problem
*Example:* $3 \times 8 = 24$
↑ product

**Q**

**quadrilateral** [kwäd•ri•lat'ər•əl] **cuadrilátero** A polygon with four sides and four angles
*Example:*

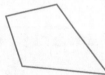

**quarter** [kwôrt'ər] **moneda de 25¢** A coin worth 25 cents and with a value equal to that of 25 pennies; 25¢
*Example:*

**quarter hour** [kwôrt'ər our] **cuarto de hora** 15 minutes
*Example:* Between 4:00 and 4:15 is one quarter hour.

**quotient** [kwō'shənt] **cociente** The number, not including the remainder, that results from division
*Example:* $8 \div 4 = 2$
↑ quotient

## R

**ray** [rā] **semirrecta** A part of a line, with one endpoint, that is straight and continues in one direction
*Example:*

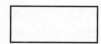

**rectangle** [rek'tang•gəl] **rectángulo**
A quadrilateral with two pairs of parallel sides, two pairs of sides of equal length, and four right angles
*Example:*

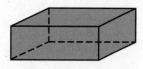

**rectangular prism** [rek•tang'gyə•lər priz'əm]
**prisma rectangular** A three-dimensional shape with six faces that are all rectangles
*Example:*

**regroup** [rē•grōōp'] **reagrupar** To exchange amounts of equal value to rename a number
*Example:* 5 + 8 = 13 ones or 1 ten 3 ones

**related facts** [ri•lāt'id fakts] **operaciones relacionadas** A set of related addition and subtraction, or multiplication and division, number sentences
*Examples:* 4 × 7 = 28      28 ÷ 4 = 7
                    7 × 4 = 28      28 ÷ 7 = 4

**remainder** [ri•mān'dər] **residuo** The amount left over when a number cannot be divided evenly

**results** [ri•zults'] **resultados** The answers from a survey

**rhombus** [räm'bəs] **rombo** A quadrilateral with two pairs of parallel sides and four sides of equal length
*Example:*

**right angle** [rīt ang'gəl] **ángulo recto** An angle that forms a square corner
*Example:*

**round** [round] **redondear** To replace a number with another number that tells about how many or how much

## S

**scale** [skāl] **escala** The numbers placed at fixed distances on a graph to help label the graph

**side** [sīd] **lado** A straight line segment in a polygon

**sixths** [siksths] **sextos**

These are sixths

**skip count** [skip kount] **contar salteado** A pattern of counting forward or backward
*Example:* 5, 10, 15, 20, 25, 30, . . .

**solid shape** [sä'lid shāp] **cuerpo geométrico**
*See* three-dimensional shape.

**sphere** [sfir] **esfera** A three-dimensional shape that has the shape of a round ball
*Example:*

**square** [skwâr] **cuadrado** A quadrilateral with two pairs of parallel sides, four sides of equal length, and four right angles
*Example:*

**square unit** [skwâr yo͞o′nit] **unidad cuadrada**
A unit used to measure area such as square foot, square meter, and so on

**standard form** [stan′dərd fôrm] **forma normal**
A way to write numbers by using the digits 0–9, with each digit having a place value
*Example:* 345   ← standard form

**subtraction** [səb·trak′shən] **resta** The process of finding how many are left when a number of items are taken away from a group of items; the process of finding the difference when two groups are compared; the opposite operation of addition

**sum** [sum] **suma o total** The answer to an addition problem
*Example:* 6 + 4 = 10

⬆—sum

**survey** [sûr′vā] **encuesta** A method of gathering information

**tally table** [tal′ē tā′bəl] **tabla de conteo** A table that uses tally marks to record data
*Example:*

| Favorite Sport | |
|---|---|
| **Sport** | **Tally** |
| Soccer | ⷮⷮⷮⷮⷮ ||| |
| Baseball | ||| |
| Football | ⷮⷮⷮⷮⷮ |
| Basketball | ⷮⷮⷮⷮⷮ | |

**thirds** [thûrdz] **tercios**

These are thirds

**three-dimensional shape** [thrē də·men′shə·nəl shāp] **figura tridimensional** A shape that has length, width, and height
*Example:*

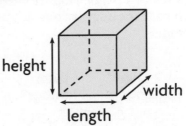

**time line** [tīm līn] **línea cronológica** A drawing that shows when and in what order events took place

**trapezoid** [trap′i·zoid] **trapecio** A quadrilateral with at least one pair of parallel sides
*Example:*

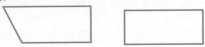

**triangle** [trī′ang·gəl] **triángulo** A polygon with three sides and three angles
*Examples:*

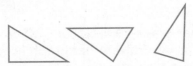

**two-dimensional shape** [to͞o də·men′shə·nəl shāp] **figura bidimensional** A shape that has only length and width
*Example:*

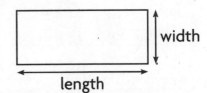

**unit fraction** [yo͞o′nit frak′shən] **fracción unitaria** A fraction that has 1 as its top number, or numerator
*Examples:* $\frac{1}{2}$  $\frac{1}{3}$  $\frac{1}{4}$

**unit square** [yo͞o′nit skwâr] **cuadrado de una unidad** A square with a side length of 1 unit, used to measure area

**Venn diagram** [ven dī'ə•gram] **diagrama de Venn** A diagram that shows relationships among sets of things
*Example:*

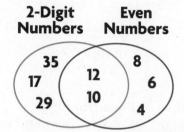

**vertex** [vûr'teks] **vértice** The point at which two rays of an angle or two (or more) line segments meet in a plane shape or where three or more edges meet in a solid shape
*Examples:*

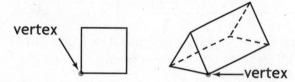

**vertical bar graph** [vûr'ti•kəl bär graf] **gráfica de barras verticales** A bar graph in which the bars go up from bottom to top

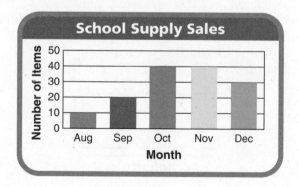

**whole** [hōl] **entero** All of the parts of a shape or group
*Example:*

$\frac{2}{2} = 1$

This is one whole.

**whole number** [hōl num'bər] **número entero** One of the numbers 0, 1, 2, 3, 4, . . . The set of whole numbers goes on without end

**word form** [wûrd fôrm] **en palabras** A way to write numbers by using words
*Example:* The word form of 212 is two hundred twelve.

**Zero Property of Multiplication** [zē'rō präp'ər•tē əv mul•tə•pli•kā'shən] **propiedad del cero de la multiplicación** The property that states that the product of zero and any number is zero
*Example:* $0 \times 6 = 0$

# Correlations

## COMMON CORE STATE STANDARDS

## Standards You Will Learn

| Mathematical Practices | | Some examples are: |
|---|---|---|
| **MP1** | Make sense of problems and persevere in solving them. | Lessons 1.2, 2.1, 2.4, 5.3, 6.3, 7.1, 9.3, 10.7, 11.2 |
| **MP2** | Reason abstractly and quantitatively. | Lessons 1.1, 1.5, 3.7, 5.5, 6.4, 7.2, 10.9, 11.4, 12.8 |
| **MP3** | Construct viable arguments and critique the reasoning of others. | Lessons 2.5, 4.7, 5.3, 7.2, 9.7, 10.4, 10.5, 11.1, 12.6 |
| **MP4** | Model with mathematics. | Lessons 1.12, 2.2, 3.2, 5.2, 6.2, 8.2, 10.3, 11.3, 12.9 |
| **MP5** | Use appropriate tools strategically. | Lessons 1.6, 2.7, 3.5, 4.9, 6.7, 7.8, 9.5, 10.6, 11.4 |
| **MP6** | Attend to precision. | Lessons 1.1, 1.4, 2.6, 5.2, 6.8, 7.1, 9.2, 10.1, 12.6 |
| **MP7** | Look for and make use of structure. | Lessons 1.1, 3.3, 3.6, 5.1, 6.5, 7.11, 11.5, 11.7, 12.6 |
| **MP8** | Look for and express regularity in repeated reasoning. | Lessons 2.2, 3.6, 4.5, 5.4, 6.9, 7.7, 9.5, 11.4, 12.3 |
| **Domain: Operations and Algebraic Thinking** | | **Student Edition Lessons** |
| **Represent and solve problems involving multiplication and division.** | | |
| **3.OA.A.1** | Interpret products of whole numbers, e.g., interpret $5 \times 7$ as the total number of objects in 5 groups of 7 objects each. | Lessons 3.1, 3.2 |
| **3.OA.A.2** | Interpret whole-number quotients of whole numbers, e.g., interpret $56 \div 8$ as the number of objects in each share when 56 objects are partitioned equally into 8 shares, or as a number of shares when 56 objects are partitioned into equal shares of 8 objects each. | Lessons 6.2, 6.3, 6.4 |

# Standards You Will Learn

| Domain: Operations and Algebraic Thinking | | |
|---|---|---|
| **Represent and solve problems involving multiplication and division.** | | |
| 3.OA.A.3 | Use multiplication and division within 100 to solve word problems in situations involving equal groups, arrays, and measurement quantities, e.g., by using drawings and equations with a symbol for the unknown number to represent the problem. | Lessons 3.3, 3.5, 4.1, 4.2, 4.3, 6.1, 6.5, 6.6, 7.1, 7.3, 7.8 |
| 3.OA.A.4 | Determine the unknown whole number in a multiplication or division equation relating three whole numbers. | Lessons 5.2, 7.8 |
| **Understand properties of multiplication and the relationship between multiplication and division.** | | |
| 3.OA.B.5 | Apply properties of operations as strategies to multiply and divide. *Examples: If $6 \times 4 = 24$ is known, then $4 \times 6 = 24$ is also known (Commutative property of multiplication.) $3 \times 5 \times 2$ can be found by $3 \times 5 = 15$, then $15 \times 2 = 30$, or by $5 \times 2 = 10$, then $3 \times 10 = 30$. (Associative property of multiplication.) Knowing that $8 \times 5 = 40$ and $8 \times 2 = 16$, one can find $8 \times 7$ as $8 \times (5 + 2) = (8 \times 5) + (8 \times 2) = 40 + 16 = 56$. (Distributive property.)* | Lessons 3.6, 3.7, 4.4, 4.6, 6.9 |
| 3.OA.B.6 | Understand division as an unknown-factor problem. | Lesson 6.7 |
| **Multiply and divide with 100.** | | |
| 3.OA.C.7 | Fluently multiply and divide within 100, using strategies such as the relationship between multiplication and division (e.g., knowing that $8 \times 5 = 40$, one knows $40 \div 5 = 8$) or properties of operations. By the end of Grade 3, know from memory all products of two one-digit numbers. | Lessons 4.5, 4.8, 4.9, 6.8, 7.2, 7.4, 7.5, 7.6, 7.7, 7.9 |

© Houghton Mifflin Harcourt Publishing Company

# Standards You Will Learn

## Domain: Operations and Algebraic Thinking

### Solve problems involving the four operations, and identify and explain patterns in arithmetic.

| | | |
|---|---|---|
| **3.OA.D.8** | Solve two-step word problems using the four operations. Represent these problems using equations with a letter standing for the unknown quantity. Assess the reasonableness of answers using mental computation and estimation strategies including rounding. | Lessons 1.12, 2.1, 2.6, 3.4, 4.10, 7.10, 7.11 |
| **3.OA.D.9** | Identify arithmetic patterns (including patterns in the addition table or multiplication table), and explain them using properties of operations. | Lessons 1.1, 4.7, 4.10, 5.1 |

## Domain: Number and Operations in Base Ten

### Use place value understanding and properties of operations to perform multi-digit arithmetic.

| | | |
|---|---|---|
| **3.NBT.A.1** | Use place value understanding to round whole numbers to the nearest 10 or 100. | Lessons 1.2, 1.3, 1.8 |
| **3.NBT.A.2** | Fluently add and subtract within 1000 using strategies and algorithms based on place value, properties of operations, and/or the relationship between addition and subtraction. | Lessons 1.4, 1.5, 1.6, 1.7, 1.9, 1.10, 1.11, 2.2, 2.3, 2.4, 2.5, 2.7 |
| **3.NBT.A.3** | Multiply one-digit whole numbers by multiples of 10 in the range 10–90 (e.g., $9 \times 80$, $5 \times 60$) using strategies based on place value and properties of operations. | Lessons 5.3, 5.4, 5.5 |

**Domain: Number and Operations—Fractions**

**Develop understanding of fractions as numbers.**

| | | |
|---|---|---|
| **3.NF.A.1** | Understand a fraction $1/b$ as the quantity formed by 1 part when $a$ whole is partitioned into $b$ equal parts; understand a fraction $a/b$ as the quantity formed by $a$ parts of size $1/b$. | Lessons 8.1, 8.2, 8.3, 8.4, 8.7, 8.8, 8.9 |
| **3.NF.A.2** | Understand a fraction as a number on the number line; represent fractions on a number line diagram. | |
| | a. Represent a fraction $1/b$ on a number line diagram by defining the interval from 0 to 1 as the whole and partitioning it into $b$ equal parts. Recognize that each part has size $1/b$ and that the endpoint of the part based at 0 locates the number $1/b$ on the number line. | Lesson 8.5 |
| | b. Represent a fraction $a/b$ on a number line diagram by marking off $a$ lengths $1/b$ from 0. Recognize that the resulting interval has size $a/b$ and that its endpoint locates the number $a/b$ on the number line. | Lesson 8.5 |

# Standards You Will Learn

## Domain: Number and Operations—Fractions

### Develop understanding of fractions as numbers.

| 3.NF.A.3 | Explain equivalence of fractions in special cases, and compare fractions by reasoning about their size. | |
|---|---|---|
| | a. Understand two fractions as equivalent (equal) if they are the same size, or the same point on a number line. | Lesson 9.6 |
| | b. Recognize and generate simple equivalent fractions, e.g., 1/2 = 2/4, 4/6 = 2/3. Explain why the fractions are equivalent, e.g., by using a visual fraction model. | Lesson 9.7 |
| | c. Express whole numbers as fractions, and recognize fractions that are equivalent to whole numbers. | Lesson 8.6 |
| | d. Compare two fractions with the same numerator or the same denominator by reasoning about their size. Recognize that comparisons are valid only when the two fractions refer to the same whole. Record the results of comparisons with the symbols $>$, $=$, or $<$, and justify the conclusions, e.g., by using a visual fraction model. | Lessons 9.1, 9.2, 9.3, 9.4, 9.5 |

**Domain: Measurement and Data**

**Solve problems involving measurement and estimation of intervals of time, liquid volumes, and masses of objects.**

| | | |
|---|---|---|
| **3.MD.A.1** | Tell and write time to the nearest minute and measure time intervals in minutes. Solve word problems involving addition and subtraction of time intervals in minutes, e.g., by representing the problem on a number line diagram. | Lessons 10.1, 10.2, 10.3, 10.4, 10.5 |
| **3.MD.A.2** | Measure and estimate liquid volumes and masses of objects using standard units of grams (g), kilograms (kg), and liters (l). Add, subtract, multiply, or divide to solve one-step word problems involving masses or volumes that are given in the same units, e.g., by using drawings (such as a beaker with a measurement scale) to represent the problem. | Lessons 10.7, 10.8, 10.9 |

**Represent and interpret data.**

| | | |
|---|---|---|
| **3.MD.B.3** | Draw a scaled picture graph and a scaled bar graph to represent a data set with several categories. Solve one- and two-step "how many more" and "how many less" problems using information presented in scaled bar graphs. | Lessons 2.1, 2.2, 2.3, 2.4, 2.5, 2.6 |
| **3.MD.B.4** | Generate measurement data by measuring lengths using rulers marked with halves and fourths of an inch. Show the data by making a line plot, where the horizontal scale is marked off in appropriate units—whole numbers, halves, or quarters. | Lessons 2.7, 10.6 |

**Domain: Measurement and Data**

**Geometric measurement: understand concepts of area and relate area to multiplication and to addition.**

| | | |
|---|---|---|
| **3.MD.C.5** | Recognize area as an attribute of plane figures and understand concepts of area measurement. | Lesson 11.4 |
| | a. A square with side length 1 unit, called "a unit square," is said to have "one square unit" of area, and can be used to measure area. | Lesson 11.4 |
| | b. A plane figure which can be covered without gaps or overlaps by *n* unit squares is said to have an area of *n* square units. | Lesson 11.5 |
| **3.MD.C.6** | Measure areas by counting unit squares (square cm, square m, square in, square ft, and improvised units). | Lesson 11.5 |
| **3.MD.C.7** | Relate area to the operations of multiplication and addition. | Lesson 11.6 |
| | a. Find the area of a rectangle with whole-number side lengths by tiling it, and show that the area is the same as would be found by multiplying the side lengths. | Lesson 11.6 |
| | b. Multiply side lengths to find areas of rectangles with whole-number side lengths in the context of solving real world and mathematical problems, and represent whole-number products as rectangular areas in mathematical reasoning. | Lesson 11.7 |
| | c. Use tiling to show in a concrete case that the area of a rectangle with whole-number side lengths *a* and *b* + *c* is the sum of *a* × *b* and *a* × *c*. Use area models to represent the distributive property in mathematical reasoning. | Lesson 11.8 |
| | d. Recognize area as additive. Find areas of rectilinear figures by decomposing them into non-overlapping rectangles and adding the areas of the non-overlapping parts, applying this technique to solve real world problems. | Lesson 11.8 |

## Standards You Will Learn

**Domain: Measurement and Data**

**Geometric measurement: recognize perimeter as an attribute of plane figures and distinguish between linear and area measures.**

| | | |
|---|---|---|
| **3.MD.D.8** | Solve real world and mathematical problems involving perimeters of polygons, including finding the perimeter given the side lengths, finding an unknown side length, and exhibiting rectangles with the same perimeter and different areas or with the same area and different perimeters. | Lessons 11.1, 11.2, 11.3, 11.9, 11.10 |

**Domain: Geometry**

**Reason with shapes and their attributes.**

| | | |
|---|---|---|
| **3.G.A.1** | Understand that shapes in different categories (e.g., rhombuses, rectangles, and others) may share attributes (e.g., having four sides), and that the shared attributes can define a larger category (e.g., quadrilaterals). Recognize rhombuses, rectangles, and squares as examples of quadrilaterals, and draw examples of quadrilaterals that do not belong to any of these subcategories. | Lessons 12.1, 12.2, 12.3, 12.4, 12.5, 12.6, 12.7, 12.8 |
| **3.G.A.2** | Partition shapes into parts with equal areas. Express the area of each part as a unit fraction of the whole. | Lesson 12.9 |

© Houghton Mifflin Harcourt Publishing Company

# Index

© Houghton Mifflin Harcourt Publishing Company

**Connect,** 29, 119, 223, 313, 427, 476, 593, 643, 670, 709, 729, 747

**Correlations,**
  Common Core State Standards, H13–H20

**Counting**
  back
      on clocks, 562–564, 579–582
      on number lines, 55–58, 326–328, 371–373, 377–379, 384, 579–582, 585–588
    elapsed time, 573–576, 579–582, 585–588
    equal groups, 139–142, 145–148, 151–154, 191–194, 301–304, 307–310, 313–316, 319–322, 333–336, 339–342, 345–348, 365–368, 383–386, 389, 395–398, 403–406, 415–418
    number lines, 23–25, 151–154, 573–576, 579–582, 585–588
  on
      on clocks, 561–564, 573–576
      on number lines, 23–26
    skip counting, 192
      equal groups, 139–142, 145–148, 151–154, 301–304
      by fives, 197–200, 204
      by sixes, 203–206
      by tens, 197–200, 278–284
      by threes, 203–206
      by twos, 192–194
    tens and ones, 23–25, 55–58
    time intervals, 573–576, 579–582, 585–588
  up
      by fives, 377–379
      on number lines, 55–58, 378–379, 579–582, 585–588

**Counting numbers,** 281, 562, 574, 625

**Cross-Curricular Activities and Connections**
  Connect to Reading, 58, 128, 218, 354, 542, 678, 726
  Connect to Science, 238, 582
  Connect to Social Studies, 430

**Customary units**
  for length
    feet, 151, 634, 638, 664
    inches, 126, 593–596, 631–649
  for weight, ounces, 148

## D

**Data, represent and interpret**
  bar graphs, 107–110, 113–116, 119–122
    making, 113–116
    using, 107–110, 119–122
  collect data, 126
  dot plots. *See* Line plots
  experiments, 100, 115
  frequency tables, 87–90
  generating measurement data, 126, 593–596
  key, 93
  line plots, 125–128
    making, 125–128
    using, 125–128
    shape of, 126
  make a table, 87–90, 247–250
  organizing data, 87–90
  picture graphs, 93–96, 99–102, 114, 374
    making, 99–102
    using, 93–96
  scale, 107
  solving problems, 119–122
  surveys, 93, 95, 100, 108, 113, 125
  tally tables, 87–90, 101
  use a table, 14, 20, 38, 52, 64, 70, 151, 168, 180, 200, 206, 217, 237, 243, 261–264, 270, 283, 304, 310, 322, 342, 348, 368, 386, 392, 412, 490, 510, 582, 665

**Decagons,** 710–712

**Denominators,** 461
  comparing fractions with same, 513–516, 525–528
  defined, 461
  fraction greater than 1, 475–478
  ordering fractions with same, 533–536

**Diagrams.** *See also* Graphic Organizers
  Draw a Diagram, 73–76, 159–162, 275–278, 493–496, 585–588, 741–744
  Venn diagrams, 4, 364, 624, 741–744

**Digital clocks,** 563, 568–569

**Distributive Property**
  area, 669–672
  multiplication, 209–212, 215, 241, 275–278, 669–672

**Divide,** 307

**Dividend,** defined, 320

modeling, 539–542, 545–548
on a number line, 540–541
to whole numbers, 546–548
find part of a group, 481–484, 487–490
fourths, 443
fractions greater than 1, 475–478,
482–483
of a group, 481–484, 487–490
halves, 443
linear models, 467–470, 475–478,
514–515, 533–536, 540–541
on number line, 467–470, 475–478,
514–515, 540–541
numerator of, 461
ordering, 533–536
using fraction strips, 533–536
using same denominators, 533–536
using same numerators, 533–536
part of a set, 481–484, 487–490
part of a whole, 443–446, 455–458,
461–464
related to shapes and area, 747–750
related to whole numbers, 475–478
representing
equal to 1, 539–542, 545–548
equal to whole number, 475–478
greater than 1, 475–478, 482–483
less than 1, 455–458, 461–464, 467–470
on a number line, 467–470
representations of fraction equivalence,
539–542, 545–548
set models, 481–484, 487–490
sixths, 443
thirds, 443
unit fractions, 455–458, 487–490,
493–496, 747–750
of a whole, 443–446, 461–464
writing, as whole numbers, 461–464,
475–478, 482–483

**Fractions greater than** 1, 475–478,
482–483

**Frequency tables,** 87–90

**G**

**Geometric patterns,** 663–666
**Geometry**
angles. *See* Angles
attributes of shapes, 697–700, 703–706,
709–712, 715–718, 723–726, 729–732,
735–738, 741–744, 747–750

classifying plane shapes, 697–700,
741–744
closed shapes, 698–700
comparing plane shapes, 697–700,
723–726
decagons, 709–712
describing plane shapes, 697–700
drawing, 729–732
endpoints, 697
hexagons, 709–712
lines
defined, 697
intersecting, 715–718
parallel, 715–718
perpendicular, 715–718
line segments, 697
open shapes, 698–700
partitioning shapes to make equal areas,
747–750
plane shapes, 697–700, 703–706, 741–744
*See also* Two-dimensional shapes
points, 697
quadrilaterals
angles of, 723–726
classifying, 723–726
drawing, 729–732
rectangles, 723–726, 729–732
rhombuses, 723–726, 729–732
sides of, 723–726
squares, 723–726, 729–732
trapezoids, 723–726, 729–732
rays, 697
triangles
angles of, 735–738
classifying, 735–738
modeling, 735
sides of, 723–724, 735–738
two-dimensional shapes. *See also*
Two-dimensional shapes

**Glossary,** H1–H12

**Go Deeper,** In some Student Edition lessons.
Some examples are: 11, 116, 217, 328,
398, 478, 516, 564, 658, 738

**Grams**
defined, 605
as metric unit, 605–608
solving problems in, 605–608, 611–614

**Graphic Organizers.** *See also* Tables and
charts
Bubble Map, 86, 300, 442
Flow Map, 506

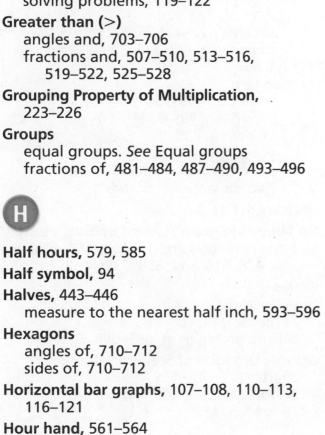

counting back on, 55, 326–328, 371–374, 377–380, 384
counting up on, 55, 378–379
dividing with, 325–328, 371, 377–380, 384
elapsed time. *See* Time
fractions greater than 1, 495–501
fractions on, 467–470
multiplying with, 151–154, 197–200, 235, 281–284
number line for hours in a day, 567
round numbers and, 11–14
skip counting, 151–154
    by eights, 235
    by fives, 197–198
    by sixes, 151
    by tens, 197–198
    time intervals. *See* Time
    by twos, 192
subtracting with, 55–58
take away tens and ones, 55–58
use to represent
    distances, 467–470
    elapsed time, 573–575, 579–582, 585–588
whole numbers on, 467–470, 475–478

**Number patterns,** 5–8, 229–232, 242, 261–264

**Numbers**
compatible, 17–20, 24–25, 49–52
counting, 281, 562, 438, 625
even, 5–8, 229–232, 235–236
expanded form of, 24, 35–38, 42, 56
fractions, 443–446, 449–452, 437–440, 455–458, 467–470, 475–478, 481–484, 487–490, 493–496, 507–510, 513–516, 519–522, 525–528, 533–536, 539–542, 545–548
hundreds, 11–14, 18–20, 35–38, 41–44, 50–52, 56–57, 61–64, 67–70, 281–284, 287–290
odd, 5–8, 229–232, 235–238
ones, 23–26, 29–32, 35–38, 41–44, 50–52, 55–58, 61–64, 67–70, 177–180, 351–354
ordering, 533–536
rounding, 11–14, 17–20
standard form of, 36
tens, 11–14, 23–26, 29–32, 35–38, 41–44, 55–58, 61–64, 67–70, 197–200, 287–290
unknown, 63, 193, 199, 225, 267–270, 367, 390–391, 396–397, 404–405, 410–411, 417, 429
zero, 177–180, 351–354

**Numerators,** 461
comparing fractions with same, 519–522, 525–528
defined, 461
fractions greater than 1, 476–478
ordering fractions with same, 533–536

## O

**Octagons**
angles of, 709–712
sides of, 709–712

**Odd numbers,** 5–8, 229–232, 235–236

**Ones,** 12–14, 23–26, 29–32, 35–38, 41–44, 50–52, 55–58, 61–64, 67–70, 177–180, 287–290

**On Your Own,** In most lessons. Some examples are: 7, 43, 379, 411, 731, 744

**Open shapes,** 698–700

**Ordering**
fractions, 533–536
fraction strips, 533–536
liquid volume, 600
mass, 606

**Order of operations,** 427–430

**Organize data,** 87–90

## P

**Parallel lines,** 715–718

**Partitioning**
fractions, 443–446, 449–452
shapes, 747–750

**Patterns**
addition, 5–8, 261–264
on the addition table, 5–8
arithmetic, 5–8, 229–232, 261–264
defined, 5
describing, 261–264
explaining using properties, 5–8, 229–232, 236
finding, 663–666
multiplication, 229–232, 242, 261–264
on the multiplication table, 229–232
with nine, 241–244
number, 5–8, 229–232
in a table, 261–264

© Houghton Mifflin Harcourt Publishing Company

**Pentagons**
    angles of, 710–712
    sides of, 710–712

**Perimeter**
    area related to, 643–646
    defined, 625
    estimate and measure, 631–634
    find unknown side length, 637–640
    modeling, 625–628
    of polygons, 637–640
    of rectangles, 675–678
        same area, different perimeters, 681–684
        same perimeter, different areas, 675–678
        solving problems, 643–646

**Perpendicular lines,** 715–718

**Personal Math Trainer,** In all Student Edition chapters. Some examples are: 3, 52, 96, 137, 231, 290, 299, 398, 505, 602, 672, 695

**Picture graphs**
    defined, 93
    drawing, 99–102
    half symbol, 94
    key, 93
    making, 99–102
    read and interpret data in, 99–102
    solving problems, 93–96, 99–102

**Place value**
    addition and, 17–20, 23–26, 29–32, 35–38, 41–44
    expanded form, 24, 35–38, 42, 56
    hundreds, 11–14, 17–20, 35–38, 41–44, 50–52, 56–57, 61–64, 67–70, 282–284
    multiplication and, 281–284, 287–290
    ones, 12–14, 23–26, 29–32, 35–38, 41–44, 50–52, 55–58, 61–64, 67–70
    rounding and, 12, 17–20, 49–52
    standard form, 36
    subtraction and, 49–52, 55–58, 61–64, 67–70
    tens, 11–14, 23–26, 29, 35–38, 41–44, 55–58, 61–64, 67–70

**Plane shapes.** See Two-dimensional shapes

**P.M.,** 567–570

**Points,** 697

**Polygons**
    angles of, 710–712, 715–718
    classifying, 709–712
    comparing, 710
    decagons, 710
    defined, 709
    describing, 709
    hexagons, 710
    identifying, 709–712
    line segments of, 709–712
    octagons, 710
    pentagons, 710
    perimeter of, 637–640
    quadrilaterals, 710
    sides of, 709–712, 715–718
    triangles, 710

**Pose a Problem,** 76, 102, 380, 398, 429, 464, 536, 608

**Pounds,** 52

**Practice and Homework**
    In every lesson. Some examples are: 9–10, 91–92, 305–306, 565–566
    Practice: Copy and Solve, 37, 43, 63, 69, 225, 289, 321, 353, 385, 391, 595, 613, 731

**Prerequisite skills**
    Show What You Know, 3, 85, 137, 189, 259, 299, 363, 441, 505, 559, 623, 695

**Problem solving applications.** See also Cross-Curricular Activities and Connections
    Investigate, 333–336, 427–430, 539–542, 625–628, 747–750
    Pose a Problem, 102, 109, 154, 237, 322, 342, 348, 374, 380, 398, 429, 464, 536, 608
    Real World Problem Solving, In most lessons. Some examples are, 14, 52, 374, 412, 732, 750
    Real World Unlock the Problem, In most lessons. Some examples are: 11, 41, 377, 409, 669, 741
    Think Smarter problems, In every lesson. Some examples are: 7, 43, 374, 411, 732, 750
    Try This!, In some lessons. Some examples are: 12, 42, 390, 444, 709, 716
    What's the Error?. See What's the Error?

**Problem solving strategies**
    act it out, 301–304, 421–424, 507–510
    draw a diagram, 73–76, 159–162, 275–278, 493–496, 585–588, 741–744
    find a pattern, 663–666
    make a table, 87–90, 247–250

© Houghton Mifflin Harcourt Publishing Company

on a number line, 573–576, 579–582, 585–588

subtracting, 573–576, 579–582, 585–588

measure in minutes, 561–564

to minute, 561–564, 567–570

number line, 567, 573–576, 579–582

P.M., 567–570

reading time, 561–564

time lines, 567

telling time, 561–564, 567–570

writing time, 561–564, 567–570

**Time intervals.** *See* Elapsed time; Time

**Trapezoids**

angles of, 723–726

drawing, 729–732

sides of, 723–726

**Triangles**

angles of, 698–699, 736–738

classifying, 735–738

comparing, 736–738

describing, 735–738

drawing, 735–738

modeling, 735

sides of, 710–711, 735–738

**Try Another Problem,** 74, 88, 160, 248, 276, 302, 422, 494, 508, 586, 664, 742

**Try This!,** In some lessons. Some examples are: 12, 42, 390, 444, 709, 716

**Two-digit numbers**

addition, 18–20, 23–26, 29–32

subtraction, 49–52, 55–58

**Two-dimensional shapes**

angles. *See* Angles

area. *See* Area

attributes of, 697–700, 703–706, 709–712, 715–718, 723–726, 729–732, 735–738, 741–744, 747–755

classifying, 697–700, 723–726, 741–744

comparing, 695–700, 723–726

defined, 698

describing, 697–700

draw a diagram, 741–744

drawing, 698, 712, 716, 729–732

partitioning shapes to make equal areas, 747–750

perimeter. *See* Perimeter

plane shapes, 697–700, 703–706, 741–747

circles, 698, 709, 712

decagons, 709–712

hexagons, 709–712

octagons, 709–712

open or closed shapes, 698–700, 709–712

pentagons, 709–712

polygons, 709–712

quadrilaterals, 709–712, 723–726

rectangles, 723–726

rhombuses, 723–726

squares, 723–726

trapezoids, 723–726

triangles, 709–712, 735–738

polygons. *See* Polygons

quadrilaterals, 709

angles of, 723–726

classifying, 723–726

drawing, 729–732

rectangles, 723–726, 729–732

rhombuses, 723–726, 729–732

sides of, 723–726

squares, 723–726, 729–732

trapezoids, 723–726, 729–732

sides

defined, 709

describing, 715–718

of polygons, 710–712

of quadrilaterals, 710–711, 723–726

of triangles, 710–711, 735–738

vertex, 703

**Two-step problems,** 73–76, 159–162, 421–424, 427–430

**U**

**Understand Vocabulary,** 4, 86, 138, 190, 260, 300, 364, 442, 506, 560, 624, 696

**Unit fractions,** 455–458, 461, 467–470, 487–490, 493–496, 747–750

**Unit squares,** 643

**Units**

customary units

for area

square feet, 656–658, 663–666, 669

square inches, 649, 651

for length

feet, 151, 634, 638, 664

inches, 593–596, 631–633

for liquid volume and capacity, cups, 217

for mass, grams, 605–608

for weight, ounces, 148

# Table of Measures

| METRIC | CUSTOMARY |
|---|---|

## Length

1 centimeter (cm) = 10 millimeters (mm)

1 decimeter (dm) = 10 centimeters (cm)     1 foot (ft) = 12 inches (in.)

1 meter (m) = 100 centimeters    1 yard (yd) = 3 feet, or 36 inches

1 meter (m) = 10 decimeters    1 mile (mi) = 1,760 yards, or 5,280 feet

1 kilometer (km) = 1,000 meters

## Capacity and Liquid Volume

1 liter (L) = 1,000 milliliters (mL)    1 pint (pt) = 2 cups (c)

1 quart (qt) = 2 pints

1 gallon (gal) = 4 quarts

## Mass/Weight

1 kilogram (kg) = 1,000 grams (g)    1 pound (lb) = 16 ounces (oz)

## TIME

1 minute (min) = 60 seconds (sec)    1 year (yr) = 12 months (mo), or about 52 weeks

1 hour (hr) = 60 minutes

1 day = 24 hours    1 year = 365 days

1 week (wk) = 7 days    1 leap year = 366 days

1 decade = 10 years

1 century = 100 years

## MONEY

1 penny = 1 cent (¢)

1 nickel = 5 cents

1 dime = 10 cents

1 quarter = 25 cents

1 half dollar = 50 cents

1 dollar ($) = 100 cents

## SYMBOLS

< is less than

> is greater than

= is equal to